More praise for *Private Security in Afr*

'Ranging from secret societies in Sierra Leone to private security companies in South Africa, this important book provides a major contribution to the theory and practical understanding of the everyday experience of private security across Africa.'

Paul Jackson, University of Birmingham

'Higate and Utas have produced a cohesive collection of insightful essays on the politics of private security in Africa (and beyond). Theoretically sophisticated and empirically informed, this impressive volume will be the baseline for future scholarship for years to come.'

Kevin Dunn, Hobart and William Smith Colleges

'The global trend of privatising security has received little systematic attention. This highly recommended book starts to close this gap and raises important questions about what this means for the role of the state in this age of uncertainty.'

Morten Bøås, Norwegian Institute of International Affairs

'Through the adoption of an ethnographic lens, this volume provides a compelling account of everyday private security practices and the kaleidoscopic configurations within which they blend and assemble.'

Daniel C. Bach, Sciences Po Bordeaux (emeritus)

Africa Now

Africa Now is published by Zed Books in association with the internationally respected Nordic Africa Institute. Featuring high-quality, cutting-edge research from leading academics, the series addresses the big issues confronting Africa today. Accessible but in-depth, and wide-ranging in its scope, Africa Now engages with the critical political, economic, sociological and development debates affecting the continent, shedding new light on pressing concerns.

Nordic Africa Institute

The Nordic Africa Institute (Nordiska Afrikainstitutet) is a centre for research, documentation and information on modern Africa. Based in Uppsala, Sweden, the Institute is dedicated to providing timely, critical and alternative research and analysis of Africa and to co-operation with African researchers. As a hub and a meeting place for a growing field of research and analysis the Institute strives to put knowledge of African issues within reach for scholars, policy makers, politicians, media, students and the general public.

www.nai.uu.se

Forthcoming titles

Anders Themnér (ed.), *Warlord Democrats in Africa*

Mimmi Söderberg Kovacs and Jesper Bjarnesen (eds), *Violence in African Elections*

Atakilte Beyene (ed.), *Agricultural Transformation in Ethiopia*

Titles already published

Fantu Cheru and Cyril Obi (eds), *The Rise of China and India in Africa*

Ilda Lindell (ed.), *Africa's Informal Workers*

Iman Hashim and Dorte Thorsen, *Child Migration in Africa*

Prosper B. Matondi, Kjell Havnevik and Atakilte Beyene (eds), *Biofuels, Land Grabbing and Food Security in Africa*

Cyril Obi and Siri Aas Rustad (eds), *Oil and Insurgency in the Niger Delta*

Mats Utas (ed.), *African Conflicts and Informal Power*

Prosper B. Matondi, *Zimbabwe's Fast Track Land Reform*

Maria Eriksson Baaz and Maria Stern, *Sexual Violence as a Weapon of War?*

Fantu Cheru and Renu Modi (eds), *Agricultural Development and Food Security in Africa*

Amanda Hammar (ed.), *Displacement Economies in Africa*

Mary Njeri Kinyanjui, *Women and the Informal Economy in Urban Africa*

Liisa Laakso and Petri Hautaniemi (eds), *Diasporas, Development and Peacemaking in the Horn of Africa*

Margaret Lee, *Africa's World Trade*

Godwin R. Murunga, Duncan Okello and Anders Sjögren (eds), *Kenya: The Struggle for a New Constitutional Order*

Lisa Åkesson and Maria Eriksson Baaz (eds), *Africa's Return Migrants*

Thiven Reddy, *South Africa: Settler Colonialism and the Failures of Liberal Democracy*

Cedric de Coning, Linnéa Gelot and John Karlsrud (eds), *The Future of African Peace Operations*

Tobias Hagmann and Filip Reyntjens (eds), *Aid and Authoritarianism in Africa*

Henning Melber (ed.), *The Rise of Africa's Middle Class*

Private security in Africa

From the global assemblage to the everyday

edited by Paul Higate and Mats Utas

Zed Books
LONDON

Private Security in Africa: From the Global Assemblage to the Everyday was first published in association with the Nordic Africa Institute, PO Box 1703, SE-751 47 Uppsala, Sweden in 2017 by Zed Books Ltd, The Foundry, 17 Oval Way, London SE11 5RR, UK.

www.zedbooks.net
www.nai.uu.se

Typeset in Minion Pro by seagulls.net
Index by Rohan Bolton
Cover design by Alice Marwick
Cover photo © Marc Shoul/Panos

A catalogue record for this book is available from the British Library.

ISBN 978-1-78699-026-6 hb
ISBN 978-1-78699-025-9 pb
ISBN 978-1-78699-028-0 pdf
ISBN 978-1-78699-027-3 epub
ISBN 978-1-78699-029-7 mobi

Printed and bound by CPI Group (UK) Ltd, Croydon, CR0 4YY

Contents

Acknowledgements

In December 2013 a workshop entitled 'Private Security Providers in Conflict Environments – Transitional Actors or Active Influencers' was held at the Crowne Plaza Hotel in Nairobi. The workshop brought together a number of established scholars and practitioners with expertise on the provision of private security on the continent of Africa. While we would have very much liked to have included all of the excellent contributions from the workshop, this has not been possible as we selected those pieces that chimed most closely with the theme of the global security assemblage. The event was generously supported by the World Bank and the Center on Conflict, Security and Development and the Nordic Africa Institute. Much was learned over those few days, not least that the continent remains largely overlooked from an ethnographic perspective when it comes to questions of private security provision. The editors would like to thank the following whose input, help and assistance – either directly or indirectly – have made the current volume possible: Rita Abrahamsen, Peter Albrecht, Lydia Amedzrator, Maya Mynster Christensen, Markus Derblom, Tessa Diphoorn, Susanna Dukaric, Annika Franklin, Marsha Henry, Mathias Krüger, Marcus Mohlin, Ruth Mwangi, Henri Myrttinen, Jacob Rasmussen, Will Reno, Peer Schouten and Leila Stockmarr. We would also like to thank Nivi Manchanda and Ilmari Käihkö for commenting on earlier drafts of the introduction and epilogue and, finally, Ken Barlow at Zed for his patience and work on the manuscript.

Paul Higate
Mats Utas

Note: A version of Chapter 4 by Maya Christensen appeared in *African Affairs* with the same title, 'The underbelly of global security: Sierra Leonean ex-militias in Iraq', *African Affairs*, doi: 10.1093/afraf/adv055.

Introduction

Paul Higate

While the wider literature on private security provision has developed both theoretically and empirically in recent years, the nefarious activities of Executive Outcomes and its mercenary operatives in Sierra Leone through the 1990s are rarely far from discussion of private security on the continent of Africa. Here, the mercenary caricature continues to loom large in elements of this literature in ways that align private security with force, militarism and violence. Inflected with the spectre of the fragile state, and seen through the lens of profit, narcissm, underdevelopment and ungovernability, these narratives function at the level of common sense to constitute a crude inside/outside binary where the (African) latter is incomplete and found wanting as a distant entity with which 'we' have little in common (Abrahamsen and Williams 2011: 37). Within mainstream IR, Security Studies and Development Studies literatures, state-building instigated by actors in the global North is invariably seen as the de facto panacea to failure and, consequently, sight of the global as one analytical field configured through myriad connections across time and space is lost (ibid.: 4–12). Taken together, then, these framings can occlude a wider focus on the conditions under which new geographies of power and security emerge in the region. Yet this is not the only narrative in circulation around private security provision on the continent, and though the literature is no longer solely preoccupied with mercenarism, it does nonetheless lag behind developments on the ground, where private security provision has proliferated exponentially in both the rural and urban contexts. One way in which to counter the speculation, silences and cultural stereotyping around private security provision on the continent of Africa as invoking militarized and mercenary-driven activities is to investigate its current empirical character. To these ends, the current volume is informed by ground-up approaches, and authors focus on the everyday dimensions of security that include experiences of both consumer and provider. Conceived through the ethnographic lens, their concern is with non-militarized elements of security, the development and impact of which can be explained by localized historical and cultural legacies manifest in traditional structures. A total of seven sub-Saharan countries are brought under the critical spotlight and, rather than seeing Africa as a unique periphery floating free of its global Northern influences, authors respond directly to the call for the continent to be studied both in its own right, and as an entity enmeshed in wider relationships. As one way in which to analyse localized manifestations of power with seemingly distant, yet nonetheless immediately present, national and international normativities, the volume engages the global assemblage framework (ibid.: 38–146). Complex and fluid networks through and by which assemblages are configured are largely invisible to consumers and perhaps less so providers, yet remain visceral in their sometimes violent materiality. Ultimately, these hybridized forms of governance seek order in the name of capital accumulation, a logic that comes into sharpest relief when we consider the resource extraction sector in Nigeria and Sierra Leone. Here we note extreme forms of explicitly militarized private security provision in contexts of inequality, social injustice and violence (ibid.).

Taking a step back and locating Africa in a global context, it is clear that the growth in private security provision across many regions of the world continues unabated and exerts an inconsistent influence on countless millions. Avoiding the influence of private security in either its direct or indirect guise is a challenge, and the extent to which provision is embedded in everyday security landscapes is exemplified by the ubiquity of the G4S employee to be found in the government, resource extraction, transport, energy, utility, leisure and retail sectors of numerous states in both the global North and the global South. It is not simply that the state *appears* to have little to do with security in contemporary times as outsourcing has intensified, and become increasingly normalized, but rather that private security has gained an unstoppable momentum in its reconfiguring of the state's public institutions. To put this differently, rarely if ever are privately delivered services taken back into government ownership, yet in theoretical and empirical terms, the story is not simply one of the state being supplanted by the market, as authors argue below.

To date, scholars across the social sciences have analysed private security and its contracting workforce from a range of substantive and theoretical perspectives. Over the last two decades we have learned a great deal about the genesis of the industry in regard to its mercenary heritage (Singer 2003; Kinsey 2007; Percy 2007), its ethical, legal and civil–military dimensions (Alexandra et al. 2008), how far and in what kinds of ways it is regulated (Percy 2006), the unintended consequence of regulation (Leander 2010), the complex and fluid manner through and by which it connects with state structures (Abrahamsen and Williams 2011), its impact on local populations (Higate 2012b), its racial and gendered constitution (ibid.; Chisholm 2013, 2014; Stachowitsch 2013; Eichler 2015), the questionable nature of the business case as a key rationale for outsourcing (Krahmann 2010), representations of the security provider as an 'expert' who may in part be driving the demand for services (Abrahamsen and Williams 2007; Berndtsson 2012), and the moral dilemma private security poses from a philosophical perspective (Pattison 2010). However, significant lacunae prevail in this literature, and as is the case across the social sciences more broadly, scholarly interest trails in the wake of recent developments as the sector has proliferated territorially and 'matured' in industry parlance. In more specific terms, and widening the concern from mercenarism on the continent as indicated, Africa-focused literature has considered: the external factors that facilitate developments in private security provision (Cilliers and Mason 1999), critical considerations of industry regulation (ibid.; Gumedze 2007; Berg and Nouveau 2011), arguments for the positive benefits of private security in supplementing both state and international forces in the region (Brooks 2000), and questions of policing, albeit with a disproportionate focus on South Africa (Baker 2002; Minnaar and Ngoveni 2004; Minnaar 2005; Kempa and Singh 2008; Berg 2010). Other more topical concerns invoke private security and the maritime industry (Affi et al. 2016), alongside the provocative figure of the Somali pirate, of whom little has been heard in recent years as the industry has evolved to counter this particular threat (see Bueger 2015).

The assemblage approach

In terms of generating innovative theoretical perspectives, cutting-edge concepts and their potential corollary – enlivening allied fields of study – mainstream elements of the private security literature parallel that of IR in that it is argued they are intellectually limited (Lisle 2013). It is also the case that pioneering theoretical interventions are now forging fruitful directions of scholarly travel through applying the assemblage framework to private security (Abrahamsen and Williams 2009, 2011). For example, it has been used to illuminate the airport/security nexus where Berndtsson and Stern (2011) have focused on the company Securitas at Stockholm's Arlanda airport, Lippert and O'Connor (2003) have considered airport security in the wake of profound shifts in security post-2001, and Schouten (2014) has drawn on actor-network theory to analyse the role of non-human elements of airport security at Amsterdam's Schiphol airport. In a broader sense, this approach has also begun to develop critical traction through challenging reified conceptions of the international. Rapid social change demands fresh perspectives able to illuminate complexity and transformation, and in light of technological developments and hybridity, between the material and biological (Acuto and Curtis 2013). In parallel with many of the key concepts within the social sciences – with security as the most pertinent example here – assemblage thought can be eclectic, diverse and at times contested. That said, there are a number of commonly held perspectives coalescing around the framework, and put succinctly these invoke the importance of materialist approaches, a focus on social interaction, creativity, deconstruction, relationalism, non-linearity, and a sensitivity to the processual and fluid (ibid.). This thinking can be deployed in an explicitly normative sense as an analytical tactic where, for example, the idea of a financial market stands as an unhelpful abstraction that demands not just destabilization, but disaggregation into specific elements open to reflexive analysis (Sassen 2013). Here we see the influence of numerous basic tenets of sociological thought that concern themselves with a priori social relations as the building blocks of institutions, networks and connectivities of various kinds, shaped by contingency and dynamism. In order to do the social complexities of private security explanatory justice it is argued that the approach provides for a nimble resource unhindered by fixity, and open to revision in light of the empirically novel. Moving from the theoretical as point of departure in assemblage thought, Abrahamsen and Williams (2013) assume an explicitly inductive stance (see also Bueger 2013), where attempts to account for, and explain, the empirical have been followed by reflection on the limitations of traditional state-oriented, theoretical frames that fail to capture the dynamics at play in a number of African countries. Rather, their response has been to foreground and further enhance the assemblage framework through co-opting key Bourdieusian concepts into analysis. Consequently, key nodes within the assemblage are argued to exert forms of capital power, understandings of which reveal the complex and inconsistent nature of connectivity and the political struggles that shape their interactions. In a more substantive sense, their influential contributions have focused on decentralization, sensitive to citizens and security in the network of relationships shaping private security in particular African case studies. Reassembly is characterized by novel arrangements of hybridized security that are beyond straightforward categorization and therefore may be conceived of (somewhat counter-intuitively perhaps) as *both* private and public (Abrahamsen and Williams 2013). An alternative approach to the framework is considered by Srnicek (2013), who focuses on why it is that particular assemblages are deemed 'acceptable' in an explicitly political sense, alongside how interventions of various kinds are supported, or at least viewed as inevitable. To be sure, scholarly responses to private security – particularly from 2003 and the occupation of Iraq – can be usefully considered through this approach, with an earlier critical literature questioning the legitimacy of private security quickly losing momentum in the face of the rapid growth of the industry. Invoking the sociologist Tony Giddens' metaphor of modernity as a 'juggernaut', private security tends to be implicitly imbued with unstoppable momentum in both lay and academic commentary. Resonant in some sense with the mantra that certain financial sectors of the industrialized economies are 'too big to fail' is the rarely questioned belief that there is no alternative to private security in the face of its ubiquity and relevance in contemporary times. Similarly, feminist and activist approaches that were initially critical of the growth of private security (Richards 2006) soon adopted problem-solving approaches focused on ethical concerns within the industry (for example, Higate and Stachowitsch

2013). Unsurprisingly, the International Code of Conduct for Private Security Services (ICoC) also proceeds from a normalization of this form of provision that plays out within a context of self-regulation. Chiming with Srnicek's interests, and perhaps invoking a particular aspect of neoliberalism in regard to private security, Lisle (2013) raises the question of by what rationales assemblages are brought into play. Alongside a focus on the conditions that make possible configurations of various kinds is the call to practise what she calls 'creative ethnography'. Following earlier appeals by scholars working on the critical fringes of IR (Lutz 2006; Vrasti 2008) is the argument that slowing down and paying attention, as Lisle puts it, are necessary precursors to the generation of anthropologically oriented thick description, vital for capturing the social contingencies and complexities of the networks under scrutiny. Picking up on a key element of assemblage thinking as indicated above, Chandler (2013) urges us to reflect on the ontological status of the nodes or units considered relevant within the wider network. In turn, this raises questions around method: how does one render legible the messiness of the social world? By what ontological criteria are particular aspects of the assemblage considered relevant in contrast to those deemed less so, or others ignored altogether? Notwithstanding these philosophical concerns, discussion now turns to an overview of the chapters in the volume with a particular focus on how authors have rendered the assemblage approach legible through the lens of ethnography.

Organization of the volume: thinking with the assemblage

Rita Abrahamsen and Michael Williams open the volume with their chapter 'Golden assemblages: security and development in Tanzania's gold mines', which provides a succinct exposition of the theoretical framework taken up and applied to different substantive cases by subsequent authors. As point of departure, their example is provocative and considers the death of six young men killed by police at one of African Barrick Gold's (ABG) mines in Tanzania. They argue that the mine's security strategies are illustrative of novel global security assemblages that engage a diversity of private, public, community and ABG actors. Attempts to secure the mines are not just manifest through the razor wire, CCTV and frequent patrolling of resource extraction sites such as these, but also in terms of winning hearts and minds locally through encouraging local communities and NGOs to play a role in mine security. One way to reflect on a key dynamic at play here is to locate it within a series of nodes made possible by the demands of distant consumers procuring the precious metal – a rare substance imbued with relatively stable value in times of global financial volatility. This observation reminds us of the possibility of extending assemblage thinking far beyond the immediate orbit of mine security, as one way to broaden a field of analysis that reaches into the everyday lives of those at the point of production, and others far distant and often oblivious to these conditions.

Chapter 2, 'Failed, weak or fake state? The role of private security in Somalia', shifts the regional focus north-east from Tanzania to Somalia, where William Reno focuses on the African Union Mission in Somalia (AMISOM) through the growth of private security networks associated with this multilateral peacekeeping operation. He argues that private security firms and commercial ventures provide new opportunities for local and external actors to redefine relationships between governance and commerce. Those emergent relationships that come under the spotlight are illustrative of the global security assemblage that engages individuals and groups from domestic and overseas governments, international organizations and commerce, whose services are taken up by foreign actors. More than that, these relationships are refracted through pre-existing kinship networks that play out at the highest levels of the Somalian government, where US aspirations to bring the 'failed state' into line are thwarted through a problematic Security Sector Reform (SSR) programme.

In Chapter 3, 'Private security beyond the private sector: community policing and secret societies in Sierra Leone', Peter Albrecht considers the role of policing in this post-conflict context. Everyday, non-militarized forms of policing play out through traditional leaders and vigilante groups who deal with the vast majority of disputes in their communities. Framed as beyond market logic, the relationship between Local Policing Partnership Boards (LPPBs) in Sierra Leone and the Poro or secret society is oriented towards delivering and enforcing security in ways that almost entirely exclude the government. As Albrecht notes, this assemblage is shaped by competing forms of authority, a myriad of both informal and formal rules and the functioning of power that overlaps, coexists and intertwines with local and distant actors. Boards are distinctive hybridized orders, the emergent qualities of which are made possible through particular configurations of history, culture and tradition against the backcloth of the resources made available to its key actors.

Staying with Sierra Leone, Maya Christensen's contribution in Chapter 4 reminds us of the continued exploitation of Third Country Nationals (TCNs) in 'The underbelly of global security: Sierra Leonean ex-militias in Iraq'. In the intensified attempt to drive down labour costs, and in collaboration with the Sierra Leonean authorities, the British Private Military and Security Company (PMSC) Sabre set about recruiting former West Side Boys for their base-guarding operations in Iraq. The process is shown to be fraught – both bureaucratically and more poignantly emotionally – for impoverished actors hoping to break out of the situation in Sierra Leone, which offers only a marginal possibility of employment. In turn, their commitment to the company and the opportunities they promise are heightened, and made all the more potent, through investing in a colonial narrative of beneficence in regard to Sabre and its revered white

Western hierarchy. Yet, as Christensen shows, the reality in Iraq falls far short of the promise and as such jars with the allied expectations expressed by the men at the centre of the study. Specifically, Sabre's duty of care to its employees was found wanting, a challenging situation further exacerbated by low levels of remuneration and the risks to which they were exposed whilst deployed in Iraq. This assemblage blends private and public actors across two post-conflict contexts. As such, it is illustrative of wider trends in the industry, where cheap labour is sought and encouraged to migrate for relatively high wages, but often at damaging cost to themselves. Specifically, mental health can be put on the line – for example through the development of Post Traumatic Stress Disorder – though in keeping with wider trends in the sector, firms' duty of care is far from adequate. As Christensen puts it, the complex matrix at play in this situation is comprised of entangled national and transnational networks imbued with a veneer of legitimacy through the Sierra Leonean government's narrative of 'youth employment', where Sabre are presented as 'saving' impoverished men. This framing serves Sabre's economic aims well yet, through Christensen's ethnography, we are shown the significance of affect (hope), race and migration to the assemblage under scrutiny. Thus, from being disconnected and excluded, these former West Side Boys become somewhat unwitting vectors of foreign policy through their role in the controversial occupation of Iraq.

Chapter 5 by Tessa Diphoorn, 'Who do you call? Private security policing in Durban, South Africa', is the second to explore policing through an ethnographic focus, though in this instance it involves private armed response officers in Durban, South Africa. The group she studies is located at the interface of state and non-state policing and practises punitive, disciplinary and exclusionary approaches to those deemed to be a threat to community security – often through threats of, or actual, face-to-face violence. While this focus on policing in South Africa has attracted wider interest noted above, Diphoorn's contribution captures the visceral and gendered dimensions of an assemblage that has gained considerable commercial success in recent years, such that the state police force are rarely seen as the default security provider. It is routine for many in urban areas to purchase security provision, even for those who can barely afford to do so, yet require some kind of protection from acquisitive crime. Following on from the ethnographic moments she details so well is discussion of the key nodes of the assemblage that turn on (justifiable) fear of crime and the prevailing dynamics of an old boys' network. Both are linked to the enduring legacy of apartheid, where in the former, the state's transition to majority rule plays out against stark inequality. As she puts it, 'the political and financial connections between the industry and the apartheid state [exist] at both national and local levels' (p. xx) with this configuration of actors giving rise ultimately to forms of racialized violence theorized through the lens of 'twilight policing'.

Liberia is the focus of Chapter 6, 'Security Sector Reform as Trojan horse? The new security assemblages of privatized military training in Liberia', where Marcus Mohlin moves from the everyday to the institutional level in the case of the US PSC Dyncorp's interaction with local power brokers and government actors. He argues that their presence can be seen as a key moment in a security assemblage that shapes national security policy in Liberia according to the geostrategic interests of US foreign policy. SSR, then, provides something of a smokescreen for the interests of a hegemonic power whose imperatives may be at sharp odds with the security needs of a post-conflict state in an unstable region of the world. Common to assemblages in general, as Mohlin argues, is the ability of SSR in this context to 'obfuscate its political origins very effectively' (p.xx) such that the influence of the USA within the Liberian Ministry of Defence, right down to the individual unit, is hidden in plain sight. Crucially, though Liberian defence is reassembled, it is not actually weakened but rather, as he states, 'signals a new mode of global governance'. As we note below, this approach has considerably wider applicability and calls for renewed scrutiny into SSR in different contexts, alongside the nature of the assemblages that make them possible.

In Chapter 7, Jacob Rasmussen applies assemblage thinking to a somewhat demonized group in 'Political becoming and non-state emergence in Kenya's security sector: Mungiki as security operator'. In contrast to the commercial policing activities supporting the relatively affluent in Kenyan society, the focus switches to the informal means by which the poor in the country are governed. Somewhat paradoxically, while the Mungiki challenge the authority of the state in their provision of security, their hold over particular communities is also facilitated by the state in ways that illuminate one of the numerous contradictions at the heart of this particular assemblage. Rasmussen's long-term ethnographic fieldwork shows that the disassembly of the security sector to include the Mungiki as informal and sometimes ambiguous security actors did not initially threaten the authority of the state. However, it was the intervention of the International Criminal Court that cast doubt on this element of Kenya's general security practices, which, in turn, influenced how this aspect of the assemblage was viewed. The assemblage in question is revealed to be not just political in its unorthodox modes of governance – often through the everyday, sometimes violent exercise of authority exercised by the Mungiki – but also in relation to who gets to decide what kind of 'policing' is acceptable according to distant standards.

In Chapter 8, '*Parapluies politiques:* the everyday politics of private security in the Democratic Republic of Congo', Peer Schouten paints a broad-brush picture of private security provision in the DRC. As in the other chapters, the state's absent presence is evident through the myriad entanglements between private and public actors exemplified in the figure of the Armed

Forces of the Democratic Republic of the Congo (FARDC) soldier working as a security guard, in this particular instance for one of the many thousands of private security companies in the country. Elements of Congolese culture that turn on particular kinds of 'connected' relationships appear amenable to the proliferation of diverse forms of security governance that influence actors moving between, or with access to, forms of official authority. Schouten does not equate the quality of security with the nature of its provider, but unlike in other chapters stresses the centrality of capital accumulation to its foundational elements.

Mats Utas brings the volume to a close with a highly personal epilogue that nests everyday experiences of security with those broader structures and processes that make for dichotomous structures of (security) feeling. His reflective journey through particular security landscapes invites consideration of disparate literatures that also connect – though not obviously – with the immediate topic at hand. Here, the humanitarian sector is considered along with the contradictory character of security providers who at one and the same time both threaten yet guarantee the safety of local populations through deeply moral narratives. Security providers may also switch allegiance, as Utas notes in the case of the West Side Boys, thereby underscoring the influence of the limited socio-economic possibilities available to actors on the ground. The chapter is brought to a close with an anecdote that reveals a further, yet much neglected, dynamic worthy of in-depth research – that linking security with the extensive criminal networks that are hidden in plain sight in the everyday context.

Concluding comments

Though variegated in its design, implementation and impact, neoliberalization's energies are far from exhausted (Herring 2011). And, given that so-called '*out*sourcing' (itself a misnomer given the hybridized character of security assemblages that renders meaningless the in/out distinction), we can expect to see the continued proliferation of private security providers across numerous sectors and regions. As economic growth in many areas of Africa accelerates, a concomitant burgeoning of private security will be its corollary, and as such stands as a crucial area for future research.

Notwithstanding opening comments above, lines of enquiry sparked by this volume could further develop understandings of particular, highly militarized assemblages as one way to both update and complement the concern with non-militarized companies in the African context; a focus on both elements is desirable. How far and in what kinds of ways do militarized and non-militarized assemblages differ? Do common patterns exist between the two forms? Militarized firms often recruit white, Northern expertise that attracts higher premiums, particularly those ex-special forces personnel whose presence is made possible through an assemblage shaped by colonial undertones. In turn, questions might be raised about the role of these actors in perpetuating long-standing inequities around race and gender, as key nodes in an assemblage that suppresses wages for local employees who are often placed in the riskiest roles when it comes to security work. How might we understand the political-economic repercussions of highly privileged (white) men in this context? Will assemblages shaped by these markers of power evolve to harness cheaper labour from the global South? Or is this feature of the assemblage likely to remain tenacious and so maintain the gendered and raced status quo of the private security presence?

At first glance SSR might be seen as something of a franchised model, whereby training by outside (often private) companies is oriented towards modernizing and professionalizing militaries and other security services, including the police force. Features of the franchise could include set formulae around unit strength, skill training and so forth. Rather less is known about the actors involved in such initiatives in regard to their private/public and local/national affiliations and amorphous derivatives thereof. What are the conditions of political, economic and perhaps cultural possibility that provide for assemblages of distinct kinds involved in SSR? How far do local conditions frame relations with international actors? Who are stakeholders with whom 'business can be done', and on what basis are they selected in those countries designated as in need of SSR? What kinds of intra-kin/clan/tribal relations pre-exist the SSR presence and how are they shaped through an assemblage that brings them into contact with unknown others – often those from the global North?

Other questions that might inform a future research agenda include: How might we understand the politics of the (SSR) security assemblage in terms of who wins and who gains valuable resources that include skill capital (being trained to fight), as well as resources linked to employment in the military or police? What is the role of the assemblage in mediating military and police values in contexts that may be at sharp odds with 'best practice' in the global North? The extent to which effective policing has been tied to the availability of resources with which to pay for services in South Africa also raises pressing questions around how these practices may be replicated more widely on the continent. How far are these policing assemblages territorially bounded? Seen in light of the so-called lion economies in Ghana, Nigeria and Tanzania, might the well-developed policing assemblages from the south migrate to areas of growing affluence? If so, how will they co-opt traditional forms of governance into these novel policing practices and in what kinds of ways might histories of potential enmity between groups shape who is secured and who is not?

Set against the backcloth of the insights developed below, the continent of Africa provides fertile ground for future research into the provision of private security. It is hoped that the current volume has contributed in its own modest way to helping to establish not only a sense of current arrangements, but also as a catalyst to seeing the continent as an increasingly important actor in an evolving global security assemblage.

Bibliography

Abrahamsen, R. and M. Williams (2006) 'Security Sector Reform: bringing the private in', *Conflict, Security and Development*, 6(1): 1–23.

— (2007) 'Securing the city: private security companies and non-state authority in global governance', *International Relations*, 21(2): 131–41.

— (2009) 'Security beyond the state: global security assemblages in international politics', *International Political Sociology*, 3(1): 1–17.

— (2011) *Security beyond the State: Private Security in International Politics*, Cambridge: Cambridge University Press.

— (2013) 'Tracing global assemblages: bringing Bourdieu to the field. A conversation with Rita Abrahamsen and Michael Williams', in M. Acuto and S. Curtis (eds), *Reassembling International Theory: Assemblage Thinking and International Relations*, London: Palgrave Macmillan.

Acuto, M. and S. Curtis (eds) (2013) *Reassembling International Theory: Assemblage Thinking and International Relations*, London: Palgrave Macmillan.

Affi, L., A. A. Elmi, A. Knight and S. Mohamed (2016) 'Countering piracy through private security in the Horn of Africa: prospects and pitfalls', *Third World Quarterly*, doi: 10.1080/01436597.2015.1114882.

Alexandra, A., D. P. Baker, and M. Capriani (eds) (2008) *Private Military and Security Companies: Ethics, policies and civil–military relations*, London: Routledge, Cass Military Studies.

Baker, B. (2002) 'Living with non-state policing in South Africa: the issues and dilemmas', *Journal of Modern African Studies*, 40(1): 29–53.

Berg, J. (2010) 'Seeing like private security: evolving mentalities of public space protection in South Africa', *Criminology and Criminal Justice*, 10(3): 287–301.

Berg, J. and J. P. Nouveau (2011) 'Toward a third phase of regulation: re-imagining private security in South Africa', *South African Crime Quarterly*, 38: 23–42.

Berndtsson, J. (2012) 'Security professionals for hire: exploring the many faces of private security expertise', *Millennium: Journal of International Studies*, 40(2): 303–20.

Berndtsson, J. and M. Stern (2011) 'Private security and the public–private divide: contested lines of distinction and modes of governance in the Stockholm-Arlanda security assemblage', *International Political Sociology*, 5(4): 408–25.

Brooks, D. (2000) 'Messiahs or mercenaries: the future of private international military services', *International Peacekeeping*, 7(4): 129–44.

Bueger, C. (2013) 'Thinking assemblages methodologically: some rules of thumb', in M. Acuto and S. Curtis (eds), *Reassembling International Theory: Assemblage Thinking and International Relations*, London: Palgrave Macmillan.

— (2015) 'Learning from piracy: future challenges of maritime security governance', *Global Affairs*, doi: 10.1080/23340460.2015.960170.

Chandler, D. (2013) 'The onto-politics of assemblage', in M Acuto and S. Curtis (eds), *Reassembling International Theory: Assemblage Thinking and International Relations*, London: Palgrave Macmillan.

Chisholm, A. (2013) 'The silenced and indispensable: Gurkhas in private military security companies', *International Feminist Journal of Politics*, pp. 26–47.

— (2014) 'Marketing the Gurkha security package: colonial histories and neoliberal economies of private security', *Security Dialogue*, 45(4): 349–72.

Cilliers, J. and P. Mason (eds) (1999) *Peace, Profit or Plunder?: The Privatisation of Security in War-Torn African Societies*, Pretoria: Institute for Security Studies.

Eichler, M. (ed.) (2015) *Gender and Private Security in Global Politics*, Oxford: Oxford University Press.

Gumedze, S. (2007) 'The private security sector in Africa: the 21st century's major cause for concern?', Institute for Security Studies Paper Series 133, Pretoria.

Herring, E. (2011) 'Variegated neo-liberalization, human development and resistance: Iraq and global resistance', *International Journal of Contemporary Iraqi Studies*, ericherring.files.wordpress.com/2011/05/herring-neoliberalization-iraq-11.pdf.

Higate, P. (2012a) 'Cowboys and professionals: the politics of identity work in the private and military security company', *Millennium: Journal of International Studies*, 40(2): 321–41.

— (2012b) 'Martial races and enforcement masculinities of the global South: weaponising Fijian, Chilean and Salvadoran postcoloniality in the mercenary sector', *Globalizations*, 9(1): 35–52.

Higate, P. and S. Stachowitsch (2013) 'The problem of PMSCs or PMSCs as a problem? Reflections of gender scholarship and the legitimization of violence in private security', Annual Convention of the International Studies Association (ISA), San Francisco, 3–6 April.

Kempa, M. and A. M. Singh (2008) 'Private security, political economy and the policing of race. Probing global hypotheses through the case of South Africa', *Theoretical Criminology*, 12(3): 333–54.

Kinsey, C. (2007) *Corporate Soldiers and International Security: The Rise of Private Military Security*, London: Routledge.

Krahmann, E. (2010) *States, Citizens and the Privatisation of Security*, Cambridge: Cambridge University Press.

Leander, A. (2010) 'The paradoxical impunity of private military security companies: authority and the limits to legal accountability', *Security Dialogue*, 41(5): 467–90.

— (2012) 'What do codes of conduct do? Hybrid constitutionalization and militarization in military markets', *Global Constitutionalism*, 1(1): 91–119.

Lippert, R. and D. O'Connor (2003) 'Security assemblages: airport security, flexible work, and liberal governance', *Alternatives: Global, Local, Political*, 28(3): 331–58.

Lisle, D. (2013) 'Energizing the international', in M Acuto and S. Curtis (eds), *Reassembling International Theory: Assemblage Thinking and International Relations*, London: Palgrave Macmillan.

Lutz, C. (2006) 'Empire is in the details', *American Ethnologist*, 33(4): 593–611.

Minnaar, A. (2005) 'Private–public partnerships: private security, crime prevention and policing in South Africa', *ACTA Criminologica*, 18(1): 85–114.

Minnaar, A. and P. Ngoveni (2004) 'The relationship between the South African police service and the private security industry: any role for outsourcing in the prevention of crime?', *ACTA Criminologica*,17(1): 42–65.

Onuoha, F. (2009) 'Sea piracy and maritime security in the Horn of Africa: the Somali Coast and Gulf of Aden in perspective', *African Security Review*, 18(3): 31–44.

Pattison, J. (2010) 'Deeper objections to the privatisation of military force', *Journal of Political Philosophy*, 18(4): 425–47.

Percy, S. (2006) *Regulating the Private Security Industry*, Adelphi Paper 384, London: Routledge.

— (2007) *Mercenaries: The history of a norm in International Relations*, Oxford: Oxford University Press.

Richards, L. (2006) *Corporate Mercenaries. The threat of private military and security companies*, London: War on Want.

Sassen, S. (2013) 'The carpenter and the bricoleur. A conversation with Saskia Sassen and Aihwa Ong', in M. Acuto and S. Curtis (eds), *Reassembling International Theory: Assemblage Thinking and International Relations*, London: Palgrave Macmillan.

Schouten, P. (2014) 'Security as controversy: reassembling security at Amsterdam Airport', *Security Dialogue*, 45(1): 23–42.

Singer, P. W. (2003) *Corporate Warriors*, Ithaca, NY: Cornell University Press.

Srnicek, N. (2013) 'Cognitive assemblages and the production of knowledge', in M. Acuto and S. Curtis (eds), *Reassembling International Theory: Assemblage Thinking and International Relations*, London: Palgrave Macmillan.

Stachowitsch, S. (2013) 'Military privatization and the remasculinization of the state: making the link between the outsourcing of military security and gendered state transformation', *International Relations*, 27(1): 74–94.

Vrasti, W. (2008) 'The strange case of ethnography and international relations', *Millennium: Journal of International Studies*, 37(2): 279–301.

1 | Golden assemblages: security and development in Tanzania's gold mines

Rita Abrahamsen and Michael Williams

In May 2011, five young men were killed by police at African Barrick Gold's North Mara mine in Tanzania, following an intrusion by artisanal miners and local people onto the company site. The incident generated significant national and international attention and concern, placing the security practices of one of the world's major gold-mining corporations under intense scrutiny. In response to the incident, ABG increased both hard and soft security measures at all of its Tanzanian operations. A three-metre-high security wall, complete with razor wire, now surrounds many of the company's concessions, and a raft of enhanced security measures seeks to exclude the neighbouring communities as well as potential 'intruders' from the mines. Yet at the same time, ABG expanded its community development programmes, and international NGOs, community leaders and non-state policing actors are now part of a strategy that seeks to achieve security through development and community engagement.

This chapter treats ABG's evolving security strategies as a paradigmatic example of novel global security assemblages that are emerging across Africa and the developing world. The concept of the global security assemblage has emerged as a powerful image and a productive methodology for analysing contemporary security landscapes (see Abrahamsen and Williams 2009, 2011; Berndtsson and Stern 2011). In contrast to more conventional approaches, an assemblage perspective does not frame private, non-state security actors in opposition to state authority and the public provision of security. Instead it focuses on the multiplicity of actors, the different forms of power and resources available to them, and the manner in which they come together in a contingent whole to exercise powerful effects in specific sites. This makes global security assemblages a particularly useful lens for exploring security provision and governance in complex fragile environments where the centrality of the state cannot not be taken for granted, and where plurality of security actors is nothing new but where the context and conditions of their existence are changing and interacting with novel, global dynamics.

Few places evince this plurality and globality more strikingly than resource extraction sites in Africa. While frequently remote from capital cities and major urban centres, in these zones the local and the everyday are nevertheless always already global by virtue of resource extraction's relationship with assemblages that inhabit local settings but are stretched across national boundaries in terms of actors, knowledges, technologies, norms and values. Because extraction frequently takes place in conflictual and highly unequal environments, security is at a premium and a plethora of security actors come to coexist, cooperate and compete in the delivery and governance of security. Resource extraction sites are also places where multiple norms and values come to clash; profit motives exist side by side with demands for local development, security logics rub shoulders with community relations discourses. As we argue in this chapter, it is the dynamic interactions of these multiple and varied actors, norms and transformations that explain the novel global security assemblages that are emerging in contemporary resource extraction sites. As exemplified by ABG's gold mines in Tanzania, these assemblages not only incorporate the traditional security providers such as the public police, private security companies and in-house security specialists, but also a range of development specialists, human rights educators and local community leaders. They represent the coming together of a plethora of different actors, norms, agendas and interests – some local, some global, some public and some private – in close but often tension-filled relationships. They give rise to new security institutions, practices and forms of cooperation and conflict, while simultaneously serving to ensure and facilitate the continuation of resource extraction in complex fragile environments.

Theorizing global security assemblages

To set the scene for the ensuing analysis of ABG and the other chapters in this volume, we begin with a brief exploration of the concept of global security assemblages and of assemblage thinking more generally.[1] This is no simple task, as there is no unified or single assemblage theory or methodology. Instead assemblage thinking is diverse and dispersed, having emerged from a range of different disciplines and scholarly traditions (see Acuto and Curtis 2014). This said, its various forms can all be said to proceed from a similar starting point, namely a dissatisfaction with the dominant ontologies that have informed social theory, including anthropology, political science, sociology and International Relations. Over time these disciplines have come to operate with more or less well-established theories that see the world as consisting of a range of discrete units or objects: the state, the nation, the city; or capitalism, religion, science, etc. When studying the global, the nation-state is generally approached as a unit that contains society, which in turn is separate from the unit of the international or the global. Assemblage thinking rejects such fixed and stable ontologies, and replaces essentialism and reification with a flat ontology. It does not, in other words, predetermine the units or categories that make up the world, but instead treats every social formation or 'unit' as consisting of complex assemblages of different elements and seeks to discover how elements of many different kinds come together to function as systems or contingent wholes.

Assemblage approaches are thus relational; the focus is on provisional and historically contingent relations between elements, both human and non-human, rather than totalities and reified units of analysis (Latour 2007; Bueger 2014). This entails a recognition of change and difference, as relations are not fixed and stable, nor are they always and everywhere the same. Categories like the state or society cannot therefore be defined by their substance or essential properties, but are constituted by the multiple and diverse relations that make them function together as a system or an assemblage. In this way, substantivist modes of thought give way to a relational approach, where it is the specific relations within each particular configuration that give access to and insights into the object of analysis, not any predetermined or inherent properties.

The relations and elements that make up the assemblage are not only human, but also non-human or material. In contrast to most conventional social science methods where the material world provides a passive context within which individuals and people act, here the material is seen to interact with people in producing the social world. Physical objects, cultural artifacts, technologies, ideas and so on are thus considered as active, formative parts of the assemblage. An assemblage discussion of security must therefore pay attention not only to the agency of human actors like the police, the army and the private security guards, but also the various technologies – barbed wire, fences, surveillance devices, site designs, etc. – as well as the ideas, norms and values that inform and stimulate actors and actions. The assemblage consists of the interactions and co-functioning of all these various elements.

Importantly, these interactions can be simultaneously local, national and global, and in this sense assemblage thinking is multi-scalar. Breaking with the conventional social science terminology of 'levels of analysis', the local, the national and the international are not stacked one on top of the other as discrete spheres or separate spaces, nor is the 'macro' any more important or real than the 'micro', or vice versa (see DeLanda 2006). Instead, different elements within the same assemblage can inhabit either the local or the global, or both simultaneously. The local, in other words, is multi-scalar and need not necessarily run through the national to function at the global level. By the same token, the global is not simply imposed in a top-down manner on the local, but is partly produced in articulation with local dynamics. As Sassen (2006) has observed, the global is in important ways constituted inside the national, and globalization erodes traditional spatial divisions and gives rise to new assemblages that both territorialize and deterritorialize. Thus, a resource extraction site in Tanzania, Ghana or South Africa is a local setting or entity, infused with local traditions, norms and relationships, but it is simultaneously part of global markets and global discourses and normativities. In this way, assemblages can at one and the same time mark new territories, spaces and boundaries (of, for example, security governance) and deterritorialize or rescale by eroding or destabilizing existing spaces or spheres of authority (of, for example, the nation-state or national justice). An assemblage is accordingly not wholly determined by its location within national settings but is instead indicative of the formation of new geographies of power that can only be grasped by approaching the social world as one analytical field rather than a series of neatly divided levels of analysis marked by international boundaries.

Taken together these key features have made assemblage thinking a productive technique for challenging accepted theories, categories and understandings and for capturing change, fluidity and the emergence of new institutions, practices and forms of authority. In discussions of security and security privatization, the concept of the global security assemblage has proved particularly instructive in drawing attention to the deficiencies of accounts that proceed from a strict Weberian definition of the state and highlighting instead transformations, differences and contestations in how security is delivered and governed. Two shortcomings of such accounts are worth highlighting in this context. First, most conventional analyses of contemporary security privatization depart from a conception of the state as possessing a monopoly on the legitimate use of force. While there is much to commend this starting point, it simultaneously risks blinding us to deeper structural transformations of the state and the relationship between the public and the private, the global and the local. Approached from a statist perspective, the growth of private and non-state security actors must necessarily come at the expense of the power and authority of national public actors, giving rise to two possible sets of interpretations. In the most pessimistic scenario, the state is losing its sovereignty and authority, heralding the end to any notion of public safety and the public good. This has been a particularly influential narrative in discussions of security privatization in Africa, where non-state security provision is often seen as both cause and effect of state weakness and state failure. In a more optimistic scenario, the state is not necessarily losing power, but outsourcing and sharing it with the private, be it through networked governance, multilevel governance, rule at a distance or partnerships with non-state actors. In both interpretations, however, the basic nature of the state remains unaltered – it might be weaker or stronger, it might share power and authority, but as a basic unit, category or assumption it remains unchanged or ontologically intact, as do the distinctions between the public and the private, the global and the local.

A focus on how security provision and governance are assembled in particular locations, however, reveals much more profound and diverse transformations that cannot be adequately captured in a vocabulary that speaks only in terms of a weaker or stronger state. Instead the multiple processes of security privatization give rise to new security relationships, institutions, practices and authority, and the construction of the state proceeds apace with – and in relationships with – a multitude of other actors within global security assemblages. These assemblages inhabit specific local and national settings but they are simultaneously stretched globally across territorial divides, and the state is being assembled, or reassembled, not from scratch, but in ways that alter and challenge many preconceived notions of the public/private and the global/local divides (see Abrahamsen and Williams 2011). In this way, the notion of the global security assemblage allows us to make visible the complexity and specificity of contemporary security provision and governance, and this in turn can allow us to theorize the state, state formation and security anew.

Second, unlike analyses that proceed from a strict Weberian conception of the state, a focus on the assembly of security acknowledges that assemblages are almost infinitely diverse. Rather that starting from the assumption that the state is always and everywhere the same, the approach opens up the possibility that the state and the security field might be differently assembled in different places, and as such it is not only more sensitive to place and specificity, but also allows for a deeper understanding of the politics of security and the forces and histories that produce different global security assemblages. In this sense assemblage thinking is associated with a critical stance regarding the social world. It embodies an ethos that is sensitive to difference and heterogeneity, and this places it in opposition to the more familiar social science methodology of comparison. Whereas comparative methodology proceeds from established categories and units of analysis, an assemblage methodology entails a more open-ended exploration or an 'experimental realism oriented towards process of composition' (Anderson et al. 2012: 171). Unlike the variables of comparative social sciences, in assemblage thinking there are no a priori claims about the order of social formations. Instead, these are to be discovered through careful tracing of the processes by which specific orders emerge and endure (ibid.). Methodologically and politically, this makes it possible to account for difference and multiplicity, while avoiding the often implicit universalism and Eurocentrism of most comparative approaches, where difference often becomes a code word for some kind of deviance from a norm (see Hagmann and Hoehne 2009).

This attention to difference and change makes global security assemblages particularly useful for examining security in so-called 'failed' or 'fragile' states and environments. While there is no denying that some states are more capable of protecting their citizens than others, approaching the issue from the prior claim of what the state is or should be may blind us to the different processes through which social and political (dis)orders are actually assembled. Such an approach is likely to find institutions and practices that fail to fit the Weberian model wanting, pathologizing them as deviant forms of an ideal, instead of focusing on the possibility that states can be differently assembled in different places and emerge from different processes at different times. An assemblage approach can also help make visible the global processes that shape seemingly discrete national and local institutions, capturing the specificity of states by 'de-abstracting' them and theorizing from the ground up, without a prior, implied standard or norm. In this sense, assemblage thinking allows us to escape the comparative trap and sustain a more open, experimental and yet concrete and detailed orientation towards the social world.

Analysing global security assemblages accordingly calls for empirically grounded theory: that is, a careful analysis of how different security actors, discourse, values, technologies, and so on, are assembled and brought together in different localities. Tracing such global security assemblages frequently involves both attention to global transformations and detailed engagement with specific localities and the relationships between humans, discourses, technologies and all manner of ideational and material elements. It requires attention to seemingly mundane, everyday practices that serve to make assemblages function together and that ground, for example, global discourses, values and technologies in local settings. Such ethnographic investigations will likely show that the local is not simply the passive recipient or victim of global dynamics and actants, nor completely disconnected from the global, however seemingly 'remote' the location (see Piot 1999). Instead the local translates, adapts and modifies global dynamics, and in this way the local is productive and the global is shaped and articulated through interactions with localities.

The remainder of this chapter draws on these insights to show how security provision and governance in Africa's resource extraction sites are best analysed and understood from a global assemblage perspective. Centred on ABG's Buzwagi gold mine in Tanzania, it shows how this assemblage draws together a multiplicity of actors in response to evolving security challenges and changing global norms and discourses concerning Corporate Social Responsibility, human rights and development. The result is the emergence of novel security institutions, practices and forms of security governance, in a global security assemblage that marks important transformations in the relationship between security and development, and the relationship between states, multinationals and development organizations.

Widening security, expanding the assemblage

Africa's resource extraction sites are in many ways paradoxical; frequently remote and enclaved, they are simultaneously deeply integrated into the global economy. Frequently surrounded by poverty, deprivation and relatively voiceless populations, they are hypermodern displays of abundance, technology and connectivity. In part for these reasons, resource extraction is often conflictual, with local populations contesting their exclusion from the wealth derived from their soil, development and human rights organizations arguing for more inclusive and just practices, and transnational companies and governments concerned to ensure continued commercial activity and profitability.

This makes extraction sites particularly salient locations for the study of global security assemblages. Not only are these sites where a multiplicity of local and global security actors come together to provide and govern security, they are also the location for novel technological arrangements as well as numerous normative discourses and social strategies concerning business, development and human rights. In today's business environment, Corporate Social Responsibility has become a competitive necessity for many transnational companies, with campaigners, shareholders and consumers pressing for greater social accountability and respect for human rights in business relations (Avant and Haufler 2014). Such pressures have been particularly strong in the extractive sector, where abuses of human rights by security forces have been frequent (Viego Rating 2011; PRI 2015). At the same time, resource extraction – if responsibly managed and governed – has been identified by the World Bank, bilateral donors and African governments as a route to development and growth (see Campbell 2003; World Bank 2003; Africa Progress Panel 2013). This multiplicity of actors, interests and agendas is crucial to understanding the emergence of novel global security assemblages across African resource extraction sites.

African Barrick Gold (ABG) in Tanzania provides a good illustration of these broader dynamics, and their particular articulation with local settings.[2] While Tanzania is a peaceful country, mining activities have frequently encountered local resistance. There are numerous reasons for this, one being competition between artisanal miners and multinational corporations, another the prevailing sense that local populations receive few benefits and ample discomforts from mining operations (see Lange 2011; Revenue Watch Institute 2013). Since the mid-1990s the country has promoted resource extraction as a route to development and growth, and the mining sector's contribution to GDP more than tripled in the period to 2012 (Revenue Watch Institute 2013). Today Tanzania is Africa's third-largest gold producer, after South Africa and Ghana, and in 2011 the value of mineral exports reached $2.1 billion, more than 95 per cent of which came from six gold mines (ibid.). Yet even after the adoption of a new mining law in 2010 the royalties on gold and other precious metals are a meagre 4 per cent, and approximately 30 per cent of the population live below the poverty line.

In 2012 Tanzania was one of the first African countries to join the Extractive Industries Transparency Initiative (EITI), an initiative designed to improve transparency and hence ensure that government income derived from resource extraction is used for public development rather than private benefit. Despite its early membership, however, Tanzania has been severely criticized both by domestic civil society organizations and international NGOs for the lack of transparency and accountability in the management of its mineral wealth, and especially for failing to translate export earnings into benefits for local communities near the mines (Lange 2011; Revenue Watch Institute 2013). The country received a weak score on the Resource Governance Index in 2013, ranking 27 out of 58, in large part because of the opaque nature of contract negotiations with multinational companies and the lack of a freedom of information law. In September 2015 Tanzania was suspended from the EITI after failing to submit its 2012/13 report on time.

At first glance, the prevailing sense of local exclusion and social injustice goes a long way towards explaining the security arrangements at ABG's three Tanzanian gold mines. In many ways, arrangements at the Bugwazi, Bulyanhulu and North Mara mines appear classic cases of fortress or enclave security, focused on exclusion and perimeter defence. Indeed, to the extent possible, the concessions are surrounded by a three-metre-high concrete wall, drawing a prison-like barrier between the company on the inside and the local communities on the outside.[3] There is, however, much more to these security strategies than first meets the eye; this is a complex and evolving global security assemblage that consists of a range of different actors, with different normativities, objectives and forms of power.

The events that took place at ABG's North Mara mine on 16 May 2011 provide an instructive entry point for unpacking the evolving dynamics of this global security assemblage. On this day, as on almost every other day prior to the building of the perimeter wall, large groups of villagers and migrant artisanal miners had entered the concession to search the massive piles of waste rock for small amounts of leftover gold. On most days, the artisanal miners would be allowed onto the concession, reflecting informal arrangements with the mine and Tanzanian police assigned to control the perimeter. But on 16 May, the police opened fire as a large group of people, perhaps as many as 1,500, entered the concessions, killing at least five and injuring many more. The exact circumstances of the shootings are unclear and contested, especially as regards ABG's culpability and legal responsibility for the actions of a national police force assigned to protect its assets. What is certain, however, is that the company confronted an unprecedented security and public relations crisis, and a barrage of international criticism and intensified scrutiny of its operations and practices.[4]

In response Barrick Gold embarked on a significant review and restructuring of its security strategy.[5] Parts of this strategy involved traditional, 'hard' dimensions of security; the three-metre-high security walls, complete with barbed wire, being its most striking and visible outcome. But at the same time the company was forced to recognize the limits of a primarily exclusionary and coercive security approach. The shootings at the North Mara mine demonstrated that a narrow, coercive security strategy risked backfiring, increasing rather than reducing the company's conflictual relations with the local communities. The shootings also highlighted the company's ambiguous and dangerous relationship with the Tanzanian police over security practices and the use of force, and the resulting international criticism demonstrated the reputational risks and potential damage to shareholder and government relations that could follow from allegations of human rights abuses. Both security and commercial logics thus pushed the company towards revising its security strategy, combining 'hard' security measures with 'softer' development and community relations programmes.

As a result, the security arrangements at ABG mines now include the usual suspects of an in-house security department and a global private security company, Group4Securicor.[6] At the Buzwagi mine, the in-house security force comprises 250 guards, complemented by 60 G4S personnel, reduced from 85 after the building of the perimeter wall. While the G4S contingent is unarmed, the in-house security force is issued with firearms and strategically placed around the concessions. At night they patrol heavily armed, wearing body armour, and accompanied by guard dogs. The Tanzanian police are now strikingly absent from the security arrangements and the mining concessions. Following the events of May 2011, ABG is reluctant to trust the police. The company has negotiated a Memorandum of Understanding (MoU) with the police at each concession, restricting their access to the mine site and requiring them to use minimum force and comply with international standards on human rights and the use of force. To facilitate this, ABG is providing human rights training to the Tanzanian police, thus seeking to avoid future abuses and violations. The human rights training started after Barrick Gold – belatedly – became the first Canadian mining company to sign the Voluntary Principles on Security and Human Rights, an international set of guidelines for the extractive industries.[7] The Principles oblige signatories to investigate and report any credible information about human rights abuses at their workplaces, and ABG now provide human rights training not only to the police but to all employees and security forces involved with security at and around the concessions. By 2013, more than six thousand individuals had received training under this programme and all security officers on the concessions carry cards reminding them of the need to respect human rights and the conditions under which force can be used. The police assigned to protect the concession are also provided with food, accommodation and transport, the latter enabling ABG to exercise some control over their movements and operations.

Alongside these usual suspects, ABG's security strategy now involves a series of more surprising actors and elements. The company's security review not only resulted in a significantly expanded community relations department and the appointment of a community relations manager, working alongside the security manager, but also the hiring of an NGO to work with local communities on ABG's behalf.[8] Specializing in conflict resolution and conflict prevention, the US-based NGO Search for Common Ground (SFCG) has since 2011 been tasked by ABG to improve community relations and facilitate peaceful and constructive communication between ABG and local communities. To this end, NGO staff conduct human rights training with communities surrounding the three mine sites, and run various conflict management sessions with youth and women. The NGO also support regular so-called 'multi-stakeholder' meetings between ABG, local government, village leaders and community members, and provide training on the Voluntary Principles and on human rights to the police. The function of SFCG thus straddles the domains of security and development, as well as the commercial and not-for-profit sectors, and as such the NGO's work with ABG is paradigmatic of an expanded security strategy that seeks to increase security in part through development, community relations and partnerships with a wide range of actors.

Another relative new feature of ABG's security arrangements is the Sungusungu; local, informal community police forces or 'vigilantes' that have a quasi-legal status in rural Tanzania.[9] ABG now liaises with chiefs from surrounding villages, who take turns in organizing and providing patrols for the outer perimeter of the concession. In return the Sungusungu receive a modest compensation, as well as human rights training. Their participation in security patrols, however, is as much a community relations strategy as a security strategy: it provides some employment for local villagers, compensating for the fact that the mines otherwise require mostly skilled labour and hence employ very few local people. It provides some opportunity for interaction and dialogue with local communities, as well as access to information and local intelligence about security issues.

Despite these revisions to ABG's security strategy since the violent incidents of May 2011, its operations remain conflictual and contentious, as do those of many other mining enterprises in Tanzania. In 2014, as many as ten people were killed by police and security forces around the North Mara mine and at Buzwagi civil society organizations are protesting against damage to their houses from explosions at the mine, as well as against environmental damage (Schneider 2014; York 2014). In the UK, where ABG has corporate offices, the All Party Parliamentary Group on international Corporate Social Responsibility has expressed severe concern over continued violence at North Mara, claiming that sixteen people have been killed by the police in the last six years (McVeigh 2014). Following claims against ABG at the London high court by the British law firm Leigh Day, the company has agreed to an out-of-court settlement for several victims of violence at the North Mara mine in 2008 (Vidal 2015). Accordingly, it is important to emphasize that the point of our discussion is not to suggest the success (or failure) of ABG's security strategy, but rather to analyse the actors, dynamics and politics that inform these transformed security strategies and the resulting global security assemblages.

Transformation, contestation and difference

The concept of the global security assemblage has proved instructive in drawing attention to the deficiencies of security analyses that proceed from a strict Weberian definition of the state, highlighting instead transformations, differences and contestations in how contemporary security is delivered and governed. This can be seen clearly in the case of the security assemblages at ABG's gold mines in Tanzania, and this closing section is dedicated to an elaboration of these three themes of transformation, contestation and difference and their multi-scalar instantiations.

The global security assemblages at ABG's Tanzanian operations are far from static, but have undergone significant transformations since the violence of 2011. These transformations have brought together a multiplicity of diverse actors, values, norms and technologies that function as a contingent whole, irreducible to a single centre or common logic. Capturing these transformations requires attention to numerous pressures and dynamics, both at the global and the local levels. In particular, they can be traced to the numerous initiatives to join 'business and human rights' and promote a more ethical business environment, spearheaded by multilateral organizations like the UN, various coalitions of multinational companies, governments and NGOs, as well as local activists and protests in poor countries like Tanzania. The resource sector, because of its notoriety as an abuser of human rights, has been a key target of such campaigns, and the pressure for CSR and a more development-oriented extractive sector has opened the door for new partnerships between multinational companies, NGOs and governments. The result at mine sites like Buzwagi is a particular blend of corporate business strategies and development agendas, conjugated with security logics.

The reformed security strategy by no means reflects a simple 'normative' shift or a moral awakening; it arises equally from the failure of purely coercive security strategies and from the realization that security failures (as in the case of North Mara) can have severe implications not only for the company's public image, but also for the bottom line. Put differently, hard-nosed business interests are also behind the change in security approach. For this reason, the new security strategies cannot be dismissed as simply empty rhetoric. While we must always mind the gap between declaration and reality – and reality on the ground rarely looks as one-dimensional as in glossy corporate brochures – these new approaches nevertheless mark substantial transformations in corporate security practices. More important for the argument we are making here, they provide the basis for novel global security assemblages. In order to ensure continued operations and profitability, these security assemblages draw development and community actors that are often informed by different values and normativities to those that have traditionally dominated the sector.

In the past, the extractive industries have generally been the adversaries of NGOs; the villains in stories of underdevelopment, exploitation, resource curse, conflict minerals and environmental degradation. Today, by contrast, NGOs are increasingly partnering with resources companies, providing community liaisons, delivering development programmes, and suggesting that they can provide the bridge between the pursuit of corporate profit and broad-based development. SFCG's relationship with ABG is far from unique. The company has another partnership with White Ribbon, an NGO that works to prevent gender-based violence, and many other NGOs such as International Alert, PACT and Care International Canada have partnered with major multinational extractive companies. The results are complex global assemblages centred on security but with a strong normative emphasis on development and human rights. The actors and the forms of power that interact and compete within these assemblages are historically contingent, traceable to multiple dynamics that span the global and the local. They give rise not only to new security practices and institutions, such as human rights training and community dialogues, but also to new forms of competition and contestation.

It is easy to see that the resource companies have much to gain from bringing NGOs into their security arrangements. According to the 2014 Edelman Trust Barometer, NGOs are the world's most trusted institutions – for the seventh year in a row.[10] Dubbed the 'new super brands' (Wooliff and Deri 2001), NGOs can give much-maligned corporations a more developmental, humanitarian face vis-à-vis communities, shareholders and concerned publics. In corporate terms, they come cheap. Yet for these security strategies to function effectively, NGOs must retain a substantial distance from direct control by the company, since their legitimacy as agents of development – and thus their effectiveness as community security actors – depends upon not being seen simply as tools of corporate agendas. This creates complex tensions and challenges within the assemblage: the mining company finances the activities of not-for-profit actors that it does not (and cannot) directly control and yet needs to manage, and NGO actors depend upon the company for contracts for their activities, yet must retain considerable autonomy over those activities.

These tensions are intensified by the fact that in many ways the stakes for NGOs within the assemblage are higher than those for the mining company. On the one hand, partnering with extractive industries provides an alternative source of income at a time when public funding is decreasing and development policy has eagerly embraced 'public–private partnerships'. In an increasingly competitive NGO world, corporations provide an alternative revenue stream, and one that is frequently more long-term than government funding. There is thus a clear political economy to the 'NGO scramble' for shrinking resources (Cooley and Ron 2002), and as one of our interviewees put it, 'corporate partnerships are the future'. On the other hand, partnering with resource companies poses a risk to the reputation of NGOs as trusted and value-driven institutions. By working with and for corporations, being paid by them to improve security and company–community relations, NGOs come to occupy a different position. In terms of security, the result might well be a move towards more humane strategies that are more respectful of human rights and more conducive to development, but it nevertheless draws NGOs as development actors into global assemblages centred on security.[11] Within ABG, for instance, the partnership with SFCG has involved a not always easy attempt to coordinate the new development and community initiatives with the more traditional, exclusionary security practices.

This new form of contestation is instructive; one of the key insights arising from research on global security assemblages has been the problematic nature of the public/private distinction, and the manner in which this distinction is not only historically and geographically contingent, but also a symbolic distinction bestowing forms of capital on actors involved in struggles over who has the right to provide and govern in the security field (see Abrahamsen and Williams 2011). Our analysis here draws attention to another problematic distinction, but one that operates within the private, between the corporate and the benevolent, indicating how the domain of the private is not only historically contingent but is also an arena of struggle between actors over the legitimate forms of capital required to act authoritatively in specific fields. Contemporary global security assemblages are thus rearticulating the distinction between the corporate and the benevolent.

The global security assemblage at ABG's gold mines also points towards important forms of contestation between the public and the private. As mentioned, ABG has negotiated an MoU with the police at all its mine sites, preventing them from entering the concessions and seeking to control their use of force in the communities surrounding the mines through guidelines and human rights training. At the same time, the Tanzanian public police retain the legitimate monopoly on force, and the company's ability to influence their decisions and practices is limited to strategies of discipline (human rights training) and avoidance (preventing them from entering the concessions). New forms of public/private contestation are also emerging along the lines of the formal police and the informal Sungusungu. While the former is strikingly absent from ABG's security, the latter is arguably being empowered and gaining legitimacy, albeit in a relatively small way, by their incorporation into the security strategies of a multinational company. By receiving training, compensation and a limited role in security provision, the Sungusungu are a local anchor point for global discourses of inclusive security strategies. They are, in other words, one of the ways in which the global is translated and produced by the local, drawing attention to the multi-scalar existence of the security assemblage.

At the time of our fieldwork, it was still too early to tell how the contestation between the formal and informal policy would evolve, and what the effects would be for security, politics and social relations. The relative absence of the public police and the presence of an informal policing agent in the global security assemblage, however, provide a clear illustration of our final point; namely the importance of recognizing that security can be differently assembled at different times and in different places. While more state-centric analyses of security would expect to find (and/or seek to place) the public at the heart of security provision and governance, our investigation of how security is assembled seeks instead to understand how this specific security situation emerged, how (in)security and (dis)order are established, and with what consequences. Historically, of course, the state's monopoly on security in Africa has arguably always been more real in theory than in practice, reflecting in part the colonial origin of the state and its police forces. Paradoxically, however, the growing exclusion of the police from ABG's security arrangements has been reinforced at a time when global development discourses and practices otherwise seek to strengthen states and the centrality of their security apparatuses. As such, our analysis shows not only the multiple, and often contradictory, influences of the global, but also its complicity in the production of what is often referred to as weak or failed states. It underscores the need for empirically grounded theory to capture how security and insecurity are assembled in real places, and what forms of power and authority inform and underpin different global security assemblages.

In the specific case of ABG's Tanzanian gold mines, as well as at numerous other extraction sites across Africa and the developing world, novel global security assemblages are evolving as a result of multiple transformations, both globally and locally. Resource extraction sites are places where opposing norms and values collide, and this is increasingly so as a profit-hungry extractive industry is subjected to growing pressures to do business in a just and socially responsible manner. As the distinctions between the values of business and the values of development have narrowed, new actors have been drawn into security strategies, resulting in new struggles and contestations over the meaning of both security and development. In the process, practices and institutions of security are being reshaped, imbued with a 'softer' developmental touch, but never entirely devoid of their 'harder' coercive potential.

Acknowledgement

Research for this chapter was supported by the Social Sciences Research Council of Canada, grant number 410-2010-2121.

Notes

1 This section draws on Abrahamsen and Williams (2011: ch. 3) and Abrahamsen (2016).

2 At the time of our fieldwork and the events discussed here, ABG was majority-owned by the Canadian company Barrick Gold, one of the world's largest gold companies. In November 2014 ABG changed its name to Acacia Mining, but it is still 64 per cent owned by the Canadian gold giant. Acacia Mining operates three mines in Tanzania, and has further explorations in Tanzania, Kenya and Burkina Faso. For the sake of clarity we refer to the company as ABG throughout the chapter, despite the name change.

3 Owing to the size, terrain and location of the concessions, completely surrounding the mine sites is impossible, much as the company might desire it. This is especially true at North Mara.

4 For a good account of the May 2011 events at North Mara, see York (2011).

5 Interviews; see also Barrick Gold Corporation (n.d).

6 The fieldwork for this section was undertaken at the Buzwagi mine, but the general structure of ABG's security strategies is the same across their three Tanzanian mines.

7 The company has subsequently played an increasingly active role in the initiative.

8 For an overview of the company's investments in community projects, see the website of Acacia Mining (www.acaciamining.com).

9 On the origins and activities of the Sungusungu, see Abrahams (1987) and Heald (2002).

10 www.edelman.com/insights/intellectual-property/2014-edelman-trust-barometer/.

11 In a different context, Joachim and Schneiker (2015) have noted how NGOs find it increasingly difficult to criticize private security companies.

Bibliography

Abrahams, R. (1987) 'Sungusungu: village vigilante groups in Tanzania', *African Affairs*, 86(343): 179–96.

Abrahamsen, R. (2016) 'Global assemblages', in G. Xavier and P. Bilgin (eds), *Handbook of International Political Sociology*, London: Sage.

Abrahamsen, R. and M. C. Williams (2009) 'Security beyond the state: global security assemblages in international politics', *International Political Sociology*, 3(1): 1–17.

— (2011) *Security beyond the State: Private Security in International Politics*, Cambridge: Cambridge University Press.

Acuto, M. and S. Curtis (eds) (2014) *Reassembling International Theory: Assemblage Thinking and International Relations*, London: Palgrave Macmillan.

Africa Progress Panel (2013) *Equity in Extractives: Stewarding Africa's Natural Resources for All*, Africa Progress Report 2013, www.africaprogresspanel.org/wp-content/uploads/2013/08/2013_APR_Equity_in_Extractives_25062013_ENG_HR.pdf, accessed 1 December 2015.

Anderson, B., M. Kearnes, C. McFarlane and D. Swanton (2012) 'On assemblages and geography', *Dialogues in Human Geography*, 2(2): 171–89.

Avant, D. and V. Haufler (2014) 'The dynamics of private security practices and their public consequences: transnational organizations in historical perspective', in J. Best and A. Gheciu (eds), *The Return of the Public in Global Governance*, Cambridge: Cambridge University Press.

Barrick Goold Corporation (n.d.) *Barrick Security Management System*, s1.q4cdn.com/808035602/files/security/Barrick-Security-Management-System.pdf, accessed 1 December 2015.

Berndtsson, J. and M. Stern (2011) 'Private security and the public–private divide: contested lines of distinction and modes of governance in the Stockholm-Arlanda security assemblage', *International Political Sociology*, 5(4): 408–25.

Bueger, C. (2014) 'Thinking assemblages methodological: some rules of thumb', in M. Acuto and S. Curtis (eds), *Re-assembling International Theory. Assemblage Thinking and International Relations*, Palgrave Macmillan, pp. 60–68.

Campbell, B. (2003) 'Factoring in governance is not enough: mining codes in Africa, policy reform and corporate responsibility', *Minerals and Energy – Raw Materials Report*, 18(3): 2–13.

Cooley, A. and J. Ron (2002) 'The NGO scramble: organizational insecurity and the political economy of transnational action', *International Security*, 27(1): 5–39.

DeLanda, M. (2006) *A New Philosophy of Society: Assemblage Theory and Social Complexity*, London: Continuum.

Hagmann, T and M. V. Hoehne (2009) 'Failures of the state failure debate: evidence from the Somali territories', *Journal of International Development*, 21(1): 42–57.

Heald, S. (2002) 'Domesticating Leviathan: Sungusungu groups in Tanzania', Paper presented at the DESTIN/Crisis States Programme seminar, London, 17 May.

Joachim, J. and A. Schneiker (2015) 'NGOs and the price of governance: the trade-offs between regulating and criticizing private military and security companies', *Critical Military Studies*, 1(3): 185–201.

Lange, S. (2011) 'Gold and governance: legal injustices and lost opportunities in Tanzania', *African Affairs*, 110(439): 233–52.

Latour, B. (2007) *Reassembling the Social*, Oxford: Oxford University Press.

McVeigh, T. (2014) 'Killings at UK-owned gold mine in Tanzania alarm MPs', *Guardian*, 19 July, www.theguardian.com/world/2014/jul/19/killings-uk-owned-gold-mine-tanzania-concern, accessed 1 December 2015.

Piot, C. (1999) *Remotely Global. Village Modernity in West Africa*, Chicago, IL: University of Chicago Press.

PRI (2015) 'Human rights and the extractive industry: why engage, who to engaged, how to engage, principles for responsible investment', UNDP Finance Initiative, 2xjmlj8428u1a2k5034l1m71.wpengine.netdna-cdn.com/wp-content/uploads/PRI_Human-rights-extractive-industry_part01.pdf, accessed 1 December 2015.

Revenue Watch Institute (2013) 'The Resource Governance Index: Tanzania', www.resourcegovernance.org/countries/africa/tanzania/overview, accessed 17 November 2015.

Sassen, S. (2006) *Territory, Authority, Rights: From Medieval to Global Assemblages*, Princeton, NJ: Princeton University Press.

Schneider, V. (2014) 'Tanzania's gold rush and housing crush', Al Jazeera News, 20 January, www.aljazeera.com/indepth/features/2014/01/tanzania-gold-rush-housing-crush-201412011841529140.html, accessed 1 December 2015.

Vidal, J. (2015) 'British gold mining firm agrees settlement over deaths of Tanzanian villagers', *Guardian*, 10 February, www.theguardian.com/environment/2015/feb/10/british-gold-mining-settlement-deaths-tanzanian-villagers, accessed 1 December 2015.

Viego Rating (2011) 'The CSR challenges facing the extractive industries in weak governance zones', Transparanecy International France, www.vigeo.com/csr-rating-agency/images/PDF/Publications/vigeo_extractive%20industry_en.pdf, accessed 1 December 2015.

Wooliff, J. and C. Deri (2001) 'NGOs: the new super brands', *Corporate Reputation Review*, 4(2): 157–64.

World Bank (2003) *Striking a Better*

Balance. The Extractive Industries Review, Washington, DC: World Bank.

York, G. (2011) 'Blood and stone: extreme capitalism at Barrick's North Mara mine', *Globe and Mail Report on Business Magazine*, 29 September, www.theglobeandmail.com/report-on-business/rob-magazine/barricks-tanzanian-project-tests-ethical-mining-policies/article559188/?page=all, accessed 1 December 2015.

York, H. (2014) 'Deadly clashes continue at African Barrick Gold mine', *Globe and Mail*, 26 August, www.theglobeandmail.com/report-on-business/international-business/deadly-clashes-continue-at-african-barrick-gold-mine/article20216197/, accessed 1 December 2015.

2 | Failed, weak or fake state? The role of private security in Somalia

William Reno

Somalia's government is unable, and more importantly in many respects, unwilling to consolidate its authority in spite of considerable international support. This failure highlights the flaws in basic assumptions that guide most security assistance to governments in failing states. This gap between policies and outcomes creates new roles for private security firms in places like Somalia. The argument below focuses on the political reality of Somalia and other failed states that frustrate conventional security assistance, such as the persistence of militarized social divisions that shape how people fight and govern after the collapse of central authority. Conventional security assistance simply does not work in these environments. Instead, private security firms take a more prominent role in this intensely fragmented social context. These firms also face significant challenges, often partnering with local actors who provide measures of local order at the same time that they contribute to wider instability and violence.

This chapter begins with an exploration of official security assistance and the intended results in Somalia within a conventional paradigm, followed by a survey of actual developments to which official policies have had to adapt. It examines the implicit assumptions associated with the international effort to build a Somali state since the apparent expulsion of Al-Shabaab from Mogadishu in 2011. It then explains how security assistance in Somalia actually works and the new roles for private security firms in creating an alternative form of state-like governance. The critical development in this global response to state collapse in Somalia lies in the integration of ostensibly private security firms, part of what Abrahamsen and Williams (2009) call 'global security assemblages', into the on-the-ground efforts to create order in a collapsed state as it becomes apparent that a conventional strategy of security assistance has very little chance of succeeding in this environment.

Somalia is a good place to consider the role of private security in the context of changes in international responses to failing and collapsed states. State collapse in this instance, as in others, really was the collapse of a personalist authoritarian regime that up to that point ruled through strategies to fragment and cultivate the dependence of communities in a context of increasing violence and economic collapse. Boundaries between state and private violence became indistinct in this context, as personal insecurity was turned into a tool of regime control. In the absence of a semblance of effective central state authority since the collapse of the regime in 1991, Somalia's intensely fragmented and localized social context has endured for over a quarter of a century in much of Somalia. The central dilemma for those who have more recently sought to rein in and control these divisions is that the local organizations they identify as foundations for a new state, such as the army and civil administration, instead are poisoned by this social fragmentation. The constant hedging and protective tactical moves among most groups in this society work against the collective action needed to build a new state, regardless of popular desires for greater stability and the rule of law. Thus networks of personal trust in particular remain beyond the reach of efforts to build a larger administration. This is the social context and policy dilemma that shape the particular role of private security in failed states.

The promise of the conventional approach

At first glance it appears that international efforts to create security in Somalia through an incremental process of assistance to the national government have actually worked. By late 2011, African Union Mission in Somalia (AMISOM) soldiers drove Al-Shabaab militants from Mogadishu and the Transitional Federal Government (TFG) moved from Kenya to rule from the capital. AMISOM coordinated with Ethiopian forces that occupied other parts of Somalia, and by mid-2015 Al-Shabaab held no major towns. Military progress cleared the way to hold a conference in London in February 2012 that brought together dozens of governments and most major Somali political groups around a plan to create a new national government, reconstruct security and judicial institutions, and provide services to citizens. Foreign governments promised logistical and financial support for AMISOM and pressed Somali leaders to elect a new legislature and write a new constitution (Foreign and Commonwealth Office 2012; United Nations News Centre 2012). On 20 August 2012 a legislature was sworn in and on 10 September 2012 its 135 members elected a president, Hassan Sheikh Mohamud, a professor with technocratic credentials. On 17 January 2013 the USA extended diplomatic recognition to what was now called the Federal Government of Somalia (FGS), and on 25 April 2013 the UK reopened its embassy in Somalia. The UN Security Council partially lifted an arms embargo on 6 March 2013 to enable the government to begin building an army (United Nations Security Council 2013). The FGS was to have implemented human rights legislation and administrative reforms, strengthened security institutions and improved social service provision in time for elections in 2016. But in July 2015 the president announced that again only the 135 legislators would vote for a president in the 2016 election (Maruf 2015). Undeterred, international partners and Somali officials managed to expand the electorate to about 14,000 and reserved 30 per cent of the next legislature for women. Michael Keating, the UN Secretary-General's Special Representative, identified this element of social engineering as 'a major milestone in making women's political empowerment and leadership a reality' (United Nations Security Council 2016a: 2).

This institution-building path charts a parallel evolution of political and security bodies, with considerable international assistance and oversight. Private security is to play only a supplementary role. Another meeting in London, in September, 2014, brought together Somali leaders and international backers to discuss support for the Somali National Army (SNA). This conference followed the December 2013 relocation of the European Union Training Mission in Somalia (EUTM-Somalia) from Uganda's Bihunga Military Training School to Mogadishu's Jazeera training facility, and the July 2014 US announcement of training assistance to the SNA. In April 2015 Somalia's minister of defence announced the Guulwade (Victory) Plan for the long-term development of the SNA. This 10,900-person force, to include female officers, would absorb members of militias into integrated units, equipped and trained with foreign assistance to take over responsibility for security at AMISOM's withdrawal and its replacement with a UN peacekeeping mission (United Nations Security Council 2015b: 3). This effort involves a US commitment to pay these troops and UN tracking of weapons (United Nations Security Council 2016b: 6). Overall commitments are considerable: Somalia absorbed 38 per cent of US Defense and State Department Africa programme expenditures, or about $742 million for 2016, with overall Defense Department assistance to Africa rising 775 per cent from 2014 ($161.9 million) to 2016 ($1.4 billion) (Security Assistance Monitor 2016).

Coordination between the FGS and international actors was part of an integrated stabilization strategy that combines defence, basic social service delivery, and rebuilding the country's judiciary and police, and local government institutions. The deepening of cooperation and Al-Shabaab's expulsion from towns reinforced the impression of success. 'Why is it coming together and why is it being successful?' asked Nicholas Kay, Special Representative of the Secretary-General and head of the UN Assistance Mission in Somalia (UNSOM). He supplied his own answer: 'Because it is firstly a Somali-led and owned process and the result of a unique partnership between the African Union, UN, and the Federal Government' (United Nations News Centre 2015).

The desert of the real

Actual developments tell a dramatically different story. In reality, the government exercises tenuous control in its capital city and is a frequent target of attacks.[1] A survey of attacks in 2015, what Somalia's government promised would be 'the year of delivery' (United Nations Security Council 2015c: 4), illustrates the limited nature of government control. On 22 January, a car bomb exploded in front of the SYL Hotel where FGS officials were meeting a Turkish delegation, killing two policemen. A repeat attack at the same hotel a year later killed at least ten people (Ibrahim 2016). On 20 February Al-Shabaab suicide bombers and gunmen killed twenty-eight people, including two legislators and Mogadishu's deputy mayor, in an attack on the Central Hotel. On 12 March, Al-Shabaab gunmen attacked UN and government administration offices in Baidoa, killing at least eight people. On 27 March, a car bomb and Al-Shabaab gunmen at the Maka Al-Mukarama Hotel killed at least fourteen, including Somalia's representative to the UN office in Geneva. On 14 April, a car bomb and seven Al-Shabaab gunmen attacked the ministries of education and natural resources, killing at least eight people. On 20 April, Al-Shabaab attacked a UN vehicle in Puntland, killing seven, including four staff members of UNICEF. The next day, an Al-Shabaab car bomb attack on a restaurant near Mogadishu's Central Hotel killed at least ten people. On 23 May Al-Shabaab gunmen in Mogadishu killed a legislator, and three transportation ministry workers were killed in separate drive-by shootings.

At least a dozen died in a 25 July truck bomb attack on the Jazeera Hotel, several hundred metres from the airport and host to the embassies of China, Qatar and Egypt. On 1 November militants attacked the Sahafi Hotel, situated at the central crossroads of the capital, killing a legislator, a general and at least thirteen others in a complex operation that lasted several hours. Outside the capital, Al-Shabaab fighters overran AMISOM's Janale base in southern Somalia on 1 September, killing more than fifty Ugandan AMISOM soldiers, two months after attackers killed at least fifty Burundian AMISOM soldiers at their Leego base and ten days after a car bomb attack in Kismaayo killed eighteen SNA personnel.[2] Then, on 15 January 2016, Al-Shabaab overran a Kenyan AMISOM base at El Adde and killed or captured as many as 150 Kenyan soldiers as nearby SNA soldiers failed to respond.

Insurgent infiltration of Somali government security and intelligence agencies contributes to the effectiveness of these attacks. The January 2013 French attempt to rescue a hostage who had been held captive since 2009 (among other French hostages) illuminated the extent of infiltration. Since French rescuers needed detailed information to locate their hostage, held in a remote area, they enlisted the help of the Somali government's National Intelligence and Security Agency (NISA),[3] organized with US Central Intelligence Agency assistance from 2008 (Gettleman et al. 2011). But insurgent infiltration into the intelligence service provided warning of the operation and led French rescuers into a trap (Africa Confidential 2013: 11). Heavily armed Al-Shabaab fighters greeted the French rescuers and fought with them for several hours, after which a French official announced that two French soldiers and the hostage were killed in the failed operation (BBC 2013a).

Other attacks point to infiltration, such as the assault on the Somali intelligence chief Khalif Ahmed Ilig's vehicle on 18 March 2013 and a former intelligence service employee's 20 January 2013 suicide bomb attack on the prime minister's home inside the presidential compound.[4] UN experts believe that Al-Shabaab infiltrates the FGS at the highest levels, which 'includes sensitive Government agencies, such as the National Intelligence and Security Agency (NISA) and various levels within the Presidential Palace' (United Nations Security Council 2014: 64). These experts also believe that Al-Shabaab infiltration of police and NISA plays a role in the hotel bombings, and that suspected infiltrators in security services, including NISA, are often later released without charge (United Nations Security Council 2015a: 185). The bomber of Daallo Airlines flight 159 on 2 February 2016 after its departure from Mogadishu reportedly stayed at the house of a government minister for several weeks, lending credence to concerns that Al-Shabaab infiltrates intelligence and other government security services (Africa Confidential 2016: 2016, 10).

Against this backdrop of attacks and infiltration, FGS officials appear to lack a sense of urgency in building state institutions, and many of them disregard conventional distinctions between their public duties and personal interests. Frustrated UN observers concluded that 'the systematic misappropriation, embezzlement and outright theft of public resources have essentially become a system of governance' as private individuals, inside and outside the government, make personal demands on state resources that officials cannot resist, owing to obligations of kinship or political clientage (United Nations Security Council 2012: 12). In 2014 UN officials estimated that 70 to 80 per cent of Central Bank of Somalia payments went to private individuals (United Nations Security Council 2014: 29), while a private expert characterized the Central Bank as 'not only mired in corruption allegations but [operating] more like an ATM rather than a public financial institution' (Fartaag 2014: 11). A World Bank report observed that 'although a Central Bank was in existence, with a main building in Mogadishu ... it apparently was (and continues to be) largely circumvented by the TFG executive branch and their key staff' (World Bank 2012: iv), a finding that UN investigators reiterated in late 2015 while noting that no charges had been successfully brought against any government official for corruption since the current transition began in 2011 (United Nations Security Council 2015a: 23–4).

The actual strength, structure and composition of Somalia's army are difficult to determine, and as one becomes familiar with the overall situation, one suspects that pronouncements from foreign embassies and official media outlets concerning successful army operations overstate the army's role in these operations. Opaque official accounts and budget procedures require continuous efforts to weed out officers collecting pay for non-existent troops in an army that on paper has a complement of 22,000 but in reality contains more like 10,000 (United Nations Security Council 2016b: 6). The army also provides politicians with rent-seeking opportunities, as when the United Arab Emirates recruited actual Somali soldiers (and soldiers from Eritrea, Sudan and Colombia) to fight Houthi rebels in Yemen, for which the UAE's government allegedly pays Somalia's government $2,500 per soldier per month (Africa Confidential 2015a: 11). These activities leave soldiers and police unpaid, except when foreigners provide 'stipends' to soldiers that are often their only incomes. This situation creates continuous problems years after the start of the supposed transition, such as when a European Union training mission was 'halted for several weeks because trainers worried that Somali troops who hadn't been paid might hold them hostage to bring attention to their plight' (Sieff 2016).

AMISOM forces that are supposed to protect Somalia's government also combine military and commercial activities, with Kenya's army accused of collaborating with Al-Shabaab to smuggle up to 150,000 tons of sugar per year into Kenya. 'Rather than taking the fight to the Shabaab', Kenyan forces were 'sitting in bases while senior commanders are engaged in corrupt business practices with the Jubaland administration and al-Shabaab', claimed a Kenyan journalists' organization (Journalists for Justice 2015: 2).

Adjusting expectations

Conventional approaches to building states while fighting insurgents rest upon two core principles that are absent in Somalia. First, there must be a government with the political will and capacity to undertake reform and effectively engage citizens, and second, there must be an indigenous armed force with the ability to protect the government and provide security to civilians (Galula 1964; Kilcullen 2006; Thompson 1966; United States Army & Marine Corps 2007). These principles presuppose that state collapse is temporary, and that key local actors view the state's restoration as feasible and desirable. Moreover, political reform and security assistance policies are based upon assumptions that clear distinctions exist between the authority of the state and other types of authority. These assumptions presume that a territorially defined state authority ordinarily plays the dominant role in shaping how political life is organized. Private security acts in a supplementary role in this context to support the consolidation of indigenous security forces, and in some instances to protect foreign business operations that generate state revenues. Here, private security is subordinate to state sovereignty rather than a challenger to or a replacement for it.

These basic assumptions do not fit the political terrain of collapsed states. The norms and practices of kinship ('clan') and other social networks overshadow bureaucratic codes of behaviour. These networks provide security and other services to members, but usually without an accompanying interest in administering territory. Groups within these networks devote considerable energy to infiltrating one another, particularly when close to the levers of power associated with sovereign status or to control connections with foreign actors and their resources. In this context, physical and political boundaries are hard to identify when armed groups associated with these networks simultaneously infiltrate one another and their members selectively collaborate with other groups. This collaboration can occur even at the same time that the members of these groups fight one another in other places. Concepts such as 'rebel control' and 'government control' apply very imperfectly in this environment. It is difficult to separate 'licit' and 'illicit' behaviour when rent-seeking on the part of government officials is the basis of their strategies for exercising authority within these networks. This context rather than efforts to build or challenge a state shapes how most people in these societies use violence and with whom they decide to cooperate. People who want to build a state, whether members of a foreign intervention force, private security firms or armed insurgents, find themselves caught in this social environment that disrupts their efforts to engage local groups, build stable institutions and administer territory.

This distinctive political terrain of state collapse reflects the pre-collapse dictator's instrumental uses of violence against citizens to develop kinship-based networks of clients and then subject them to interlocking patterns of insecurity that central authorities then mediated. The aim of this strategy of deinstitutionalization was to make even targets of state-instigated violence dependent upon the regime for protection. Manipulating personal and family tensions to fragment communities that otherwise might mobilize to challenge the government requires intensive knowledge about local-level disputes, such as conflicts over land, commercial rivalries and personal grudges among important people. Leaders tolerated and even promoted militias under the personal control of local politicians who sought to protect their supporters and remain politically relevant, so long as these militias helped foster local tensions and competition for regime favour. This strategy enabled rulers to suppress potential challenges without having to entrust regime safety to strong security agencies and military forces that might otherwise overthrow the regime instead of reliably repressing citizens on the regime's behalf. Thus, clan-based and personal armed forces in Somalia, as in most failing and collapsed states, became integral to this changed logic of politics, which blurred the distinctions between the exercise of violence in support of state authority versus for personal or local community interests, well before the actual collapse of central authority.

Somalia's President Siad Barre (1969–91) mastered this divisive strategy after an attempted coup d'état in 1978 nearly succeeded. After a massive purge of the military, Barre instigated communal violence as a political instrument to secure his regime's hold on power. He exercised authority through using kinship networks ('clans') as vehicles for patronage to political supporters, and to foster rivalries and incite conflicts between neighbouring groups that previously had close social relations. Even Barre's closest political supporters were targets of this instrumental cultivation of insecurities (Kapteijns 2013: 71–130). This system of control explicitly targeted and weakened customary conflict resolution practices, which further intensified social fragmentation in a more general pattern of 'clan warfare' that is more accurately seen as conflict between 'neo-clans' that are products of the collapsing system of authority that earlier replaced formal state institutions as the primary instrument in the regime's exercise of authority.

Persistent social fragmentation and the militarization of these networks shape how Somalis deal with insecurity and engage with externally driven Security Sector Reform. The case of the kidnapped French agents noted earlier shows how this logic of politics intersected with security assistance in an international attempt to support a reconstructed Somali central government. The seizure of the French operatives was allegedly masterminded by a relative of the interior minister and a deputy leader of the Islamic Courts Union (ICU), a predecessor to Al-Shabaab. These two men were part of a December 2008 power-sharing agreement that created a transitional government under the leadership of the ICU head Sharif Sheikh Ahmed.[5] This appointment gave the ICU an opportunity to position operatives in the TFG security services.[6] This pattern of simultaneous alliance and opposition facilitated sharing of information and collaborative operations. For example, Hizbul Islam emerged among ICU members that rejected the 2008 power-sharing deal with the TFG and merged with Al-Shabaab in December 2010. In 2009 these groups fought together against the TFG in Mogadishu at the same time that they fought each other in Kismayo (Filiu 2009). This situation points to the difficulties of applying rigid political labels to groups that collaborate in some areas and on some issues while fighting one another elsewhere in the service of kinship obligations.

This event sheds light on yet other family and clan considerations guiding the captors. Hizbul Islamiyya's capture of the French hostages drew Al-Shabaab onto the scene, which left Hizbul Islamiyya with only one hostage to sell back to the French. This ransom activated yet more cleavages as the original kidnappers and the recipients of the ransom quarrelled over how the seizure, involving about forty fighters arriving at the Sahafi Hotel where the French were staying, and the distribution of the ransom would affect the power of factions within the larger collection of Islamist groups. This reflected the complex nature of the Islamists' selective participation in the TFG while still benefiting from the ransom.[7] The story only gets more complicated from there, and illuminates the extent to which personal and wider kinship networks overwhelm efforts to establish a distinct sphere of state interest.

'Private' security firms amidst state collapse

At least some private security firms in Somalia play key roles in which they substitute for state capacities in an environment that lacks a solid social basis for state institutions. In doing so, these firms need to address the problems of information leakage that accompany the hedging and mutual infiltration that come with short-term survival strategies in this social environment. The compartmentalization of information is critical for gaining dominance in the exercise of coercion, particularly in the capacity to target other groups to subordinate them to 'state' authority. Private firms thus have to devise a way to create alternative social environments for their local employees to ensure that they privilege their relationship to the firm over their obligations to kinship networks. This requires a degree of social engineering that exceeds the interests or capabilities of the great majority of foreign private security firms. It also requires a high degree of coordination between private security firms and foreign political actors who coordinate with these firms in an effort to maintain the illusion that a conventional conflict resolution and state-building exercise is successful and deserves continued international support. This process highlights the central role of private security firms in this global security assemblage that is focused on addressing the problem of state collapse.

There are two categories of private security firm that operate in this context. The first category is the state substitution firm. This category includes foreign firms that undertake or support state-like tasks in place of effective state institutions. Though legally subordinate to Somali sovereign authority, in fact they systematically violate elements of this hierarchy, occasionally in direct defiance of key politicians. But even when they do so, these firms are careful to preserve the outward illusion that the Somali government is able, or at least trying, to exercise effective control over armed actors within its own borders. State substitution firms thus perform critical roles in foreign strategies, particularly US counter-terrorism strategies. These in turn provide an illusion of domestic sovereign control in lieu of an effective indigenous Somali capacity to undertake, much less refrain from undermining, an effective counter-insurgency programme.

The second category of private security firm is the alternative indigenous network. This category includes local private security firms, with Somali employees under the command of Somali bosses, but often under the supervision of foreign contractors. Though these firms are legally subordinate to domestic official regulations, their relationships to political authorities are based upon the personal connections of their heads. This arrangement gives foreigners the opportunity to use these firms to create autonomous 'indigenous' social networks to collect information and exercise coercion in the fluid social context of the collapsed state. In doing so, these firms need strategies to manage kinship obligations and discipline the behaviour of their employees while still being able to collect intelligence. In effect, these firms need to behave like a clan militia in an environment of competing militias. Those that are most effective co-opt elements of that political environment to a more stable logic of territorial control and centralized authority. In many respects, the place of these firms in the global and local security assemblages of this region resembles that of the warlords that US officials recruited in the 2000s, noted in the next section, as proxies to oppose Islamist influence. But now the alternative indigenous network firms need to adhere to global standards of corporate practice, at least in form, to reassure domestic and foreign observers that they are playing acceptable roles in the international diplomatic effort to create a new Somali state.

State substitution

Foreign-backed proxies that can be described loosely as private providers of security have long played important roles in place of state security forces in Somalia. In 2004, for example, some Nairobi-based Somali businessmen reported that Americans recruited them to return to Mogadishu to do business while also using their heavily armed personal security forces in coordination with American advisers to target specific individuals (International Crisis Group 2005: 10–14). Joining up with local businessmen and militia leaders (popularly called warlords), this Alliance for Restoration of Peace and Counter-Terrorism was not part of a transitional government, which was based outside the capital at the time, and it received money and advice from American intelligence operatives.[8] Following the 1998 bombings of US embassies in Kenya and Tanzania, American officials tracked militants that they suspected had taken refuge inside Somalia, where they benefited from the absence of a central state authority. 'We need to recognize that Somalia is a front line in the broader fight against terrorism,' said US Senator Russell Feingold in 2006, 'and that it needs more than just intermittent attention' (United States Senate 2006: 2).

The central dilemma for the Americans and Somalia's neighbours who had suffered attacks and other consequences of Somalia's internal turmoil was that no officially recognized sovereign Somali forces could provide foreigners with credible security guarantees. This situation convinced many American officials that they had to rely on these militias to at least track and kill militants, despite the recognition among at least some officials that these proxies worsened Somalia's political fragmentation, contributed to a humanitarian crisis, and convinced many Somalis that they were better off under the rule of the Islamists that the warlords opposed (United States Embassy, Nairobi 2006). Somalis got their chance in June 2006 to see whether this was true after Islamic Courts Union (ICU) forces chased the warlords out of Mogadishu. As it turned out, the ICU was better at maintaining order, though their harsh rhetoric and suspicions that they harboured terrorists alarmed foreign officials.

The involvement of the private security firm Select Armor, Inc. illuminated the difficulties of crafting a policy to create order in a collapsed state as well as the disarray of US policy towards Somalia. The head of this firm boasted of contacts with the CIA and British private security firms and of a plan to help the warlords fight the ICU (Africa Confidential 2006: 2). Over the next several years she convinced assorted officials and journalists of her elaborate plans to control piracy and pacify Somalia through the development projects of a non-profit organization, Oasis Foundation for Hope, and a dizzying array of other entities. 'It's pretty sad when a horse-country socialite has more sway in Somalia than the whole U.S. government,' said a senior US official (Kloor 2013), highlighting the extent to which foreign efforts to address the problem of state collapse tended to become intertwined in the personal and commercial networks that were predominant in the collapsed state environment.

Despite these problems, foreign security firms still had a role to play in substituting for state capabilities in the absence of an even minimally capable central government. This strategy centres on NISA and special army units that receive US security assistance, including through private security contractors. Despite the problems of infiltration noted above, foreign security firms support elements of the security agency and armed units that operate independently of AMISOM and EU-trained Somali military forces. Private security firm assistance with budgeting, staff and command structure insulates the security agency and these armed units from the rest of the Somali government and associated social pressures on their behaviour. This assistance builds a local cadre who deal directly with foreign counterparts and who can be integrated into security networks as mutually recognized experts; it is believed that they are less likely to share information with people outside the organization. This relationship is more intensive and complex than a foreign power's episodic use of local armed groups as proxies in conflicts. Instead the relationship prescribes and shapes standards of governance. It presupposes that the governance endpoint is a level of order that will guarantee the security of other states, an alternative mode of engagement that signals a shift in how international actors conceptualize and define effective governance (Bayart 2004; Mandel 2013; Mattelart 2010).

This relationship appeared in 2011 during the AMISOM offensive against Al-Shabaab in Mogadishu. Local residents reported that well-trained Alpha (also called Danab) fighters appeared with foreign support. 'We initially thought that Alphas were foreign soldiers. Even when we discovered that definitely they are Somalis, we can't tell where they come from. They are completely covered so you can't see even their faces and they don't interact with army or AMISOM.'[9] A US official acknowledged US government support for special units to fight Al-Shabaab. 'The aid we provide includes training support for the Somali advanced infantry company, also known as "Danab" – the Lightning

Force. This is a 150-person unit that we believe can become a source of future leadership for the entire army' (Sherman 2014).

Foreign contractors and US Special Forces apparently train and support these fighters separately from other Somali forces (McCormick 2015). The lack of information about the specifics of this support reflects the interests of US and other foreign officials in limiting appearances of influence in Somalia, and most likely in avoiding distracting attention from a narrative that presents the conventional internationally supported state-building effort as more successful than it is in fact.[10] Nevertheless, evidence of substantial logistical support is visible. The most significant is Bancroft Global Development, which is registered as a charity in the USA. It is considered a private security firm by UN monitors, who note that the firm has been active in Mogadishu since 2007, including periods when most of the city was under Al-Shabaab control, to provide training and mentoring in a variety of projects involving AMISOM and Somali armed forces (United Nations General Assembly 2013: 11–14). Bancroft Global Investments and a number of other companies also provide secure accommodations and organize armed protection in the Somali capital, which otherwise is very risky for foreign visitors (Stewart 2013).

Some Somali officials and well-connected establishment figures express the view that much of the foreign-supported security apparatus is kept separate from the rest of the Somali government and AMISOM. One notable figure observed of a NISA director: 'He must be better linked to you [Americans] than to [TNG president] Sharif,' in light of instances when the security agency was able to target politically connected individuals.[11] An aide to a former defence minister reported that his boss was told that he was 'not authorized' to enter a compound housing private security forces near the Alpha compound and speculated that 'Americans there hesitate because they aren't confident about the Somali government's reliability' with regard to Al-Shabaab infiltration of even the highest levels of the government.[12] A senior Somali government official complained that it was typical for new private security and military companies to simply appear in Somalia and that security was 'not in the hands of the state'.[13] A foreign official present during the July 2014 Al-Shabaab attack on government offices praised the efficiency of Somali special units, attributing this to US training and their segregation from the influence of government officials.[14]

This insulation of effective security forces from the rest of the government of Somalia enables foreigners to claim that the sovereign government is able to provide credible guarantees that it has the capacity to maintain domestic order and prevent groups from using Somali territory to organize attacks outside of Somalia. Private security firms that provide direct and indirect support to Somali intelligence and Special Force units support elements of a Somali government, but these elements are effective only insofar as they are socially and operationally separate from the wider context of interlocking networks that share information. The foreign security firms that support this substitution for the (indigenous) state's capacity to control (if not administer) its domestic realm are distinct from a much larger array of private security firms that engage directly with the networked social structures of the collapsed state.

Alternative indigenous networks

Most private security firms in Somalia are closely connected to existing patronage networks. These firms and their politician partners exploit the commercial opportunities associated with the formal aspects of transition at the same time that they contribute to the conditions that undermine its progress. While these firms ostensibly aim to increase state capacities to fight Al-Shabaab and provide public order, their presence really is a reflection of the fact that it has become more lucrative to collaborate with Somalia's government than with Al-Shabaab. Some local private security firms benefit from the skills and resources provided by formal security assistance programmes, such as a firm run by a former police commissioner who recruited fellow kinsman from the foreign-trained police force.[15]

These firms can utilize the personal connections of their members, what might look like corrupt relationships from a conventional external perspective, to gain influence over individual militants. For example, members of small sub-clan groups that historically suffered from encroachment by stronger neighbours have been favourable recruiting grounds for Al-Shabaab. Prominent businessmen from such groups are also good targets for recruitment into Mogadishu-based private security networks if they are offered opportunities to win contracts. This arrangement amounts, in the words of a former diplomat from the region, to 'sending the good al-Qaeda [to whom Al-Shabaab's leadership had sworn fealty in 2012] to chase the bad al-Qaeda'.[16] In these instances, the presence of a core of state substitution security forms and local security professionals can manipulate existing indigenous networks in a broader project to consolidate control over coercion, despite the inevitable infiltrations and leakages of information that these relationships entail. The mechanics of this process are intensely complex and require detailed knowledge of the past political histories and family connections of numerous individuals.

The chart below illustrates some of the interconnections between a sampling of local private security firms and other elements of Somalia's networks of authority in the creation of this security assemblage.

Company connections to the broader political environment

TURKSOM SECURITY COMPANY Local private security/personal protection firm is reportedly a partner with a Turkish private security firm

ILAALO SECURITY COMPANY The owner of the firm was police commissioner until 2011 and kinsman of the prime minister. Some of the firm's employees are former police officers who bring the benefits of training programmes with them. The owner was later appointed ambassador to the UAE.

DUGAF ENTERPRISE SECURITY SERVICES Provides security services to companies and international organizations. Head is a journalist.

SABAH GENERAL SERVICE Owner was noted in a 2013 UN report as having been identified by senior security officials as an agent for Al-Shabaab and responsible for political violence; kinsman of Al-Shabaab spokesman.

PEACE BUSINESS SERVICE The proprietor, a businessman and owner of the Peace Hotel (open since 2005 and to date not a target of attack), is a kinsman of many high government officials. Security firm secured contracts with international organizations and other foreigners.

SomSec The proprietor also runs a consultancy in the UK where he is based and has worked with other European security firms to provide security to the European compound. He has served as an adviser to the president of the Galmudug region of Somalia.

Local private security firms represent a sort of battleground for hegemony of information and coercion. These firms are subject in varying degrees to the infiltration and information-sharing that characterize other networks of the collapsed state. An example of how cross-cutting allegiances can link these firms, government and Al-Shabaab rebels appears in a UN report that noted how a fellow kinsman who was an adviser to the president maintained relations with the army chief of logistics and was responsible for setting up a private security company in Mogadishu that was implicated in 'leakage' of government weapons to Al-Shabaab (United Nations Security Council 2014: 33).

The sharing of information across kinship networks can be a problem for Al-Shabaab too. The rebel group also has to struggle in this environment to pursue a broad programme at the same time that it has to juggle disparate clan agendas that centre on immediate kinship and community issues that have nothing to do with their broad political programmes (Hansen 2013). These problems have left Al-Shabaab and its predecessors exposed to the tendency to reflect the fragmented yet densely networked social environment of the collapsed state. While these armed groups are resilient, they, like the formal internationally mediated transition and the alternative indigenous networks in which most private security firms are embedded, are not transformers of Somali politics (Watts et al. 2007).

Many of the proprietors of these firms are people who have significant histories of involvement in Somalia's various conflicts. They fit into the clientelist structure of local politics, and connect their foreign business partners to the social networks and local political deals that are essential for foreign firms to get contracts. In an illustration of the extensive nature of this military clientelism, Somalia-Fishguard, a subsidiary of the British security firm Saladin, was charged with ensuring maritime security of the Somali coast and to be the sole agent for the sale of fishing licences as an agent of Somalia's government (United Nations Security Council 2015a: 61). This particular arrangement was related to a series of resource exploration and construction deals that involved several British politicians who offered to address Somalia's weak capacity to regulate its own territory in exchange for favourable commercial agreements (Africa Confidential 2015b).

A similar arrangement between local political networks, a foreign private security firm and militias appeared in the semi-autonomous Puntland Authority in northern Somalia. Sterling Corporate Services took over a military training programme to support the Puntland Maritime Police Force (PMPF) in the largest military facility in Somalia outside the AMISOM headquarters in Mogadishu. Financed through the UAE, this operation played a role in the political strategies of Puntland's president Farole, as PMPF personnel were reported to be used against his political rivals (United Nations General Assembly 2013: 10). The firm left PMPF in disarray as UN investigators named the firm for possible violations of sanctions (Mazzetti and Schmitt 2012). Somali Security Services appeared in 2015 to provide coastguard services. The head of the firm, involved in coastal security in Puntland in the 2000s, was a former taxi driver and sales clerk from Toronto and a close personal associate of Puntland's president Abdiweli Mohamed Ali 'Gaas', the former opposition politician who in 2012 was the target of the PMPF (United Nations Security Council 2015a: 84; Gatehouse 2009).

Situations such as this one in Puntland illustrate the tendency for these politician–private security firm partnerships to become subordinate to the existing social networks and subject to the political tensions between them. As conduits for new external resources, they can become alternative indigenous networks, as demonstrations of the attractiveness of their politician partners as patrons. It is difficult to label such forms as private, at least in the sense of operating in a separate realm from the dominant political authority of the region. Instead, they function more as intermediaries to tap international resources that can be added to kinship patronage networks.

These alternative networks can also act as proxies for external actors, but their role is very different from the state substitution security firms in the last section. The local partners of foreign private security firms in this category can tap into extensive reserves of military expertise among their employees with previous careers as highly trained soldiers in the US and UK militaries, among others. But firms such as Sterling and Saladin's subsidiary tend to become subordinate to the political agendas of their Somali partners, which contributes to the further fragmentation of the Somali political scene. Indeed, a few of the indigenous Somali private security firms are more successful than some of the foreign firms in socially insulating their operations. These few Somali firms then become effective partners of state substitution security firms in centralizing the exercise of coercion.

Conclusion

Private security firms in the context of state collapse in Somalia play direct roles in the reconfiguration of political authority. In one sense, they play an important role in what Abrahamsen and Williams identify as a process in which

> the very distinctions between the public and the private, the global and the local are rearranged, producing new practices and forms of power that cannot be neatly contained within the geographical boundaries of the nation-state. (2011: 3)

This is true particularly when politicians integrate private security firms into existing networks in Somalia to serve their personal agendas. While these firms can serve as proxies for outsiders to collect information and to supply and train local armed forces that can pursue individuals, this particular configuration of a security assemblage does little to contribute to, and occasionally even undermines, the creation of stable political authorities that administer territory and control the flows of information.

Private security firms that substitute for the state through insulation from Somalia's sovereign authorities are much more effective in addressing global concerns about the capacity of Somalia's government to control and reliably certify that its territory and people within it do not pose security threats beyond its borders. Insofar as these firms have clandestine or visible connections to US government agencies, they fit Jean-François Bayart's general observation on how the US pursuit of security through this hybridity of state and private security assists in the territorialization of power in what he called 'the fusion between the processes of state formation and those of globalization, on the basis of systematic hybridization of the private and the public' (Bayart 2004: 75). This strategic use of private security firms concentrates the exercise of coercion in the hands of indigenous actors who satisfy their foreign friends of the credibility of their domestic capacity to impose order. The strategy's success requires the social transformation of the local participants in this relationship, integrating them into a global network of security professionals while benefiting from the participant's insider knowledge of how the intricate social networks within the collapsed state environment really work and how these relationships can be used as tools for creating order on the ground.

This survey of the failure of conventional international approaches to state-building in a collapsed state does not necessarily produce conclusions that accord with global norms of justice, self-determination and human rights. It is also realistic about a fundamental problem of collapsed states: the logic of the exercise of political authority within them renders political actors incapable of extending security guarantees to outsiders. A quarter-century of repeated international efforts to help reconstruct the state in Somalia also suggests that it is unrealistic to depend on Somalia's current government to engage effectively in state-building tasks. This incapacity reflects the basic fact that there is no government that has the political will or capacity to directly engage the population through the provision of public services, and there is no armed force that is willing or able to protect such a government. Powerful international actors want Somalis to be governed by an effective state authority, not out of altruism but out of concern that Somalis perform these tasks for mutual benefit. The Somalia case helps to demonstrate how private security firms under certain circumstances can promote that goal in a collapsed state. It remains to be seen whether this strategy is sustainable.

Acknowledgement

The author thanks the Norwegian Research Council "Jihadist War Economies Project" for generous support.

Notes

1 The author observed the security situation in visits to Mogadishu in 2012, 2013 and 2014.

2 List compiled from the author's database and accounts readily retrievable from reliable media.

3 Somalis refer to this agency variously as NSA, NSS and NIIS in line with previous official labels.

4 The author observed that the latter blast scene required attackers to pass through multiple checkpoints. See also BBC (2013b).

5 This perspective was expressed in author's discussions with a Somali official, 4 July 2012.

6 Some TFG officials and militia leaders revealed in discussions with the author their personal concerns about security owing to perceived Al-Shabaab infiltration into security services. Mogadishu, June/July 2012.

7 Discussions with the owner of the Sahafi Hotel, Mogadishu, August 2013 and August 2014. See also Hassan and Sheikh (2009).

8 Interview and informal discussions with A.R.I., Mogadishu, 19 August 2013 and after, and Mazzetti (2006).

9 Interview with a well-placed lady in a niqab, Dagmada Shangaani, Mogadishu, 1 July 2012.

10 The author encountered multiple instances of foreign specialist support to NISA and other security personnel in repeated visits to Mogadishu, including NISA headquarters, beginning in 2012.

11 Interview, Osman Ali Atto, Mogadishu, 1 July 2012.

12 Discussion with Somali informants, Mogadishu, 18 August 2013.

13 Interview, State Minister for the Presidency, Mogadishu, 17 August 2013.

14 Interview with J.I.H., Villa Somalia, Mogadishu, 13 August 2014.

15 Author's personal observation and discussions in Mogadishu.

16 Frequent discussions with a former diplomat. This observation has been endorsed in numerous conversations with Somali politicians and businessmen.

Bibliography

Abrahamsen, R. and M. Williams (2009) 'Security beyond the state: global security assemblages in international politics', *International Political Sociology*, 3: 1–17.

— (2011) *Security beyond the State: Private Security in International Politics*, Cambridge: Cambridge University Press.

Africa Confidential (2006) 'Mission Mogadishu', *Africa Confidential*, 47(18), 8 September.

— (2013) 'French Somalia raid "was a trap"', *Africa Confidential*, 54(2), 18 January.

— (2015a) 'AMISOM loses friends', *Africa Confidential*, 56(20), 9 October.

— (2015b) 'The Brits are coming', *Africa Confidential*, 56(24): 7–9.

— (2016) 'Somalia: Amison Struggles', *Africa Confidential*, 57(6), 4 March.

Bayart, J.-F. (2004) *Le Gouvernement du monde. Une critique politique de la globalization*, Paris: Fayard.

BBC (2013a) 'Second French soldier dies after Somalia raid – rebels', 14 January, www.bbc.com/news/world-africa-21009364.

— (2013b) 'Suicide blast by offices of Somali president and PM', 29 January, www.bbc.com/news/world-africa-21241751.

Fartaag, A. (2014) *Their Own Worst Enemy: How Successive Governments Plundered Somalia's Public Resources and Why the World Looked On*, Fartaag Research & Consulting, Nairobi, www.keydmedia.net/download-files/Their-Own-worst-Enemy-Fartaag-Report-2014.pdf.

Filiu, J.-P. (2009) 'Lesson from Kismayo', *Jihadica*, 6 October, www.jihadica.com/lesson-from-kismayo/.

Foreign and Commonwealth Office (2012) 'London Conference on Somalia communiqué', 23 February, www.europarl.europa.eu/meetdocs/2009_2014/documents/sede/dv/sede200312londonconference_/sede200312londonconference_en.pdf.

Galula, D. (1964) *Counterinsurgency Warfare: Theory and Practice*, New York: Praeger.

Gatehouse, J. (2009) 'This cabbie hunts pirates', *Maclean's*, 12 January, www.macleans.ca/news/world/this-cabbie-hunts-pirates/.

Gettleman, J., M. Mazzetti and E. Schmitt (2011) 'US relies on contractors in Somalia conflict', *New York Times*, 10 August, www.nytimes.com/2011/08/11/world/africa/11somalia.html.

Hansen, S. J. (2013) *Al-Shabaab in Somalia: The History and Ideology of a Militant Islamist Group, 2005–2012*, London: Hurst & Co.

Hassan, A. and A. Sheikh (2009) 'Qaeda linked Somali group takes one of French hostages', Reuters, 16 July, www.reuters.com/article/us-somalia-conflict-idUSTRE56F1Y520090716.

Ibrahim, M. (2016) 'Shabaab militants claim deadly attack on hotel in Somalia', *New York Times*, 26 February, www.nytimes.com/2016/02/27/world/africa/shabab-gunmen-attack-hotel-in-somalia.html.

International Crisis Group (2005) *Counter-Terrorism in Somalia: Losing Hearts and Minds*, Nairobi: ICG.

Journalists for Justice (2015) *Black and White: Kenya's Criminal Racket in Somalia*, Nairobi: Journalists for Justice, www.jfjustice.net/userfiles/file/Research/Black%20and%20White%20Kenya's%20Criminal%20Racket%20in%20Somalia.pdf.

Kapteijns, L. (2013) *Clan Cleansing in Somalia: The Ruinous Legacy of 1991*, Philadelphia: University of Pennsylvania Press.

Kilcullen, D. (2006) 'The three pillars of counterinsurgency', US Government Counterinsurgency Conference, Washington, DC.

Kloor, K. (2013) 'Pirates and warlords aside, Michele Ballarin believes she can turn Somalia around', *Washington Post*, 4 October, www.washingtonpost.com/lifestyle/magazine/pirates-and-warlords-aside-michele-ballarin-believes-she-can-turn-somalia-around/2013/10/04/117ef754-0102-11e3-9a3e-916de805f65d_story.html.

Mandel, R. (2013) *Global Security Upheaval: Armed Nonstate Groups Usurping State Stability Functions*, Palo Alto, CA: Stanford University Press.

Maruf, H. (2015) 'Somalia: no popular elections in 2016', *VOA News: Africa*, 29 July, www.voanews.com/content/somalia-says-no-popular-elections-in-2016/2883749.html.

Mattelart, A. (2010) *The Globalisation of Surveillance*, Cambridge: Polity Press.

Mazzetti, M. (2006) 'Efforts by C.I.A. fail in Somalia, officials charge', *New York Times*, 7 June, www.nytimes.com/2006/06/08/world/africa/08intel.html?_r=1.

Mazzetti, M. and E. Schmitt (2012) 'Private army formed to fight Somali pirates leaves troubled legacy', *New York Times*, 5 October, www.nytimes.com/2012/10/05/world/africa/private-army-leaves-troubled-legacy-in-somalia.html?_r=0.

McCormick, T. (2015) 'U.S. operates drones from secret bases in Somalia', *Foreign Policy*, foreignpolicy.com/2015/07/02/exclusive-u-s-operates-drones-from-secret-bases-in-somalia-special-operations-jsoc-black-hawk-down/.

Security Assistance Monitor (2016) securityassistance.org/blog/4-charts-spike-us-military-and-police-aid-africa.

Sherman, W. (Under-Secretary for Political Affairs, US Department of State) (2014) 'U.S. foreign policy in Somalia', Remarks before the United States Institute of Peace, 3 June, iipdigital.usembassy.gov/st/english/texttrans/2014/06/20140612301214.html#ixzz47MoV1HgZ.

Sieff, K. (2016) 'Somalia's president says al-Qaeda-backed rebels are "resurgent"', *Washington Post*, 10 April, www.washingtonpost.com/world/africa/somalias-president-says-al-qaeda-backed-rebels-are-resurgent/2016/04/09/56be207c-faa3-11e5-813a-90ab563f0dde_story.html.

Stewart, C. (2013) 'A bet on peace for war-torn Somalia', *Wall Street Journal*, 26 April, www.wsj.com/articles/SB10001424127887323820304578410573747048086.

Thompson, R. (1966) *Defeating Communist Insurgency: Experiences from Malaya and Vietnam*, New York: Praeger.

United Nations General Assembly (2013) *Report of the Working Group on the use of mercenaries as a means of violating human rights and impeding the exercise of the rights of peoples to self-determination*, A/HRC/24/45/Add.2, New York: UN, 1 July, documents-dds-ny.un.org/doc/UNDOC/GEN/G13/153/79/PDF/G1315379.pdf?OpenElement.

United Nations News Centre (2012) 'UN and partners issue warning against Somali peace process spoilers', 1 May, www.un.org/apps/news/story.asp?NewsID=41890#.VytzW-Q2Erc.

— (2015) 'Somalia: UN envoy applauds successes as country "comes together"', 8 June, www.un.org/apps/news/story.asp?NewsID=51089#.

United Nations Security Council (2012) *Report of the Monioring Group on Somalia and Eritrea pursuant to Security Council resolution 2002 (2011)*, S/2012/544, 13 July, www.securitycouncilreport.org/atf/cf/%7B65BFCF9B-6D27-4E9C-8CD3-CF6E4FF96FF9%7D/Somalia%20S%202012%20544.pdf.

— (2013) *Resolution 2093 (2013)*, S/

RES/2093 (2013), www.refworld.org/docid/5139a40e2.htm.
— (2014) *Report of the Monitoring Group on Somalia and Eritrea pursuant to Security Council resolution 2111 (2013): Somalia*, S/2014/726, 13 October, www.securitycouncilreport.org/atf/cf/%7B65BFCF9B-6D27-4E9C-8CD3-CF6E4FF96FF9%7D/S_2014_726.pdf.
— (2015a) *Report of the Monitoring Group on Somalia and Eritrea pursuant to Security Council Resolution 2182 (2014): Somalia*, S/2015/801, 19 October, www.securitycouncilreport.org/atf/cf/%7B65BFCF9B-6D27-4E9C-8CD3-CF6E4FF96FF9%7D/s_2015_801.pdf.
— (2015b) *The Situation in Somalia*, S/PV/7445, 19 May, www.securitycouncilreport.org/atf/cf/%7B65BFCF9B-6D27-4E9C-8CD3-CF6E4FF96FF9%7D/s_pv_7445.pdf.
— (United Nations Security Council (2015c) *Report of the Secretary-General on Somalia*, S/2015/331, 12 May, www.securitycouncilreport.org/atf/cf/%7B65BFCF9B-6D27-4E9C-8CD3-CF6E4FF96FF9%7D/s_2015_331.pdf.
— (2016a) *7674th Meeting*, S/PV.7674, 19 April, www.securitycouncilreport.org/atf/cf/%7B65BFCF9B-6D27-4E9C-8CD3-CF6E4FF96FF9%7D/s_pv_7674.pdf.
— (2016b) *Report of the Secretary-General on Somalia*, S/2016/27, 8 January, www.securitycouncilreport.org/atf/cf/%7B65BFCF9B-6D27-4E9C-8CD3-CF6E4FF96FF9%7D/s_2016_27.pdf.
United States Army & Marine Corps (2007) *Counterinsurgency Field Manual* [FM3-24], Chicago, IL: University of Chicago Press.
United States Embassy, Nairobi (2006) 'Humanitarian crisis in central and southern Somalia', 14 June.
United States Senate, Subcommittee on African Affairs, Committee on Foreign Relations (2006) Opening statement of Hon. Senator Russell Feingold, *Somalia: U.S. Government Policy and Challenges*, 11 July, babel.hathitrust.org/cgi/pt?id=pst.000061489547;view=1up;seq=5.
Watts, C., J. Shapiro and F. Brown (2007) *Al-Qaeda's (Mis)Adventures in the Horn of Africa*, West Point, NY: Combating Terrorism Center.
World Bank (2012) *World Bank Summary of Financial Diagnostic Assessment of Audit Investigative Financial Report 2009-10*, 30 May.

3 | Private security beyond the private sector: community policing and secret societies in Sierra Leone

Peter Albrecht

The security governance debate on private security has commonly revolved around military companies as commercial enterprises and the role they play in warfare (Leander 2010). Broadening this debate is a growing body of literature that explores non-militarized, everyday forms of private security (Abrahamsen and Williams 2007, 2011). The security industry leases combatants and guards, procures equipment and provides training, working within and across state boundaries. Private security companies protect national and transnational as well as localized interests and assets. They engage in a variety of military and domestic policing operations, providing strategic planning and intelligence. But it is also the case that order-making beyond the direct management of a central government takes place outside the commercial sphere. In fact, this is mostly the case.

Rarely considered in the debate on commercial security is the myriad of institutions such as traditional leaders and locally organized security groups that are often referred to as 'non-state actors' (Albrecht 2013). On an everyday basis, they deal with an estimated 80 to 90 per cent[1] of local disputes in the global South and are as such arguably far more widespread than private security companies. More importantly, they do not primarily guard, but actively make order; indeed, they are integral to it.

They also differ from private security companies in the sense that they cannot be explained by reference to political liberalization, commercial interest or market logics alone. They have often emerged in areas where capitalist enterprise has played only an indirect and in some cases no role (Lentz 2007: 45). Yet like private security companies, they blur the distinction between the private and public in their order-making practices, drawing on authority in legislation produced by a parliament as well as rules and regulations produced by local practices and institutions. With an empirical focus on Sierra Leone, this set of actors is explored in an attempt to add further nuance to what order-making through 'private security' in the global South entails.

The current role of private security companies in Sierra Leone is generally limited to areas where commercial interest is at stake – for example, mining sites in Kono District, office buildings in Freetown and other assets that are considered in need of protection. In turn, the enforcement of order in rural areas is commonly carried out by a mix of traditional leaders, locally organized youth groups and elders. What the global security companies and locally embedded traditional leaders have in common is that they operate in spaces where centrally governed institutions, including the Sierra Leone Police (SLP), have been unwilling or unable to establish order.

In this regard, rural – and urban (King and Albrecht 2015) – Sierra Leone is characterized by a hybrid order, overseen by a diverse set of actors, constitutive of and constituted by different hierarchies, incentives and interests.[2] This results in 'hybrid structures' (Abrahamsen and Williams 2009: 8) or polycentric governance arrangements (Berg and Shearing 2015), within which there are no 'clear-cut hierarchical or vertical relationships', where authority runs in only one direction or from a clearly defined centre (Abrahamsen and Williams 2009: 8, 2011; Albrecht and Kyed 2015). As such, processes are at work that establish assemblages of diverse and competing structures of authority, sets of rules, logics of order and claims to power that coexist, overlap, interact and intertwine (Albrecht 2012: 22; Albrecht and Moe 2015; Richmond 2010).

Empirically, the chapter explores two institutions that are central to order-making in rural Sierra Leone –Sierra Leone's community policing forums, Local Policing Partnership Boards (LPPBs), and the Poro, a secret society into which most Sierra Leonean boys are initiated.[3] The two institutions have emerged under fundamentally different circumstances and serve equally distinct purposes, but they exemplify how 'the community', commonly led by paramount and lesser chiefs, is mobilized to make order at the local level.

The chapter first outlines the role of paramount and lesser chiefs in Sierra Leone, around whom considerable levels of authority revolve in rural areas of the country. Following this, LPPBs and the Poro are explored. In the case of the LPPBs, the Sierra Leone Police (SLP) negotiates with local communities to ensure ordinary people's collaboration in providing their own security. The Poro, in turn, constitutes an institution that makes order through the exclusion of non-members from decisions over land, the most coveted resource in rural Sierra Leone. Both institutions provide insights into how hybrid orders assemble and thus exemplify cases of security beyond the private sector.

Paramount and lesser chiefs in Sierra Leone

In this section, I provide insight into the sources of authority that paramount and lesser chiefs draw on, and how they both practise and embody a foundational hybrid order (Albrecht 2012). Sierra Leone's 149 chiefdoms, subdivided into a number of sections, are established in a series of legal documents. Some date from before or just after Sierra Leone's independence in 1961, including The Tribal Authorities Ordinance (1938), the Chiefdom

Treasuries Act (1938) and the Tribal Authorities (Amendment) Act (1964). Other more recent pieces of legislation include the Local Government Act (2004) and the Chieftaincy Act (2009).

The 1991 Constitution of Sierra Leone ratifies the official position of paramount chiefs by stating that 'the institution of the Chieftaincy, as established by customary law and usage' and 'its non-abolition by law' are to be 'guaranteed and preserved' (GOSL 1991: 72(1)). By law, the government thus has an obligation to restore the 'traditional role' of paramount chiefs, including their administrative and customary judicial responsibilities. With reference to the colonial era, this is done on the basis of the Ruling Houses that existed at independence in 1961 (one to three Ruling Houses exist in each chiefdom and paramount chiefs can only be drawn from these families).

The chiefdom constitutes the basic unit of local government, and paramount chiefs sit on District and Town Councils across the country. The 2004 Local Government Act stipulates that the paramount chiefs have a 'traditional function' – for instance, in preventing offences in the area over which they rule; prohibiting illegal gambling and making and enforcing by-laws (GOSL 2004: 28). At the core of their state-sanctioned power lies their legal mandate to hold the land in trust for the people of the chiefdom (ibid.). In many rural areas this means that they hold almost exclusive powers over the distribution of the most important source of income generation.

In principle, the minister of internal affairs has the legal authority to recommend the suspension of chiefs. However, in one interview a ministry official told me that the minister does not have

> much by way of a structural thing that will link him to the chiefs. Except if he decides to visit some place; but there is nothing there really [by way of representing him]. There is no requirement for the chief to communicate with him; now, there is no real requirement for the chief to communicate with anybody. (Interview, ministry official, 29 November 2008)

This point indicates that there is a basic disconnect between state legislation and state practices.

The next section explores how the hybrid order that chiefs embody and the authority of Sierra Leone's chiefs are sourced in local space outside the jurisdiction of a central government, despite the fact that they are recognized in legislation. This provides some insight into the fact that while making a split between state and society – or the public and the private – may be analytically important, it obscures our understanding of the chief's authority, and, perhaps, private security generally in fragile situations.

Chiefs and the importance of origin Apart from being reflected in legislation, it is also evident that chiefly authority has a distinctly local origin.

Fanthorpe (2001: 372) uses the concept of 'extreme localization' to denote criteria of identity and belonging in rural areas of Sierra Leone (see also Allen 1968: 306). This concept helps explain the implications of how authority is distributed in communities across rural Sierra Leone. The crucial role of chiefs in Sierra Leone has at times been explained by 'lack of state' (see Sesay 1996; Chaves and Robinson 2011), rather than by the types of capital that these hybrid organizational formations can draw upon to make order. Among those who do not interpret 'localization' as 'lack of state' per se are Hardin (1993) and Fanthorpe (2001, 2005). In her study of Kainkordu, a small town in Kono District in the eastern part of Sierra Leone, Hardin (1993) makes an important argument for what 'localization' implies, demonstrating that identity relies on ritual actions that 'locate individuals in particular spaces by giving them rights, as well as obligations, to others who share those spaces' (ibid.: 93). Localization and the authority that emanates from it are thus to be understood in rather concrete terms.

One of the key functions of articulations of localization is that it expresses an important distinction between 'natives' and 'strangers' of a locality. The distinction allows a local community to make boundaries, draw on sources of authority that have a local origin, undergo and undertake the same rites of passage in the same locale and defend the stake at stake in the locality. In fact, application of these localizations defines and defends the very existence of that locality as a habitable space against challenges from external impositions, be they from 'the state' (system) or other tribes.

Authority is mobilized to enforce a particular order in the justice and security field, and how, more specifically, the articulation of authority occurs in individual localities. At a very basic level, originating from one particular location, being a 'son of the soil' rather than a 'stranger' generates immediate authority. Those who can render probable that they descend directly from individuals who established the town as a habitable space are considered to have a proportionally greater interest in its survival, channelling earnings from diamond finds, for instance, towards upholding it. In short, they 'own' the authority.

A successful claim to 'own the authority' is not a fixed status, but must be reproduced continuously. Being a 'son of the soil', and articulating a forceful reference to this claim, is always open to manipulation. It is a status that is constantly challenged and invoked in symbolic and physical struggles, and is thus deeply political with respect to who occupies what positions vis-à-vis other contenders at any one given time. It is a position that cannot be fixed, it cannot be fetishized through written text, and thus appear with the quality of being detached from both its producers and from any specific addressees (Connerton 1989: 7; Herzfeld 1992: 118). Being a 'son of the soil' is not represented in bald, decontextualized, legal prose – and as such is an 'extremely localized' struggle over power, and ultimately resources.

What these brief deliberations imply is that chiefs embody a hybrid order, which always simultaneously assembles multiple sources of authority from sacred and other customary powers, kinship and secret society membership as well as an operative decision-making centre of government of bureaucracy and legislation (Albrecht 2012: 11). It is by extension also clear that the hybrid order, which chiefs embody and govern, is a historically constituted process, and not, as recent developments in peace and conflict studies tend to imply, a particular feature of peacebuilding processes (Richmond 2010, 2011; Boege et al. 2009a; Brown et al. 2010; Roberts 2011). Indeed, hybrid orders are the product of constantly evolving and contested, mutually antagonistic and integral sources of authority that become inseparable when subjected to empirical scrutiny. The chapter now turns to two institutions, the LPPBs and the Poro, which exemplify how 'the community', commonly led by the chiefs, is mobilized to make order at the local level.

Local Policing Partnership Boards: co-opting the private

Police reform in Sierra Leone was initiated in the late 1990s during open conflict, and the LPPBs became central to how the process was articulated locally. Brima Acha Kamara, who became Sierra Leone Inspector-General of Police in 2003, described the police's scope to enforce order in the late 1990s as policing by consensus: 'There were other forces, warring factions, RUF [Revolutionary United Front] combatants, CDF [Civil Defence Force], competition about who should really be in charge of internal security. We were not able to flex our muscle, and we were ultimately doing policing by consensus' (interview, Brima Acha Kamara, 2009). In his assertion lay the rationale of policing in the years to come, including the basis on which the LPPBs would be established in peacetime. There was a direct link between the attempt to engage combatants in the SLP's stabilization/peacebuilding efforts, and peacetime attempts to engage communities across Sierra Leone in providing their own security.

The reorganization of the justice and security field that was part of ending the conflict entailed the marginalization or elimination of these 'other forces' and 'warring factions'. But 'policing by consensus' was not simply the consequence of war and a breakdown of a centrally governed state system. Rather, it was the result of a deep-seated hybrid order that transcended the years of conflict. Logically, attempts to re-establish the 'state system' through police reform were therefore unlikely to make the principle of policing by consensus obsolete.

LPPBs became a concrete vehicle for appropriating and translating into practice the SLP's ethos of Local Needs Policing that had been formulated by British police advisers in the late 1990s.[4] Unlike the regime-preserving approach prior to and during the conflict, the SLP was oriented towards 'the community' as the space in which the interface and amalgamation of different approaches to ordering would take place. However, while the SLP used a language of benevolence and inclusion to explain the rationale of the LPPBs, their emergence was also articulated as a pragmatic response to an understanding that the 'numerical strength of the Sierra Leone Police (SLP) in coverage is smaller compared to the fast growing population for the entire nation'. The statement is taken from the *Proposed Guidelines and Codes of Conduct for Operations of the Local Policing Partnership Boards of Sierra Leone 2005* (SLP 2005), which express the common perception that LPPBs should compensate for the lack of resources within the SLP. People were to police themselves.

The 2005 Proposed Guidelines – replaced by a LPPB Constitution in 2011 that is very similar in wording – provide insight into the community-based structure that the SLP are co-opting in order to play a role in local security. As a 'community based structure' and a 'non-partisan, inter-religious, social integration development group' the LPPBs were established 'to create a peaceful and healthy police/community co-existence at all levels, with the ultimate goal to fight and reduce crime to an appreciable level and contribute to the socio-economic and political development of Sierra Leone' (ibid.). What this particular statement expresses is the extrapolation of certain representatives of the community, and their movement into an apparently neutral and depoliticized space, where the hierarchy that centres on paramount and lesser chiefs as figures of authority is muted. Nothing is stated about the chiefs' role in appointing – and managing – the individuals who get involved in the work of the LPPBs, and thus the latter's role in reproducing structures of power at the local level.

Mustapha Kambeh, who was involved in developing the LPPB concept when he was posted at police headquarters in Freetown in the mid-2000s, and later became Local Unit Commander in the eastern part of the country, explained the relevance of the LPPBs in the following way:

> [They are] critical in assisting the police to curb and mediate in conflict within the area [of the police division]. They know that [they have that role] because they're part and parcel of the community and they [the police] listen to them [the partnership board] and will as a consequence understand the situation very well. So that is helping us police our area. So what the partnership board is now doing is helping us [do] early warning, [they are an] early response mechanism to conflict, because of the resources given, and the economic trend in the country, and the whole world. The resources are inadequate if you allow conflict to erupt and grow within your areas of responsibility. The sooner we observe that conflict is about to erupt, we are able to move quickly to curb it in a timely way; it assists us in our resource.

In the early days of police reform, external advisers had been uncomfortable with engaging the 'local community', and the chiefs in particular. While the needs of the community were to be heard by the SLP, the intention behind Local Needs Policing, as envisioned by the international advisers who played a crucial role in re-establishing the SLP, was not to reproduce a system of order-making that was organized by actors other than the SLP. It was precisely to establish the imagery of vertical encompassment, a police force as separate from and yet encompassing and integrated with 'the community'. Indeed, external advisers assumed that the role of traditional leaders would diminish in importance and disappear as relics of the past and conflict once the state-building process had gathered momentum, and marginalized or toppled other makers of order (Keith Biddle, interview, June 2009).

However, simply ignoring the role of chiefs in order-making would and did not automatically lead to their marginalization. On the contrary, their position and the order they administer were consolidated through the collaborative approach that defines the LPPBs. As they have been established in many parts of Sierra Leone, the LPPBs have not constituted a fundamental reorganization of the security and justice field. Instead these organizational formations fortified and consolidated an already existing relationship between the SLP and the chief. Mustapha Kambeh urgently understood that the authority to act within the justice and security field depended on entertaining close relations with the chiefs:

> Well, for me to work effectively, you must be in cordial relationship with your traditional leaders in the area you find yourself, because if there is an amicable relationship, I mean, between the LUC and the paramount chiefs and their section chiefs, town chief, et cetera, it will go a long way to ease policing problems in that area. Because then there will be a common understanding among the chiefs and the police. They will understand the problems of the police and find ways and means how to harmonize their relationship and make sure that things work effectively to make their areas secure. We have to preserve the peace and public tranquillity and make sure that the fear of crimes is reduced to the nearest minimum within the area and make sure that people go about their normal activities without hindrance. So to achieve all these things, you must be in good relations with the paramount chief.

The SLP know their position, and that their room for manoeuvring is driven both by capacity and legitimacy vis-à-vis chiefs, who above all draw authority to act from their status as autochthons of the area over which they rule. The perception among Sierra Leonean police officers is that there is a shortage of personnel and equipment within the force, which adds to the importance of maintaining good relations with the 'local community'. The police officers – and soldiers – in Kono District bordering Guinea are unaware of what happens in many parts of the district, notably in the border regions, and the SLP is dependent on 'the community' to provide them with that information. However, as this chapter argues, 'the community' is not constituted by neutrally distributed interest groups, but by a field of power that centres on paramount and lesser chiefs.

The role of LPPBs in order-making LPPBs, as outlined above, are shaped by numerous, interrelated words, actors and things that constitute assemblages of international policy discourse on community policing, the distribution of material and financial resources within the police and the articulation of authority within the justice and security field. Paramount and lesser chiefs play a vital role in shaping how they operate, but have also been presented as an important push by the SLP towards 'increased collaboration between SLP and civilians; by NGOs that work with them' (Hanson-Alp 2008: 14; Albrecht and Jackson 2009: 189–97).

The Board's purpose is to liaise with the police to promote safety and security through consultations and joint operations. A divisional board is set up, which is headed by a chairman, a vice-chairman, a treasurer, a representative of the youth and women, two traditional chiefs, and several other positions. Five delegates from each section in the chiefdom are put forward for election, selected for their 'reputable character', and only if they are 'dedicated to the course of security and community development' (SLP 2005, 2011). Their appointment is marked by a certificate awarded by the LUC and they meet once every month (SLP 2011).

Only central executive members that are constitutive of the LPPB at police divisional level are formally elected every two years (a process that in some cases is 'statified' by having the National Electoral Commission oversee the process). In the case of individual chiefdoms, members at section and village level are appointed by the chiefs and elders. In one village, the LPPB member was first a central member of the group of elders and was then replaced with a close ally of the town chief. Only if an issue is deemed important by the LPPB member and the chief will it be brought to the Partnership Board chairman of the chiefdom, the nearest police post or station or both. Furthermore, the SLP expect the chiefs to deal with matters within their own jurisdiction, and while these cases are referred to as minor it is not always clear what constitutes a minor case. Murder, sudden deaths, severe beatings (referred to as 'blood crimes'), substantial theft and sexual abuse of children are commonly considered to be 'above' the town, and to require police involvement.

Generally, when a criminal act takes place, young men will, if necessary, support the LPPB member to make an arrest. These youth groups constitute the physical force of community security. In rural areas, they are not, however, formally part of the LPPBs or recognized as such by the SLP (in urban areas this is often the case). Rather, the youth groups represent general order-making practices that date back to before the introduction of community policing in Sierra Leone when interaction with the police was rare and feared.

LPPBs as an expression of SLP presence have thus intertwined with already existing local structures of authority and practices. For this reason it is not always evident whether LPPB members act in the capacity of being members of the LPPB or as community members of a certain status. This indicates the powers that are vested in chiefs in Sierra Leone and the point that the LPPBs are co-opted by them. Indeed, SLP officers at chiefdom level often note that they work for and take guidance from the chiefs. This might be denied at headquarter level in Freetown, but chiefdoms and villages on the border of Guinea are far away from the capital.

That said, community policing has not simply reproduced already existing chieftaincy structures. It has also reshaped the relations between communities and the SLP. Concrete interactions and negotiations over case resolution between SLP and LPPB members have an important symbolic value in signalling the novel presence of the SLP in the rural areas. And at times, investigations and intelligence are less important. This is illustrated by a case from Peyima, a small town in Kamara Chiefdom, Kono District, in eastern Sierra Leone, where an epileptic boy had drowned, owing probably to a seizure.

It was widely believed amongst Peyima's inhabitants that the devil had taken the boy. His death was seen as the ancestors' punishment of the villagers for neglecting to make offerings to them. In line with local cosmological beliefs, the boy's death was therefore followed by a number of remedying rituals. Even so – and unusual for the time prior to the introduction of community policing – it was decided that the case should also be attended to by the SLP.

The LPPB representative in Peyima, Kalilu, came to the crime scene. Acting as a police officer investigating a case, he jotted down the course of events and went to the nearest police post to report the issue and to bring back a police officer to verify that a crime had not been committed. Despite the practical difficulties of doing so and the need to pay a transport fee to the officer, this was not a question of the police investigating the case (the SLP in the headquarter town of Kamara Chiefdom has no vehicle or the technical expertise to record and store evidence). What was important was the symbolic quality of reporting to the police, because if Kalilu had not done so, the police might have suspected that a crime had in fact taken place. Before the war, Kalilu explained, the SLP would not have come, and even if their presence did not make a big difference in technical terms of investigating the death of the boy, it did so symbolically to close the case.

As the embodiment of the LPPB, Kalilu represented the combination of different notions of authority, emanating both from the locality of Peyima and organizations defined by their extra-local quality (the SLP). Kalilu referred to the inspector of police as his boss, but he had been appointed to this position by Peyima's town chief. In his hybrid capacity, Kalilu constituted the SLP's negotiation into Peyima, but it was access shaped by the chiefs, and thus on terms set at the local level rather than by a central government.

The role of the Poro in order-making

The Poro is a male secret society located on the Guinea coast, and it is its role in regulating order-making that is analysed in this section. It describes the consequences of being excluded from decision-making at the local level as a non-Poro member, a struggle that is based on authoritative articulations of autochthony that centre on claims of tribal identity, and the ability to point to a 'home land' or a 'home village' in symbolic acts of boundary-making.

In its initiation rites, the Poro provides social knowledge and instruction. Physically entering the bush and undergoing the ritual of initiation is recognized as an important educational mechanism. The objective is to turn immature boys into fully fledged members of the adult community. The boy is swallowed by a spirit when he enters the bush, and tribal marks are cut into his back, signifying the spirit's teeth. At the end of initiation, he is delivered by the spirit and reborn. Obedience to the rules of the Poro, and, by implication, to the social regulations of the community outside the bush, is stressed as the individual enters the bush.

No person can hope to occupy political office in the chiefdom without being a member of the Poro. Hence, while it is organized around local sources of authority, the Poro underpins the administrative unit of the chiefdom outlined by state law because it props up the autochthon status of the chief (see also Bledsoe 1984: 456). These local and extra-local articulations of authority are an important expression of hybrid political orders; a loose but decisive historical integrative process of different systems of social and political relations of inclusion and exclusion.

Specifically, the inclusion/exclusion, member/ non-member aspect of the Poro has a direct effect on how acts of violence and land disputes are addressed in rural Sierra Leone. Bellman (1984: 139) rightly notes that there is 'more to the expression of membership than simply a dichotomy between those who have knowledge and those who do not'. However, what is relevant in the context of this chapter is how the distinction between those who know and those who do not produces effects in order-making practices, and sets up boundaries between 'sons of the soil' and 'strangers'. The following case involving Taylor Kondeh, a young man living in Peyima, exemplifies how the Poro conditioned his ability to safeguard what he considered family property.

The Poro society and the Kondehs' loss of land Taylor Kondeh was in his early thirties. He was not a 'son of the soil', at least not fully. However, he was born and raised in Peyima, and therefore could not generate sufficient authority to lay claim to land and authority in another locale. His mother was a Kono and the first cousin of the town chief. His father, however, was a Mandingo, which put Taylor on the margins of the chiefly hierarchy, struggling to claim authority in the township. He was therefore forced to find innovative ways to make his voice heard in Peyima.

Prior to the 2007 general elections in Sierra Leone, it had become evident to him that he would not be able to establish himself in Peyima as someone with a central role in local decision-making. He therefore made the rather radical decision (to some) to support the All People's Congress (APC), which had been in opposition for a decade, but ended up winning the 2007 elections. Taylor's rationale was that supporting the opposition, if they won, would open up a source of authority that could eventually be converted into financial gain to support his family and provide him with a platform from which he could make his voice heard in Peyima. A few years later, Taylor's strategy had not succeeded; he was still struggling to make ends meet, farming instead of mining, and zealously pursuing a political career. Taylor: 'You know, our party here has become the winning party. So we are expecting jobs, we should be considered greatly. But up to now, you see, the chief is moving around with the SLPP guys.'

Because he affiliated with the APC, Taylor stood up against the political conviction of the town chief and most of Peyima's population, who supported the Sierra Leone People's Party (SLPP). This was the reason why his family had land taken away from them, Taylor argued, a case that was eventually dealt with in the Poro bush. His story describes not only the struggle and competition over access to land, but also how legitimate authority to settle conflict emerged in the town (see Lund 2008: 10).

In Peyima, explicit symbols of the state and its language and props such as contracts and deeds are not referred to and as a consequence do not figure in local decisions over land distribution, especially not among local inhabitants. Land is not exchanged by written contract, but is consolidated verbally in front of witnesses – and never in an interest-free manner. Therefore, proof of the right to mine or farm a piece of land has to be reproduced continuously and challenges to the claim are perennial. Effectively, this leaves room for both double-dealing and interpretation of rightful ownership, both of which are common occurrences in Peyima.

Essentially, this means that land is taken and given according to allegiance to the town chief with the authority he derives from articulating the hybrid order, including from local government law, which stipulates that chiefs hold 'land in trust for the people of the Chiefdoms' (GOSL 2004: 28(d)). Thus, following Juul and Lund (2002: 4–5) in their discussions of land disputes in Africa, what comes into play is the ability of chiefs to negotiate and manipulate land claims and their freedom to deploy a raft of tactics and strategies in order to solidify this claim, including their autochthon status and political party affiliation. Inevitably, it was Peyima's powerful and influential town elders who benefited from the ambiguity of land entitlements.

Land that the Kondehs had been farming since the early 1990s was taken away from them by the town chief. The family's argument that they had been using the land for almost two decades did not constitute a sufficient public claim of ownership. Normally, eviction could not have happened unless the Kondehs had committed some serious crime or without suitable compensation with alternative land. In turn, it was not a viable option to approach extra-local institutions such as the local government District Council, the police or political parties to back up Taylor's family's counter-claim (ibid.: 18). This, in short, would lead to further social exclusion in Peyima, and it was in any case not within the mandate of the SLP or other institutions of the central government to overrule decisions made by the chief, even if they found that a crime had been committed.

In dealing with the case, the town leadership subjected Taylor's family to a strategy of exclusion through the Poro society. Taylor explained:

> So when the case reaches to a point where you say: 'Now this case is not going to be decided in town,' they are going to decide it in a different world. If the issue is between two members, they know how to decide it. OK, if they know that really, you are right, you have the right on a particular issue, they will foul you by calling the secret society members out. (Interview, Taylor Kondeh, April 2009)

A by-law of the Poro stipulates that when the members are out in the town, non-initiates are not allowed to leave their houses, 'and you lock yourself inside', Taylor continued, 'while people [secret society members] stay outside and decide the matter, when it is over, they will tell you: "I'm sorry, we are sorry, this place is no more yours"' (ibid.).

Peyima town chief Gborie's decision about the land farmed by the Kondeh family was not made independently of the state, as is often the case with respect to what Lund (2006: 687) refers to as twilight institutions. Rather, in a double pull, the decision was made both within the state, because chiefs have been a part of the state formation processes since the colonial era of 'indirect rule', and beyond it (see Mokuwa et al. 2011: 343).

Both chiefly authority and the Poro are part and parcel of the continuously reproduced hybrid order that is maintained in rural Sierra Leone. This process, however, is detached from forces that could be cast as 'national' or 'statutory' in the sense that we understand these terms today, i.e. as a centrally governed political entity. The handling of justice and land allocation through Poro involvement does not take place in competition with state authorities, but fully replaces or, perhaps more accurately, fully complements state functions (see Kyed and Buur 2007: 2). In the process, Taylor was cut off from seeking alternative means of redress and grudgingly had to accept that the family's land had been lost.

At the same time, however, the symbolic power of the chief derived from being an autochthon is embedded in his descent from those who first arrived in the particular locality of Peyima (see Bledsoe 1984: 457). Drawing explicitly on local forms of authority, and implicitly on national ones, the articulation of references to the Poro thus produced effects in the field of justice and security. These effects at once excluded state intervention and made it irrelevant, but at the same time drew on long-term state formation processes, which ended up having real effects for the Kondeh family's ability to make a living.

The town chief further undermined Taylor's status. In his capacity of 'holding land in trust' and as a hegemonic figure in Peyima, he told Taylor that 'even someone who has property and land here for fifty years, I'm the only one that have the right to take it from the person". He said that before going to the swamp [to oversee his farming]. But through our hard work we tried to extend the land, the swamp then. And the swamp was not even large at the time.' The rationale was nonetheless fairly simple, as the town chief himself explained: 'OK, for an example, Peter, you want to grow rice in this swamp, and Jimmy Sahr allows you to do it, but it does not belong to you. Jimmy Sahr allows you to make the swamp here, you have been developing this swamp for five, ten, fifteen years. Then Jimmy Sahr says my friend, I want to work my land.' The town chief's rationale was that Taylor's family had no argument, and even if Taylor maintained differently, it was his word against the town chief's, and thus an argument that Taylor could never win.

By involving the Poro, the resolution of Taylor Kondeh's case was transferred into a parallel space within the justice and security field where public confrontation, discussions and action were somewhat muted owing to the hierarchy that exists in the bush. Drawing authority from the realm of the secret society where the decision to take Taylor's land was made, the chief held a position of power that Taylor could never match. Taylor's inferior position within the social space of Peyima meant that his affiliation with the ruling party was of little use to him.

Order-making – how it is articulated and by whom – produced and reproduced power relations manifested in unequal access to land. At the heart of the Kondehs' case lay the fact that the enforcement of order is a field where power was contested, authority was reconfigured and constituted, and where different actor interests were at stake over power, resources and 'clients'. These struggles took place on the symbolic boundary between Poro bush and township, rather than between inside and outside the chiefdom.

Conclusion

As its point of departure, this chapter argues for expanding the concept of private security beyond the private sector and commercial enterprise. It is suggested that this will provide a fuller picture of what order-making in fragile situations entails. Given the hybrid order that characterizes Sierra Leone, an additional argument of the chapter is that it is not possible to make clear-cut distinctions between what is private and public. Just as when speaking of 'states' and 'non-states', the distinction is empirically inaccurate. All organizations that engage in order-making, be it commercial security companies or traditional leaders, necessarily assemble authority from a multitude of sources that include legislative processes of a set of centrally governed institutions.

It is at the same time the case that while the private security industry has grown exponentially in the past decade, commercial interests in contexts such as Sierra Leone, and especially outside Freetown, are often concentrated in specific areas where natural resources are to be found. While the implications of the mining industry are felt across Kono District, security is the business of many and varied institutions that operate side by side, interact with one another, shape and are shaped by one another. The chapter shows the variation in how and by whom order is made by drawing attention to Sierra Leone's LPPBs and the Poro. While they emerged under fundamentally different circumstances and serve equally distinct purposes, they are examples of how local institutional forms mobilize to make order, materializing around paramount and lesser chiefs that assemble their authority from a multitude of local and extra-local sources.

The LPPBs have become an important way for the SLP to negotiate access to communities across Sierra Leone, but outside the main towns of the country's districts, their ability to do so is commonly controlled and shaped by the chiefs. As such, the SLP's room for manoeuvring is driven by their legitimacy vis-à-vis chiefs, who above all draw authority to act from their status as autochthons of the area over which they rule (a source of authority that is also shaped by centrally governed institutions). The SLP is conditioned by a shortage of personnel and equipment and is therefore dependent on its ability to establish relationships with those who constitute 'the community'.

In turn, the Poro shows how order is made by distinguishing between members and non-members of this particular secret society. Claims of Poro membership, combined with ancestral association, profoundly influence land tenure decisions and, in the case of this chapter, claims to secure access to land. These micro-struggles, and the role of the Poro in settling them, take place through processes of 'extreme localization' of order-making.

Notes

1 Such estimates appear in most policy-related literature on informal or non-state justice; see, for example, Chirayath et al (2005), USAID (2005), OECD (2007), UNDP (2009).

2 The concept of hybridity has a long history in socio-legal literature to describe 'legal hybridization' and 'interlegality' of different types or sources of law (Merry 1998). It has been a central concept in cultural studies (Bhabha 1994). In addition, an extensive body of literature discusses the hybrid nature of chieftaincy and traditional authority in Africa (see, for example, Van Rouveroy van Nieuwaal 1996). The novelty of hybridity in debates within political science is that it describes a sphere of political ordering beyond a set of centrally governed institutions, commonly referred to as the state. It is also only recently that it has been applied in the field of peace and conflict studies, mostly referring to the order that emerges when state-building is promoted (Boege et al. 2009a, 2009b, 2009c; Clements et al. 2007; MacGinty 2011; Richmond 2010, 2011; Roberts 2011).

3 The chapter mainly draws on ethnographic fieldwork that was carried out in 2008/09 in Peyima, a small town in Kamara Chiefdom, Kono District (subsequent shorter visits to Peyima were carried out in 2012–14). Peyima's approximately 2,000 inhabitants generate income and livelihood primarily from diamond-mining and farming. Over a hundred interviews and countless casual conversations were carried out with interviewees drawn from a broad cross-section of Peyima's population, relevant authorities in Tombodu (headquarter town of Kamara Chiefdom) and Koidu (headquarter town in Kono District). The data was organized according to general patterns of how security and justice are organized at the local level, by whom it is organized, and with what implications. The chapter also draws on my experiences as a consultant for the UK Department for International Development Access to Security and Justice Programme in Sierra Leone (see Albrecht et al. 2014) and a large body of work that explores how security sector reform has been taken forward in Sierra Leone, mainly at the national level (Albrecht and Jackson 2009, 2014; Jackson and Albrecht 2014).

4 In its basic form, Local Needs Policing is defined as: 'Policing that meets the expectations and need of the local community and reflects national standards and objectives' (Adrian Horn, quoted in Albrecht and Jackson 2009: 32). Today, all policing activities in Sierra Leone ideally, and to a degree also in practice, fall within Local Needs Policing.

Bibliography

Abrahamsen, R. and M. C. Williams (2007) 'Introduction: The privatization and globalization of security in Africa', *International Relations*, 21(2): 131–41.

— (2009) 'Security beyond the state: global security assemblages in international politics', *International Political Sociology*, 3: 1–17.

— (2011) *Security beyond the State: Private Security in International Politics*, Cambridge: Cambridge University Press.

Albrecht, P. A. (2012) 'Foundational hybridity and its reproduction: security sector reform in Sierra Leone', PhD Series, 33.2012, Doctoral School of Organisation and Management Studies, Copenhagen: Copenhagen Business School.

— (2013) 'Local actors and service delivery in fragile situations', DIIS Report 2013:24, Copenhagen: Danish Institute for International Studies (DIIS).

— (2015) 'The chiefs of community policing in rural Sierra Leone', *The Journal of Modern African Studies*, 53: 611–35.

— (2016) 'Secrets, strangers, and order-making in rural Sierra Leone', *Journal of Contemporary African Studies*, 34(4): 519–37.

Albrecht, P. and P. Jackson (2009) *Security*

System Transformation in Sierra Leone, 1997–2007, Global Facilitation Network for Security Sector Reform and International Alert, Birmingham: University of Birmingham.
— (2014) 'Securing Sierra Leone, 1997–2013: defence, diplomacy and development in action', *RUSI Whitehall Paper* no. 82.
Albrecht, P. and H. M. Kyed (2015) *Policing and the Politics of Order-Making*, Abingdon: Routledge.
Albrecht, P. and L. W. Moe (2015) 'The simultaneity of authority in hybrid orders', *Peacebuilding*, 3(1): 1–16.
Albrecht, P., O. Garber, A. Gibson and S. Thomas (2014) 'Community policing in Sierra Leone – Local Policing Partnership Boards', DIIS Report 2014:16, Copenhagen: Danish Institute for International Studies (DIIS).
Allen, P. M. (1968) 'The stratigraphy of a geosynclinal succession in western Sierra Leone, West Africa', *Geological Magazine*, 105: 62–73.
Bellman, B. L. (1984) *The Language of Secrecy: Symbols and Metaphors in Poro Ritual*, Brunswick, NJ: Rutgers University Press.
Berg, J. and C. Shearing (2015) 'New authorities: relating state and non-state auspices in South African improvement districts', in P. Albrecht and H. M. Kyed (eds), *Policing and the Politics of Order-Making*, Abingdon: Routledge, pp. 91–107.
Bhabha, H. (1994) *The Location of Culture*, New York: Routledge.
Bledsoe, C. (1984) 'The political use of Sande ideology and symbolism', *American Ethnologist*, 11(3): 455–72.
Boege, V., A. M. Brown, K. P. Clements and A. Nolan (2009a) 'Hybrid political orders, not fragile states', *Peace Review*, 21(1): 13–21.
— (2009b) 'On hybrid political orders and emerging states: what is failing – states in the global South or research and politics in the West?', in M. Fisher and B. Schmelzle (eds), *Building Peace in the Absence of States: Challenging the Discourse on State Failure*, Berghof Handbook Dialogue Series no. 8, www.berghof-handbook.net/uploads/download/dialogue8_failingstates_complete.pdf, accessed 15 October 2013.
— (2009c) 'Undressing the Emperor: a reply to our discussants', in M. Fischer and B. Schmelzle (eds), *Building Peace in the Absence of States: Challenging the Discourse on State Failure*, Berghof Handbook Dialogue Series no. 8, www.berghof-handbook.net/uploads/download/dialogue8_failingstates_complete.pdf, accessed 15 October 2013.
Brown, M. A., V. Boege, K. P. Clements and A. Nolan (2010) 'Challenging statebuilding as peacebuilding – working with hybrid political orders to build peace', in *Palgrave Advances in Peacebuilding*, London: Palgrave Macmillan, pp. 99–115.
Chaves, I. N. and J. Robinson (2011) 'The architecture of a fragile state: the case of Sierra Leone', Paper prepared for the IGC Growth in Fragile State workshop, 6/7 July, www.theigc.org/sites/default/files/presentation_slides/sierra_leone_case_study.pdf.
Chirayath, L., C. Sage and M. Woolcock (2005) *Customary Law and Policy Reform: Engaging with the Plurality of Justice Systems*, 2, July, siteresources.worldbank.org/INTWDR2006/Resources/477383-1118673432908/Customary_Law_and_Policy_Reform.pdf.
Clements, K. P., V. Boege, A. M. Brown, W. Foley and A. Nolan (2007) 'State building reconsidered: the role of hybridity in the formation of political order', *Political Science*, 59(1): 45–56.
Connerton, P. (1989) *How Societies Remember*, Cambridge: Cambridge University Press.
Fanthorpe, R. (2001) 'Neither citizen nor subject? "Lumpen" agency and the legacy of native administration in Sierra Leone', *African Affairs*, 100(400): 363–86.

— (2005) 'On the limits of liberal peace: chiefs and democratic decentralization in post-war Sierra Leone', *African Affairs*, 105(418): 27–49.

GOSL (1991) *The Constitution of Sierra Leone*, Freetown: Government of Sierra Leone.

— (2004) *The Local Government Act*, Freetown: Government of Sierra Leone.

Hanson-Alp, R. (2008) 'Security system transformation in Sierra Leone, 1997–2007: civil society's role in Sierra Leone's Security Sector Reform process experiences from Conciliation Resources' West Africa Programme', Working Paper Series, *Security System Transformation in Sierra Leone, 1997-2007*, Paper no. 12, Global Facilitation Network for Security Sector Reform (GFN-SSR) and International Alert, Birmingham: University of Birmingham.

Hardin, K. L. (1993) *The Aesthetics of Action: Continuity and change in a West African town*, Washington, DC: Smithsonian Institution.

Herzfeld, M. (1992) *The Social Production of Indifference. Exploring the symbolic roots of Western bureaucracy*, Chicago, IL: University of Chicago Press.

Jackson, P. and P. Albrecht (2014) *Reconstructing Security after Conflict: Security Sector Reform in Sierra Leone*, London: Palgrave Macmillan.

Juul, K. and C. Lund (2002) 'Introduction: Negotiating property in Africa', in K. Juul and C. Lund (eds), *Negotiating Property in Africa*, Portsmouth: Heinemann.

King, N. and P. Albrecht (2015) 'Secret societies and order-making in Freetown', in P. Albrecht and H. M. Kyed (eds), *Policing and the Politics of Order-Making*, Abingdon: Routledge, pp. 178–95.

Kyed, H. M. and L. Buur (2007) 'Introduction: Traditional authority and democratization in Africa', in L. Buur and H. M. Kyed (eds), *State Recognition and Democratization in sub-Saharan Africa: A new dawn for traditional authorities?*, New York: Palgrave.

Leander, A. (2010) 'Practices (re) producing orders: understanding the role of business in global security governance', in M. Ougaard and A. Leander (eds), *Business and Gobal Governance*, London and New York: Routledge.

Lentz, C. (2007) 'Land and the politics of belonging in Africa', in L. de Haan, U. Engel and P. Chabal (eds), *African Alternatives*, vol. 2, Brill, pp. 37–58.

Lund, C. (2006) 'Twilight institutions: public authority and local politics in Africa', *Development and Change*, 37(4): 685–705.

— (2008) *Local Politics and the Dynamics of Property in Africa*, Cambridge: Cambridge University Press.

MacGinty, R. (2011) *International Peacebuilding and Local Resistance: Hybrid forms of peace*, Basingstoke: Palgrave.

Merry, S. E. (1998) 'Legal pluralism', *Law and Society Review*, 22(5): 869–96.

Mokuwa, E., M. Voors, E. Bulte and P. Richards (2011) 'Peasant grievance and insurgency in Sierra Leone: judicial serfdom as a driver of conflict', *African Affairs*, 110(440): 339–66.

OECD (2007) *Enhancing Security and Justice Service Delivery*, Paris: OECD.

Richmond, O. P. (2010) 'Resistance and the post-liberal peace', *Millennium: Journal of International Studies*, 38(3): 665–92.

— (2011) *A Post-Liberal Peace*, London and New York: Routledge.

Roberts, D. (2011) 'Post-conflict peacebuilding, liberal irrelevance and the locus of legitimacy', *International Peacekeeping*, 18(4): 410–24.

Sesay, M. A. (1996) 'State capacity and the politics of economic reform in Sierra Leone', *Journal of Contemporary African Studies*, 13(2): 165–82.

SLP (2005) *Proposed Guidelines and Codes of Conduct for Operations of the Local*

Policing Partnership Boards of Sierra Leone, Freetown: Sierra Leone Police (not published).

— (2011) *The Sierra Leone Police Local Policing Partnership Board Constitution*, Freetown: Sierra Leone Police.

UNDP (2009) *Community Security and Social Cohesion. Towards a UNDP Approach*, New York: UNDP.

USAID (2005) *Field Study of Informal and Customary Justice in Afghanistan and Recommendations on Improving Access to Justice and Relations between Formal Courts and Informal Bodies*, Washington, DC: USAID.

Van Rouveroy van Nieuwaal, E. A. B. (1996) 'States and chiefs: are chiefs mere puppets?', *Journal of Legal Pluralism and Unofficial Law*, 107(428): 387–403.

4 | The underbelly of global security: Sierra Leonean ex-militias in Iraq

Maya Mynster Christensen

When former militia soldiers in Sierra Leone learned that a private security company would be recruiting, they believed that the demand for military labour in a new war zone would finally offer a chance to become 'a somebody'. In May 2009, Sabre International, a private British security company providing services for the American government, arrived in Sierra Leone in order to recruit 'ex-servicemen' for security contracting in Iraq. In collaboration with the Sierra Leone government, they announced on national radio that they would be recruiting up to ten thousand people to secure American military bases in what the Ministry of Labour and Social Security referred to as the 'overseas youth employment programme'.

This chapter explores the outsourcing of security at American military bases in Iraq to Sierra Leonean ex-militias. In doing so, it sheds light on the less visible yet central processes of contemporary security privatization in Sierra Leone and in a larger global economy. By offering a perspective on how the provision of global security is experienced and practised 'from below', the aim is to explore the ambiguities and tensions that characterize these processes of security privatization, and how these processes are facilitated. Sierra Leonean ex-militias are a marginalized population of militarily skilled young men that became available in the aftermath of the Sierra Leone civil war. As markets for violence and security privatization arise not just locally and regionally, but also globally, this population has come to constitute an attractive pool of labourers. The outsourcing of security in Iraq is just one of several examples of this demand for military labour.[1] It is, however, a demand that is becoming increasingly central and, therefore, an urgent focus for ethnographic scrutiny.

The supply of global security, I argue, depends on a form of local immobility: on a population that is stuck, yet constantly on the move. Sierra Leonean ex-militias constitute a population in waiting, but it is also a population that is always moving about in search of opportunities, even when these opportunities are associated with risk and uncertainty. It is this tension between fixity and motion that must be analysed if we wish to understand how the local supply of global security is facilitated.

This chapter is based on extensive ethnographic fieldwork conducted among ex-militias in Sierra Leone from January 2006 to November 2012. These ex-militias are mainly former members of the Revolutionary United Front (RUF), commonly referred to as the rebel movement, and of the West Side Boys (WSB), a splinter group of the army that fought *against* the RUF at the end of the civil war. The core interlocutors who inform this article are in many ways distinctive, mainly because they have been in prison from 2000 to 2006, owing to the central role they played in wartime politics. Their absence from public life for almost six years excluded them from the benefits of, for instance, UN-sponsored reintegration programmes designed to equip ex-militias with peacetime livelihood skills. Their release just a year before the 2007 elections must be seen in the light of their expected remobilization (Christensen and Utas 2008). This particular group of ex-militias is *not* representative of all ex-militias in Sierra Leone, especially because they were mobilized into national and regional militarized networks *after* the declaration of peace. Even though representing a somehow marginal group, their experiences are central if we wish to understand contemporary processes of security outsourcing in Sierra Leone and beyond.[2]

Tracing the trajectories of these core interlocutors and their extended networks of mobilized ex-militias positioned on the continuum from the commanders to the foot soldiers, the chapter is structured around a chronological account of how they struggle to make their way to Iraq and back home again. Since I was unable to go to Iraq owing to the restricted access to the American military bases where the Sierra Leonean ex-militias were posted, this account is based on qualitative data collection in Sierra Leone. I conducted interviews with ex-militias both prior to and after their deployment in Iraq, and carried out participant observation around spaces of recruitment in the urban ghettos where the ex-militias I trace congregated also upon return to Sierra Leone.

The account I present documents the difficulties of winning a place in the 'overseas youth employment programme' and of the suspension and prolonged waiting that shaped the process of recruitment. Moving on to take a closer look at the military training that prepared the ex-militias for a radically different environment of warfare, the chapter describes their departure to Iraq and then the return to Sierra Leone of a deceased contractor and a large group of contractors who were deported. Recruited for employment in an environment dominated by 'white man culture', the contractors come to experience a number of obstacles relating most significantly to racialization, understood as the process by which racial identities are ascribed to particular relationships and social practices, and constructed in particular contexts (Garner 2010: 21; Fassin 2011). In the chapter, I discuss how notions of race and visions of a better life overseas are appropriated as the contractors find themselves positioned at the bottom of a racial hierarchy. Against this backdrop, I conclude with an analysis of how my informants employ notions of race and slavery to make sense of their present predicament and as a moral response to exploitative relations in a context of global security outsourcing.

The outsourcing and privatization of global security have been subjects of critical scholarly enquiry, especially during the last decade. While the military and security industry grew rapidly in the wake of the Cold War, it is following 9/11 and the 2003 Iraq military invasion that security services became managed increasingly by private security actors.[3] The tendency to outsource security services to private operators has been characterized as the 'privatization of security', understood as 'a process whereby private sector actors are called upon to perform tasks traditionally construed as being the responsibility of the state and state agencies' (Berndtsson 2009: 2–3). Yet rather than simply moving security provision from state agencies to private hands, this process is characterized by *entanglements* and by *interactions* between public–private and global–local relations, by a reassembly into what Rita Abrahamsen and Michael Williams have termed 'global security assemblages' (Abrahamsen and Williams 2009; Duffield 2001). Such entanglements and interactions are paramount to the security outsourcing I explore in this chapter. As I elucidate empirically below, the outsourcing of security in Iraq to Sierra Leonean ex-militias bridges categorical divides and calls for a reassessment of clear-cut distinctions between public and private domains.

My point of departure for exploring these entanglements and interactions differs from dominant approaches to global security privatization that have focused mainly on relations between state authority, political legitimacy and global governance, and on the legal and ethical implications of private security provision (see, for instance, Singer 2003; Leander 2005; Kateri 2010). While this scholarship has contributed significant and important perspectives on the macro-level dynamics of the private security industry, it has largely neglected the ways in which this industry depends on and is shaped by so-called 'Third Country Nationals' (TCNs), a workforce of (sub)contractors from the global South. As noted by scholars within the field of gender studies, this neglect has led to an underestimation of the importance of the gendered, classed and racialized hierarchies of power in understanding the privatization of security and its effects (Eichler 2014; Higate 2012). The chapter contributes to this overlooked subject by demonstrating how Sierra Leonean ex-militias experience and negotiate their positions as private security contractors in Iraq. This new perspective on the micro-dynamics of private security provision enables us to expose the hidden underbelly of global security (see Ferguson 1999: 242), and can serve as a prism through which we can explain and anticipate emerging economies in the field of private security outsourcing.[4]

Global security from below: between recognition and racialization

To understand how the provision of global security is experienced and practised by Sierra Leonean ex-militias, it is crucial to scrutinize the relations between recognition and racialization. These relations bring the post-war trajectories and aspirations of ex-militias to the fore, and allow us to illuminate the nexus between fixity and motion that shapes their recruitment into global security assemblages.

During a transitional post-war period new possibilities for being and becoming emerge, as new spheres of recognition and of *mis*recognition are generated along with new practices of exclusion and inclusion (Hansen 2012: 2–4). Among the ex-militias I trace in this chapter, the post-war period implied a radical change in positions and possibilities, a downward movement in social mobility and esteem. When peace was officially declared in Sierra Leone on 18 January 2002, they became classified as violent perpetrators, as unwanted social beings who constituted a threat to security. Largely excluded from social and political life, they positioned themselves through negatively defined modes of being: as 'nobodies' and as 'victims of peace'. Their opportunities to contest this precarious position were highly limited, yet a number of social categories became available for them to pursue. First and foremost, these categories were civilian. The dominant logic of the internationally directed peace process was that in order to fit into post-war society, and to turn into recognized citizens, ex-militias would have to adopt civilian identities and adapt to civilian lives and livelihoods. Yet leaving behind wartime networks and identities posed significant challenges for ex-militias as their survival depended on these networks and identities during times of peace as well, not least because they constituted an attractive resource in the field of global security outsourcing precisely because of their capacity for violence (Hoffman 2011a, 2011b). In this post-war context, security contracting in Iraq was envisioned as a chance to contest this self-ascribed position as 'victims of peace' and their experience of being stuck.

While stuckness, understood here as 'a sense of existential immobility' caused by experiences of temporal suspension and social exclusion,[5] is a precondition for the contemporary forms of private security outsourcing in which the ex-militias I trace engage, it does not sufficiently explain what facilitates these processes of outsourcing. It fails to account for the ways experiences of being stuck are constituted by movement, by experiences of what it means to move, and by imaginaries about what movement can produce. Despite being caught in a prolonged state of stuckness, Sierra Leonean ex-militias aim at regaining the position of 'a somebody' of worth, recognized human beings. Their struggle to become 'a somebody' is linked to intimate and social matters, but, as will be elaborated in this chapter, it is also a search for political recognition. They argue that they have been denied the rightful benefits of their wartime sacrifices –

'bullet marks but no benefit' is a common slogan used by ex-militias to express a collective claim to compensation and political recognition. Consequently, it was highly significant to ex-militias when the Sierra Leonean government announced that it would channel the Iraq deployment.

The government, ex-militias believed, had decided to engage in this deployment of 'ex-servicemen' in order to finally compensate them for their wartime services and for their suffering in the aftermath of the war. It was therefore interpreted as a symbolic recognition of their wartime sacrifices. Of special importance in this regard was the official nature of the recruitment. Having been mobilized into militarized networks for more shadowy purposes in the post-war period, as for instance unofficial security guards for private politicians and as regional mercenaries (Christensen 2013), ex-militias were chiefly concerned about the public framing of the 'overseas youth employment programme'. The official recognition implied in such a programme would, they assumed, bring an end to experiences of social exclusion and stuckness. It would help them to achieve a sense of inclusion and connectedness not just in Sierra Leone, but also beyond the African continent in 'the world of the white man'.

The outsourcing of security in Iraq to Sierra Leonean ex-militias highlights the ruptures between inclusion and exclusion, and between recognition and *mis*recognition, as implicated in the tension between the emic notions of being a 'somebody' and a 'nobody'.[6] Whereas it can be argued that global 'interconnection is created through circulation' (Tsing 2008 [2002]: 75), the very opposite turned out to be the case for the Sierra Leonean contractors (Schiller and Salazar 2013). For them, the circulation of labour from one (post-)war zone to another resulted instead in an increasing sense of global *dis*connection and exclusion (Ferguson 2006: 14). Their experiences are not exceptional in this regard. 'Intrinsic to contemporary global economic processes are practices of exclusion, the creating of 'black holes; of zones of disinvestment and abandonment' (Inda and Rosaldo 2008 [2002]: 35), which may produce strong claims to membership and recognition (Ferguson 2006: 14).

To describe the predicament caused by the combination of an 'acute awareness of a privileged "first class" world' and an increasing sense of disconnection, James Ferguson employs the notion of 'abjection' (ibid.: 166). This notion, I propose, also captures the predicament of the Sierra Leonean contractors. For them, however, abjection is a result not only of global disconnection, it is also intimately linked to racial matters. These racial matters are expressed in the narratives of ex-militias, which link blackness with stuckness and whiteness with progress. As argued by Henrik Vigh, such narratives should not be understood as a '(re)colonialization of consciousness', but instead as a 'racialized perception of difference' enhanced by an 'increasing knowledge of uneven distributions' (Vigh 2006: 490–92). As I elaborate below, it is in this context of uneven distributions that racial narratives are employed by Sierra Leonean ex-militias.

Registering for 'overseas youth employment'

'We are not sending mercenaries to Iraq and Afghanistan, if this is what you think,' an employee at the Ministry of Labour told me a few weeks after it was announced that Sabre International would be recruiting 'ex-servicemen' for security contracting. Like other government officials he stressed that this was a programme launched by the Sierra Leone government in order to tackle the huge youth unemployment problem; an issue considered a major threat to peacebuilding in Sierra Leone.[7] He explained that at least 2,500 people were to be employed as private security guards (though the number was expected to grow to 10,000), first in Iraq and later on in Afghanistan. If this was successful it would be a major achievement for the government and a means to stabilize security, he insisted. To begin with it would be a significant step towards meeting election promises of generating youth employment. Added to that, employing some of these ex-militias who are considered troublemakers would reduce violence and crime, first because they would be out of the country for a few years and later on because they would return to Sierra Leone with money earned from their overseas employment; an incentive to keep cool and focus on future investments.

Only a few weeks after the programme was announced, thousands of aspiring recruits made their way to the ministry in order to register. None of them had seen the contract, which apart from loose formulations about the services they might be asked to provide in 'Iraq/Afghanistan', either by Sabre International or its client, also concerned important issues such as payment, insurance, contractor conduct, use of force, and termination. No one had any idea about how long they were to stay in Iraq or Afghanistan *if* employed, or what salary they might be paid. Pointing to these uncertainties, the aspiring recruits at the ministry consequently referred to the employment as 'a blind issue'. Material benefit was not the only thing the aspiring recruits had in mind, when they made their way to the ministry. Their eagerness to be included in the programme was closely connected to expectations of official recognition and to imaginations of a better life overseas.

Victor,[8] a former soldier and WSB member, was among the first aspiring recruits to enter the space around the ministerial buildings. Though a member of the All People's Congress's (APC) task force, a formation of ex-soldiers and ex-militias set up to secure APC politicians,[9] he did not hesitate to leave the party office as soon it was announced that a company was on the lookout for 'ex-servicemen' to work in Iraq and Afghanistan. His political involvement had not yet resulted in the expected benefit. The politicians instil hope but fail to honour their promises, he had learned. Like his task force companions, who equally survived mainly from occasional handouts when they hung out by the party office, Victor regarded the programme as a chance at regular employment, and thus as a chance to make up for several years of post-war marginalization and exclusion. Since the government had decided to bring this programme in, targeting specifically the 'ex-servicemen', it was to be regarded as a symbolic recognition of his wartime sacrifices, he argued. Moreover, and just as important, 'overseas employment' offered him a legitimate source of income and, he imagined, would position him as a respectable soldier also among the white (*white man dem*).

In order to go overseas, the first step was to be registered. But getting one's name on the registration list proved a tricky task. In order to get on the certified list they had to work their way through employees attached to 'Middle East Overseas Employment' at the ministry, who, to complicate things further, each had their personally attached men to assist them in administering the registration lists. 'This is *Sababu* politics,' the recruits pointed out, thereby indicating that without being connected to a Big Man (*Sababu*), and preferably one with close connections to government officials, their chances of getting on the list were fairly bad.[10]

Despite experiences of being neglected by politicians one has loyally served, *Sababu* politics often works. After all, Victor's access to the programme *was* eased by his membership of the APC task force and his day-to-day encounters with political big men at the party office. Employees at the ministry were aware that Victor was capable of acting as a gatekeeper between the aspiring recruits and the government officials. Therefore, he was given the assignment of protecting the government officials from the crowds of people seeking to bulldoze their way to the offices. This assignment made it possible for Victor to consolidate his status as a task force member, as he was therefore placed in a position to decide who was getting in. Most important to Victor, he was rewarded with a place on the registration list. Obtaining a place on the list was the first step to getting in. If one managed to get his (or her)[11] name on the list, a screening process followed in which the recruits were tested for a number of common diseases (including HIV/AIDS) and were to pass a one-week military training programme.

The first step in the screening process was to provide the following mandatory documents: a discharge book from the national army or police headquarters to document a background either as soldier or police officer; a police clearance to document a background with no criminal record; a passport to document that they were in the required age group of twenty-five to forty-four; and a yellow fever certificate. As the recruits began manoeuvring along various channels in order to get hold of the papers, *Sababus* turned out to be helpful. For other ex-militias who had no one to tap, getting hold of the documents became a matter of intensive hustling, of 'do and die business', as they said, thereby indicating the urgency of getting hold of money. Money was, however, not the sole obstacle. Even more tricky was the fact that they had to document a background as ex-soldiers or ex-police officers. The bulk of the aspiring recruits had never joined the national army, being members of militia movements instead, while many of those who *had* joined the army were dismissed from service without any official documentation. In order to overcome this obstacle, the recruits made use of two common strategies: either they would borrow a discharge book from a relative (in most cases a deceased soldier), or they would buy one of the fakes that were being produced when the programme kicked off. Given the money they would have to pay if they also needed police clearance despite having been detained or imprisoned, the registration process was not inexpensive.

Van Damme was one of the aspiring recruits who struggled to get hold of the required documents. In order to gather sufficient money to afford the documents, he had to give up the room he was renting and sell all his belongings: a TV, a mobile phone, and his bed. Being aware that he had to manipulate bureaucracy because 'politics is playing', he had also gathered money to bribe government officials in charge of the registration lists. When I asked him whether it was really worth giving up everything in which he had invested, he first echoed a general consideration shared by the recruits: when posted in Iraq, he would receive a salary to benefit his family, and likewise in case he died. But following this consideration, he replied: 'There is no benefit without struggle. Sometimes when you struggle you will benefit, at other times you will get no benefit. The programme is like gambling: we don't know our faith but our hope is to have victory on our side.'[12]

Like the majority of the aspiring recruits, Van Damme compared the programme with gambling, based on the uncertainties associated with the job in Iraq but also as a result of the difficulties of getting in. Despite the uncertainties, however, the aspiring recruits invested everything in their hope of making it overseas. This involved not only a high degree of bureaucratic manoeuvring, but also an ability to endure prolonged waiting, since the processes of registration and screening turned out to be an extremely protracted affair.

Waiting for deployment: the politics of suspension

'We are waiting like slaves' became a common statement among the recruits. Although they maintained hope of eventually winning out, the feeling of being trapped in an endless state of suspension became dominant. Government officials sought to address this temporal uncertainty. While the programme was constantly delayed, owing mainly to negotiations between the company and the government around issues of salary and delivery of weapons for the pre-deployment training, they sought not to destroy hope and visions of progress. 'We will redeem you from slavery,' they said, as they promised the recruits that they would depart for 'greener pastures' any time soon.

Van Damme was not the only recruit who had already packed his bag when the programme was launched, and he was not the only recruit who was still stuck at the ministry a year later. Van Damme was expecting to leave together with Victor, who was included in the first batch of 350 contractors travelling on a plane to Baghdad in December 2009. At that point he had gone through medical screening and military training, and he had even managed to get on board the chartered flight transporting the first batch to Baghdad. But his hope was soon dashed. When the company representatives discovered that there were not enough seats on the plane, they jokingly remarked: 'This is not a *poda poda* [minibus]'! Together with four other unlucky ex-militias, he was ordered to leave the plane and return home to wait for the next departure. Van Damme waited for a long time together with thousands of recruits who also had difficulties bargaining their way overseas. Together they found themselves in a state of limbo for an extended period of time.

In April 2010, it was with mixed feelings of anxiety and hope that Van Damme and other recruits were standing at the ferry terminal in Freetown, ready to cross the waters to the airport. A batch of 350 was to depart for Iraq. Some were dressed in so-called 'desert uniforms', while others had dressed up as 'diplomats' in decent suits, American flags and Obama badges on their bags. 'We don't want to look cheap when we are travelling – the white man should know who we are,' they explained to me. They had all been informed that they would definitely be flying out that day. Yet it was quickly rumoured that the departure might once again be delayed. This time owing to volcanic ash![13] Sitting along the road overlooking the airport, the recruits were waiting for a plane to land. The airport was dark and silent. Van Damme and his companions had been planning a big send-off party, but only a few had money left in their pockets.

The next morning it was finally announced that their departure had been cancelled – and once again they were told by the company representatives to be on stand-by. Still dressed up in their best clothes, they carried their luggage to the nearest palm-wine hangout. 'How can we return home to our families and friends once again,' they asked as they related the emotional send-off celebrations that had been held for them. It would be shameful to return home, and only few had sufficient money to buy a ticket for the Freetown ferry. Others suddenly regretted having consulted Chinese doctors to get injections 'not to feel for women', as the company representatives had advised them to forget about 'women business' while in Iraq. Being in a state of impotency, also at a symbolic level, the disappointed recruits began to lose courage and confidence that they would ever get a chance to leave Sierra Leone. Yet it was after all the 'white man' who owned the security company – and the 'white man' would not make false promises like the 'black hypocrites', they insisted.

The above scenario urges us to consider how experiences of suspension and prolonged waiting affect future prospects and hopes. Having been mobilized by politicians for both wartime and peacetime political purposes, but without achieving the expected benefits, the recruits gradually started to lose faith that they would ever be 'redeemed from slavery', as promised by the representatives from the Ministry of Labour. Yet a vague hope remained and continued to inspire action. Among the recruits, agency was inspired by specific thoughts on how their stay in the Middle East would radically improve their social and economic status. Most important here were imaginaries relating to racial politics and visions of the West as a place of modernity and endless opportunity. In this regard, hopes about migration connect to enduring images of the civilized 'white man' *contra* submissive blacks – a dominant social imaginary 'dividing the world into black and white, adept and inept' (Vigh 2008).

Pre-deployment training: learning 'white man culture'

Racial divisions were powerfully present in the recruits' narratives from the start of their enlistment, a presence that became even more dominant when they arrived at Camp Lion, a temporary military camp set up by Sabre International to train the recruits.[14] In Camp Lion they had to learn how to perform their jobs in Iraq, including the use of weapons, but perhaps just as importantly they had to learn about 'white man culture'. In this sense, the camp not only became a space for activating military skills acquired during the civil war, but also a space for learning about racial hierarchies.

'Who are we colonized by?' shouted a Ugandan training instructor. 'By the British!' the recruits answered. These lines were repeated a number of times in the presence of two middle-aged white Sabre International employees: a British ex-soldier who had been deployed in Africa on numerous occasions and his South African colleague, who was usually based in Pretoria.[15] The white men looked at me with a perplexed expression, somehow amused and somehow embarrassed. Inevitably, the question triggers reflections about the resemblance between Sabre International and the colonizer, and between the recruits and colonized subjects. When the British company representative addressed the recruits, he advised them how to behave when working at the military bases. 'The Americans and the British work with time [punctually],' he said, 'learn to understand them and follow them without asking questions.' The lesson on 'sexual harassment' was another example thereof.

I joined the class led by the Ugandan instructor, who called on two male recruits to demonstrate how they usually hug each other. He quickly corrected them: 'Do it very fast', 'do not hold each other's hands', 'do not act like if you are gays', 'follow American standards'! The recruits practised hugging in an appropriate manner according to American standards a number of times, and were then instructed on how to address their future female colleagues.

'You can harass a woman just by looking at her,' they were informed, and they were warned that they could be dismissed for doing so. In the classes led by the Sierra Leonean instructors, American rules and standards were, however, negotiated. 'Bring your dark shades,' the recruits were advised when they asked how they would be able to look at their female co-workers. A Sierra Leonean instructor was proud to announce that he had had love affairs with several female American soldiers, and he carefully advised the recruits on how best to seduce the white women. Following this, he became more serious. He explained that the Sierra Leoneans would always be inferior to their American colleagues, and he told of several incidents of humiliation caused by his attempts to bend the rules. 'The white man is tricky, he is hard to fool,' the instructor said in concluding the lesson. After intensive lessons on how to deal with American soldiers, the weapons arrived at the camp.[16] Having been forced to carry wooden sticks fitted with a nail symbolizing the trigger, the recruits were eager to get hold of the real deal and finally get to practise what they considered far more important than American military culture: 'the use of force'. Many had been boasting about their expertise, but when lined up in groups to demonstrate their weapon-handling skills, reactions were mixed. The recruits began to display anxiety and questioned me. Would the 'bullet-proofing' of their bodies, an occult technology of protection acquired through their initiation into militia movements,[17] be powerful enough when confronted with another type of warfare? Do suicide bombers have magic powers? How does one detect a suicide bomber? And why do they choose to kill themselves? Some started to cry when asked to pick up the AK47, while others trembled too much even to hold the weapon. For many, it was their first time holding a weapon since the end of the civil war. 'This is my rifle. This rifle is everything to me. This rifle is my life,' they were instructed to repeat, a motto they also used during the civil war.

Going back to war was a chief concern for the recruits throughout the training course. While the majority of the recruits were actively engaged in violence and combat throughout the ten-year civil war, they were anxious about whether their combat skills could be directly transferred to a modality of warfare that differed radically from warfare in West Africa.[18] Owing to this anxiety, they were less alert when the instructors taught them about the rules of engagement, about issues of human trafficking and the Geneva Convention. Rather than being concerned with such more abstract implications of warfare, their thoughts and questions concentrated on the concrete levels and the means of violence they would face in Iraq, and on the new type of enemy they were to confront. The danger of being involved in yet another modality of warfare in a foreign environment was temporally made less significant, though, when they eagerly debated the transformation they would undergo once they managed to escape the African continent.

Among Sierra Leonean ex-militias, the possibility of a worthy life is often located at a distance both spatially and temporally (see also Vigh 2008), in an imagined 'overseas world' where the attractions of modernity are accessible. When the aspiring recruits envisioned their departure, it was with this 'overseas world' in mind. Iraq, they imagined, would be a space of transit, a space for new opportunities to emerge. As they were to be posted to American military bases, they were going, at least almost, to 'white man country', they argued, and consequently they could make connections to a larger global world. Against this background they spoke of Baghdad as a 'junction' for numerous opportunities that, in the long run, could help them move on to even more desirable places in the world.

Therefore, it is hard to describe the excitement experienced by Van Damme and 363 other recruits when they finally made their way through airport security on 5 May 2010. At that point they were still unaware where exactly they were going, and they had not yet read the contract they had signed. But they had learned to adjust to a new culture dominated by 'white man rules', and they had been taught how to handle what they referred to as 'the bad Arab Man'. Moreover, they had been informed that they were to play a vital role in 'fighting for democracy' – among the recruits still referred to as 'demo-crazy' – but also warned not to bring along their jungle behaviour and indiscipline. Despite being anxious, the recruits were mostly concerned about the fact that they were finally on the move.

Experiences of misrecognition and degradation in Iraq

Following the departure of Van Damme, I received the following email from Victor, who took up work at Camp Shield in Baghdad in December 2009:

> Today we lost one of our brothers here in Iraq by the name of Yandy, he has been suffering from cold and pain in the body. He will be in Freetown on Sunday. [...] The job is not easy, the majority of us have become discouraged over the job, and some are even willing to return back home because there is no proper medication and the weather condition is not easy. I am telling you, it is just because of the job crisis in Freetown otherwise I should also have returned home. We are the least paid workers here and there is no good food. [...] I greet you all. May God bless you! Please do that these serious slavery days are over.

Although he was very optimistic when departing, he now referred to his life in Iraq as 'serious slavery days'. The above email perhaps indicates that difficulties adjusting to the desert climate and a longing for African food were some of the main concerns behind his discouragement. Further discussion with Victor and his companions in Iraq made it obvious, however, that it was the experience of misrecognition and degradation that triggered the frustration, the very same experience that they had attempted to escape by leaving Sierra Leone.

A few days after I had received this email, the Sierra Leonean contractors in Baghdad began striking. 'We are mocked even by the Indian workers cleaning our toilets,' they complained as they explained to me the injustices they faced. Not only were other African contractors paid a monthly salary of US$800 while the Sierra Leonean workers were paid just US$200, but their own brothers had begun to fall ill. 'We are slaves!', 'This is civilized human trafficking', the angry contractors protested, indicating that some of them had in fact read the training manual that made references to 'diplomatic human trafficking'.

On 27 May 2010, 150 Sierra Leonean contractors were deported from Camp Shield in Baghdad as a result of their strike. Though they were relieved to leave Camp Shield, their return was characterized by feelings of doubt, uncertainty, anger and fear. How would family members depending on their income receive them? they asked me. How would the government react to their protest? How would the thousands of aspiring recruits, struggling to go to Iraq, react to the deportation? Would they receive the money they had earned? What were their future prospects?

The distressed deportees eagerly discussed their grievances. Before going on strike, they had written a letter to the site manager expressing concern about the lack of medical supplies, the long duty hours and the low salary level. This letter had been ignored. 'The type of work we do in Camp Shield is worth more than US$200 because it is weapon business. And we are the first target. It is a business that involves death,' the deportees explained to me. Upon arrival they were informed that they were being subcontracted to another private security company, TORRES Advanced Enterprise Solutions, that was providing services to the US Department of Defense. While the subcontracting did not immediately raise concerns, the recruits were surprised to learn that they would be based at an American military base from where they were denied exit. Most importantly, however, they were in shock having found out about the low salary. When they were subcontracted, the deportees were promised a salary increase, but as this did not happen they began joking about whether they should join the Taliban. The joke had not been approved of.

One of the deportees, who claimed that he had been detained, tortured and injected with something by American security workers because he was responsible for writing the letter, explained to me the bewilderment he felt on arriving in Baghdad:

> They told us to sit down at the ground – even us, the retired captains! The weather was cold, it was like being inside a fridge. We were watching each other, and then we started to laugh, we thought this was a joke! They [Sabre International] learned us about human trafficking and now they

are doing the same thing to us! I am telling you, it is cheap, cheap labour! Slavery in fact![19]

Simultaneously, experiences of being betrayed by local politicians who had made promises of 'greener pastures' overseas and of being degraded to the status of slaves quickly turned into mixed feelings of anger and despair. The deportees began contacting local media to publicize the degradation to which they had been exposed. Sabre International employees were surprised by this reaction. Why would the contractors spoil the chance of making a better future for themselves? they asked me. They considered taking pictures portraying the poor lives the contractors had been living in Sierra Leone and sending them to the base in Baghdad, as a reminder of what they risked returning to if they went on the rampage. Government officials were equally surprised. During an interview, the deputy minister of labour, Moijueh Kai-Kai, emphasized that the contractors in Iraq were living a 'very good life' and had no good reasons for going on strike. They had misbehaved, he explained, because they had brought 'politics' along with them.[20]

The deportation coincided with the death of Yandy. Yandy's body was buried in Freetown on 1 June 2010. Representatives from Sabre International insisted that he had died from disease, an argument also confirmed by other Sierra Leone contractors in the camp, who stated that he had died from 'cold' as a result of being posted in the windy control towers on long-term night duties. He had been afraid to report sick, they said, as he thought he might be deported if he did so. Yet his family members were convinced that there had been foul play.[21]

During Yandy's funeral the pastor emphasized that death is at God's will and death is always to be expected. The church was full, and several influential people, including the minister of labour, were present. Company representatives had – probably wisely – not shown up. But five of their Sierra Leonean contractors, who had recently returned home to facilitate the ongoing military training of new recruits, were lined up in their brown uniforms with the Sabre International logo. One of the instructors stood up to speak. Though he seemed confused as to whether Yandy could have been saved if given medical treatment in Iraq, he addressed the family by saying that Sabre had done well by them. To honour Yandy, he concluded his speech by stressing, 'Yandy was a warrior – and he died as a warrior.'

Making sense of uneven distributions: vocabularies of race and slavery

Yandy might have died a warrior. Yet given that he was operating as a private contractor, as part of America's largely invisible army, his death was not honoured or recognized in the same way as the deaths of regular soldiers (Taussig-Rubbo 2009). And his struggle for a better future failed, as did those of many of the recruits who gave up everything in order to make it to Iraq, but instead returned to Sierra Leone as a consequence of their perception of having been treated as slaves. As such, rather than venturing into the world, transformed into recognized soldiers, they returned home degraded to cheap labouring bodies. This experienced failure calls for critical perspectives on the global interconnectedness that is assumed here and for an examination of processes of racialization and notions of slavery employed by the Sierra Leonean ex-militias.

According to the Sierra Leonean ex-militias I have traced, the world is organized into a hierarchy. This hierarchy is, to a large extent, a racial hierarchy separating the 'world of blacks' from the 'world of whites', positioning the 'first world' as inferior to the 'third world'. A consequence of such hierarchy is an internalization of racial stereotypes (Jensen 2008). This internalization was expressed in their narratives both prior to departure and when they returned to Freetown in relation to both 'pre-facto' anticipation and 'post-facto' interpretation (Vigh 2006). In different ways, these narratives explicitly linked blackness with stuckness and whiteness with progress. Before their departure, Sierra Leonean recruits spoke of 'negative blackness' as something they would escape when leaving the African continent. Morphing into the 'worlds of whites', they would gradually leave behind the negative ways of behaving associated with 'black man culture'. Corruption, mistrust and envy were some of these 'black man' practices they believed blocked them from social and economic growth in Sierra Leone. However, when they returned to Sierra Leone, they blamed the very same practices for their failure. In this regard, a phrase they repeated over and over again was: 'We don't like ourselves'. Both among the deportees and among those recruits who returned home voluntarily after their contract had ended, this phrase was used to explain to me, and to themselves, what had gone wrong in Iraq. Their examples concentrated on how they had constantly reported the 'misbehaviour' of their own Sierra Leonean colleagues to the white authorities. Such 'misbehaviour' included a wide range of activities such as sleeping on duty, keeping a mobile phone, stealing, watching porn, drinking alcohol, passing food to the civilian Iraqis through the fence, and writing letters encouraging people to strike. However, their failure in Iraq was not simply ascribed to their blackness. It was, at least to begin with, blamed on the 'white man', who gradually went from being their promoter to being their exploiter.

'We are slaves'. This phrase was predominant among the returnees, and especially among the deportees, who employed particularly powerful discourses about how they had been exploited in Iraq. Yet slavery vocabularies were not limited to discussions of exploitative relations upon their return. These registers were employed throughout the process of recruitment. Interestingly enough, they were employed not just by recruits, but also by government officials *and* by the security company, with shifting connotations and divergent perceptions of exploitative relations.

Let me draw from a few of the above discussions in order to illustrate this. 'We are slaves,' the recruits said while waiting at the ministry. At this point, the phrase was employed with reference to the government officials whom they blamed for the delays and for keeping them in check, stuck at the ministry on a daily basis without any form of payment that could help them to sustain their daily survival. The government officials, however, made promises to the aspiring recruits of 'redeeming them from slavery', implying that the lives they lived in Sierra Leone were comparable to slavery. In Camp Lion, when the recruits had lessons on human trafficking, it was the company's employees who triggered slavery discourses. Their training manual, under the topic of human trafficking, stated: 'This is the modern way of slavery in the world'. Though this was definitely not meant to inspire protest but rather to prepare them for worst-case scenarios in case they decided to stay (illegally) in Iraq after the termination of their contracts, the recruits eventually began to draw on this very phrase to express their resentment towards the company and more generally towards the 'white men'. The 'white men' had 'sold' them to another company 'like a modern form of slavery', they protested. Paradoxically, the overseas employment that was supposed to redeem the recruits from slavery was gradually conceived as yet another manifestation of (modern) slavery.

In *Memories of the Slave Trade*, Rosalind Shaw explores how experiences of modernity in Sierra Leone are configured through four hundred years of Atlantic slave trade. Her central argument is that both the Atlantic slave trade and the domestic slave trade that followed it during the colonial era 'marked a capitalist modernity as entailing the exchange of human life for wealth and power' and that memories thereof 'open a vision of the predatory nature of modernity' (Shaw 2002: 17). Memories of the predatory nature of the Atlantic slave trade and colonial modernity, Shaw argues, are imprinted on post-colonial subjects, shaping their interpretations and responses to contemporary forms of human extraction (ibid.: 262). Among the recruits, notions of slavery are employed selectively, both as a way of making sense of present circumstances and as a moral response to uneven relationships and distributions. It was sometimes the national politicians who were regarded as the predators, while at other times it was the 'white man'. Notions of slavery were not simply employed as a response to external actors, but also as a form of self-critique. Similarly to the ways in which racial hierarchies are internalized, the recruits made use of notions of slavery in order to explain their own submission.

The ways in which Sierra Leonean ex-militias I have traced made use of vocabularies of race and slavery are not unique, but rather comparable to how other TCNs of the private security industry in Iraq have responded to experiences of subordination and exploitative relationships.[22] These vocabularies disclose how the racialization of the global division of labour is reinforced in the context of security outsourcing, as contractors from the global South are positioned at the very bottom of racialized hierarchies (Eichler 2014: 607).

Conclusion: Sierra Leonean ex-militias as intrinsic to global security provision

Paradoxically perhaps, the supply of global security depends on local immobility: on people who are stuck, but urgently aspire to be on the move. As such, Sierra Leonean ex-militias constitute an attractive resource for private security companies. These ex-militias, companies have learned, continuously make themselves available for rapid recruitment, and they do so because overseas employment inspires hope and is regarded as an opportunity to gain recognition, especially in a context where private security outsourcing is channelled through public state institutions.

In this chapter I have highlighted how Sierra Leonean ex-militias' decision to take up work in Iraq was closely connected to the perception of *public* and *official* recognition granted by the government. What was perceived as a process of national acceptance and global inclusion was, however, challenged, as the apparently public character of the 'overseas youth employment' gradually faded out, positioning the Sierra Leonean ex-militias as members of an invisible army of subcontractors in an international security complex. Such entanglements and ambiguities between public and private domains produced tensions between recognition and misrecognition, as implicated in the emic notions of being 'a somebody' and 'a nobody', which eventually stirred grievances towards Sierra Leonean politicians and towards the 'white man'. The Sierra Leonean ex-militias I have traced expressed these grievances through notions of race and slavery in a context of an increased awareness of uneven distributions and racialized hierarchies. However, only a few months after the Sierra Leonean ex-militias had their contracts with Sabre International terminated, they returned to new military-strategic sites in Iraq as contractors for yet another private security company that entered the Sierra Leone market for security outsourcing.

The supply of Sierra Leonean ex-militias, I argue, should not be regarded as a phenomenon existing on the margins of official political economies. Rather, it is *intrinsic* to emerging global economies in the field of security outsourcing. While subcontractors from the global South are often represented as marginal to the private security industry, and consequently largely absent from scholarly debates on security outsourcing, it is important to keep in mind that margins are 'a necessary entailment' of the centre (Das and Poole 2004: 4). In the context of security privatization, global economies are not only organized but also sustained by the continuous supply of cheap labour from countries in the global South such as Sierra Leone. In order to explain these economies, we need to explore the hidden underbelly of global security and the ways in which 'local' micro-dynamics facilitate and sustain private security provision. When we direct our attention towards the lived realities and experiences that inform the ways in which Sierra Leonean ex-militias move and seize emergent markets for security provision, we get a sense of how these economies are shaped and will take shape in the future.

Notes

1 For a detailed exploration of the processes of violent and militarized mobilizations in which Sierra Leonean ex-militias have engaged after the civil war, including the Iraq recruitment, see Christensen (2013).

2 It is important to note that the majority of those ex-militias who were recruited for private security contracting in Iraq do not belong to this particular group. However, members of this group facilitated access to the programme for a large number of ex-militias.

3 In March 2011 more than 28,000 private security contractors worked for the US Department of Defense in Iraq and Afghanistan; Moshe Schwartz, 'The Department of Defence's use of private security contractors in Afghanistan and Iraq: background, analysis, and options for Congress' (Congressional Research Service, report prepared for members and committees of Congress, 13 May 2011).

4 For a significant contribution to the organization of militant labour in today's global economy based on fieldwork among ex-militias in Liberia and Sierra Leone, see Hoffman (2011a, 2011b).

5 In his research on Lebanese migration and white racism, Ghassan Hage defines 'stuckedness' as a 'sense of existential immobility', which is intensified by 'conditions of permanent crisis' (Hage 2009: 97).

6 By employing these notions, I approach recognition empirically in this chapter. Among Sierra Leonean ex-militias I trace being 'a nobody' as an undesirable mode of being, linked to social and political *mis*recognition, while being 'a somebody' implies a worthy life in which one is recognized also in the eyes of others. For a more detailed discussion of the tension between being 'a somebody' and 'a nobody' in the context of Sierra Leone ex-militias, see Christensen (2013).

7 'Youth employment poses latent threat to Sierra Leone's stability, top officials warn in UN Security Council Briefing', 22 March 2010, www.un.org/press/en/2010/sc9890.doc.htm, accessed 17 December 2014.

8 To protect my interlocutors, all original names have been replaced.

9 For an ethnographic account of how such political task forces were formed during the 2007 elections, see Christensen and Utas (2008).

10 The notion of *Sababu* more broadly connotes 'possibility'. On *Sababus*/Big Men and their networks as a point of departure for explaining social, political and economic dynamics in Sierra Leone, see, for instance, Hoffman (2011b).

11 Though women were equally allowed to register, it was mainly men who were attracted by the possibility of working in Iraq. Out of the first group of women who went to Iraq, several were deported owing to 'pornographic activities'. As a consequence women were temporarily banned from the programme.

12 Interview, 'Van Damme', Ministry of Labour and Social Security, Freetown, 25 June 2009.

13 The volcanic eruption of Eyjafjallajökull in Iceland caused delays to air travel in Sierra Leone also.

14 Camp Lion is located off the dust road leading to the international airport in Lungi. Perhaps paradoxically, the camp is named after a former jungle camp in eastern Sierra Leone where the RUF was

based during the civil war. Yet it is no secret to Sabre International that a large number of the recruits are former RUF members.

15 These company representatives were based at an office by the airport in Lungi together with a senior representative: a British ex-soldier who retired from the British army in 1982. This representative has since worked as a private security contractor in numerous locations, including in Sierra Leone, where he was involved in the rescue of the British troops who had been kidnapped by the WSB in 2000.

16 It was extremely difficult to obtain the weapons, as the government was afraid to equip such a large group of ex-militias with AK47s.

17 On bullet-proofing as an occult technology, see, for instance, Hoffman (2011b: 243–7).

18 A major difference relates to the presence of an identified enemy among American soldiers in Iraq. During the Sierra Leone civil war, militias did not identify themselves or act against a clearly defined enemy. See also Hoffman (2011a: 39).

19 Interview, deported ex-militia, Freetown, 7 June 2010.

20 Interview, Ministry of Labour and Social Security, Freetown, 17 June 2010.

21 In this context, it is important to highlight that the Sierra Leonean contractors were not engaged in armed combat operations, as their tasks in Iraq were limited to static security provision *within* military camps.

22 Ugandan security contractors in Iraq have, for instance, also employed the notion of slavery to explain the conditions under which they work. See Yasiin Mugerwa and Paul Amoru, 'Uganda: "Sold like slaves" to private guard companies in Iraq', *The Monitor* (Uganda), 28 August 2008; Max Delany, 'Why 10,000 Ugandans are eagerly serving in Iraq', *Christian Science Monitor*, 6 March 2009.

Bibliography

Abrahamsen, R. and M. C. Williams (2009) 'Security beyond the state: global security assemblages in international politics', *International Political Sociology*, 3(1): 1–17.

Berndtsson, J. (2009) 'The privatization of state security and state control of force: changes, challenges and the case of Iraq', Unpublished PhD dissertation, University of Gothenburg.

Christensen, M. M. (2013) 'Shadow soldiering: mobilization, militarization and the politics of global security in Sierra Leone', Unpublished PhD thesis, University of Copenhagen.

— (2016) 'The underbelly of global security: Sierra Leonean ex-militias in Iraq', *African Affairs*, 115(458): 23–43, doi: 10.1093/afraf/adv055, first published online 13 December 2015.

Christensen, M. M. and M. Utas (2008) 'Mercenaries of democracy: The "politricks" of remobilized combatants in the 2007 general elections', *African Affairs*, 107(429): 515–39.

Das, V. and D. Poole (2004) *Anthropology in the Margins of the State*, Santa Fe: School of American Research Press.

Duffield, M. (2001) *Global Governance and New Wars: The merging of development and security*, London: Zed Books.

Eichler, M. (2014) 'Citizenship and the contracting out of military work: from national conscription to globalized recruitment', *Citizenship Studies*, 18(6/7): 600–614.

Fassin, D. (2011) 'Racialization: how to do races with bodies', in F. E. Mascia-Lees (ed.), *A Companion to the Anthropology of the Body and Embodiment*, West Sussex: Blackwell, pp. 419–34.

Ferguson, J. (1999) *Expectations of Modernity: Myths and meanings of urban life on the Zambian copperbelt*, Berkeley, Los Angeles and London: University of California Press.

— (2006) *Global Shadows: Africa in the neoliberal world order*, Durham, NC, and London: Duke University Press.

Garner, S. (2010) *Racisms: An introduction*, London: Sage.

Hage, G. (2009) 'Waiting out the crisis: on stuckedness and governmentality', in G. Hage (ed.), *Waiting*, Carlton: Melbourne University Press.

Hansen, T. B. (2012) *Melancholia of Freedom: Social life in an Indian township in South Africa*, Princeton, NJ: Princeton University Press.

Higate, P. (2012) 'Martial races and enforcement masculinities of the global South: weaponising Fijian, Chilean, and Salvadoran postcoloniality in the mercenary sector', *Globalizations*, 9(1): 35–52.

Hoffman, D. (2011a) 'Violence just in time: war and work in West Africa', *Cultural Anthropology*, 26(1): 34–57.

— (2011b) *The War Machine: Young men and violence in Sierra Leone and Liberia*, Durham, NC, and New York: Duke University Press.

Inda, J. X. and R. Rosaldo (2008 [2002]) *The Anthropology of Globalization: A reader*, Malden, Oxford and Victoria: Blackwell.

Jensen, S. (2008) *Gangs, Politics and Dignity in Cape Town*, Oxford: James Currey.

Kateri, C. (2010) *Private Security Contractors and New Wars: Risk, law and ethics*, Abingdon and New York: Routledge.

Leander, A. (2005) 'The market for force and public security: the destabilizing effects of private military companies', *Journal of Peace Research*, 42(5): 605–22.

Schiller, N. G. and N. B. Salazar (2013) 'Regimes of mobility across the globe', *Journal of Ethnic and Migration Studies*, 39(2): 183–200.

Shaw, R. (2002) *Memories of the Slave Trade: Ritual and historical imagination in Sierra Leone*, Chicago, IL, and London: University of Chicago Press.

Singer, P. W. (2003) *Corporate Warriors: The rise of the privatized military industry*, Ithaca, NY, and London: Cornell University Press.

Taussig-Rubbo, M. (2009) 'Outsourcing sacrifice: the labor of private military contractors', *Yale Journal of Law & Humanities*, 2(1): 103–66.

Tsing, A. (2008 [2002]) 'The global situation', in J. X. Inda and R. Rosaldo (eds), *The Anthropology of Globalization: A reader*, Malden, Oxford and Victoria: Blackwell.

Utas, M. (2012) *African Conflicts and Informal Power: Big men and networks*, London and New York: Zed Books.

Vigh, H. (2006) 'The colour of destruction: on racialization, geo-globality and the social imaginary in Bissau', *Anthropological Theory*, 6(4): 481–500.

— (2008) 'Wayward migration: on imagined futures and technological voids', *Ethnos*, 74(1): 91–109.

5 | Who do you call? Private security policing in Durban, South Africa

Tessa Diphoorn

Introduction

Within the field of private security, a differentiation is often made between private military companies and private security companies (Foaleng 2007; Gumedze 2007; Singer 2003; Small 2006). In this distinction, private military companies are defined as companies that provide military services aimed at influencing a particular armed conflict. They are therefore often regarded as a 'direct protagonist in conflict' (Foaleng 2007: 44) and 'corporate warriors' (Singer 2003). Private security companies, on the other hand, are defined as companies primarily concerned with internal security that focus on police-like activities, such as guarding, access control and surveillance. Although it is recognized that these two types are often interlinked (Abrahamsen and Williams 2011), private military companies are generally believed to have a larger impact on security measures and thereby threaten state sovereignty, whereas private security companies are regarded as less harmful.[1] In this chapter, I present a counterclaim and argue that private security companies are key players in the larger security assemblage that influence local security dynamics and act as 'active influencers'.

I will make this claim by describing the size, history and diversity of the private security industry in South Africa and presenting two case studies from Durban, South Africa, that are based on twenty months of ethnographic fieldwork conducted between 2007 and 2010.[2] More specifically, I analyse the policing practices of a specific type of private security officer, namely armed response officers, and show that they are active players in shaping the local dynamics of security provision. Elsewhere (Diphoorn 2016), I show how armed response officers are engaged in 'twilight policing', which refers to policing practices that are punitive, disciplinary and exclusionary and operate in a twilight zone between state and non-state policing. Through engaging with anthropological studies on sovereignty and employing a pluralized perspective on policing developed in the field of criminology, I analyse twilight policing as claims to sovereign power that are neither public nor private, but are the outcome of the imbrication of these two domains through the coming together of various actors within the security assemblage. The two central empirical vignettes of this chapter are thus performances of twilight policing that highlight the pluralized nature of policing and the importance of organizing performances of security within an assemblage framework.

This chapter will highlight three main issues. Firstly, the two vignettes will show how armed response officers play a role in both the private and public spheres of security. Secondly, I will show how the role of violence – both the capacity for and actual use of violence – is fundamental to their policing practices. Thirdly, in the vignettes, we will see how other actors, particularly clients, co-shape the performance of twilight policing. This emphasizes how armed response companies interact with other (security) stakeholders and how security provision should be analysed within an assemblage framework. In the first section of this chapter, I will introduce the private security industry and the armed response sector in South Africa. The second section will analyse the two empirical vignettes. In the third and last section, I will make some concluding remarks about how such performances can best be analysed within an assemblage framework.

South Africa: the 'champion' of the industry

South Africa is often described as having a 'culture of violence' (Altbeker 2007; Kynoch 2005) due to high rates of criminal violence and the eminence of non-state policing. Neighbourhood watches, private security companies, vigilante groups, gangs, street committees, business associations and other (collective) initiatives constitute South Africa's security assemblage. Among this wide array, the private security industry is unquestionably the leading player. South Africa is globally regarded as the 'absolute "champion" in the security industry' (De Waard 1999: 169). It has the largest private security sector in the world, valued at approximately 2 per cent of the country's total GDP (Abrahamsen and Williams 2011). In 2014, there were 8,144 registered private security providers and 487,058 active registered security officers (PSIRA 2013/14).[3]

Besides its vast size, the industry is also highly diverse, being categorized into twenty-two different types of security services by the Private Security Industry Regulatory Authority (PSIRA), the quasi-state body that regulates the industry. This ranges from locksmiths to bodyguarding to cash-in-transit services. The armed response sector is one of the largest and fastest-growing sectors of the industry, accounting for 4,550 registered providers in 2014 (PSIRA 2013/14). In addition to these registered companies, there are also 'bush companies', which refers to companies that are not registered and that therefore operate in the 'bush' to evade detection by PSIRA. Most 'bush companies' are operated by single individuals, who use their own vehicles and firearms and operate in confined areas, often defined by a few street corners.

The armed reaction sector is, as one company owner stated, 'the promising horse' of the industry.[4] Expected growth rates are based on continuous technological progress, a steady demand for armed response, and an increase in both formal and informal partnerships with police officers and community initiatives. Although each company has its own unique operating procedure, all companies undertake three main tasks: alarm installation and maintenance (including technicians and sales agents); the reception and coding of signals received from these devices (the entire operations of the control room); and the provision of armed response (the armed reaction officers). This chapter is based on ethnographic fieldwork that primarily focused on the latter, i.e. the armed private security officers who patrol communities in vehicles and react and/or respond to triggers such as alarms and panic buttons that are installed on clients' premises.

In South Africa, the private security industry began in the mining sector, entered the urban centres in the 1970s, and exploded during the height of the political resistance of the late 1980s and into the political transition circa 1994. The growth of the private security industry was directly correlated with the widening protests by liberation movements and the increasing repression by the apartheid state (Grant 1989; Irish 1999; Shaw 2002; Singh 2008). With state forces increasingly called upon to deal with political unrest throughout the country, particularly due to an upsurge in strategic attacks by the ANC, supplementary manpower was needed on the ground that would not deplete state resources. This need was primarily met by extracting resources from the 'crime prevention sector' (Shaw 2002). Through various changes in legislation, tasks that had previously fallen under the remit of the state police were handed over to the private sector (Brogden and Shearing 1993; Grant 1989; Irish 1999; Singh 2008).

One of the main changes in legislation was the establishment of the National Key Points Act (NKPA) 102 of 1980. The NKPA stipulated that responsibility for security provision (predominantly guarding) at strategic sites deemed crucial for national security should be transferred to the management/owners of these sites. Although the task of providing security was reassigned to private individuals, authority and control remained in the hands of the state. The South African state utilized the manpower and public expenditure freed up by this move to strengthen the armed forces, while simultaneously maintaining control over the private agents now overseeing its strategic sites. In this process, private security firms (and the individuals they employed) formed alliances with the state.

The collaborative relationship between the private security industry and the apartheid state was further strengthened by the creation of the Security Officers Act (SOA) of 1987 and the accompanying Security Officers Board (SOB). The SOA was 'a framework for the extension of the network of a state-corporate "partnership" policing further into civil society' (Brogden and Shearing 1993: 72). After a period of exponential growth in the industry during the 1980s, there were increasing demands for a formal regulation system, particularly as a means of monitoring and controlling security officers. The SOA was thus the first step towards state regulation of the industry, currently implemented and enforced by PSIRA. In this period, however, regulation symbolized a partnership between the public and the private – a unified effort to achieve the same goal. The enactment of the SOA had 'the very purpose of developing a relationship between the state and private security companies' (Berg 2003: 179). The political and financial connections between the industry and the apartheid state – at both national and local levels of policing – created and maintained the 'old boys' network' (Singh 2008), which refers to a string of social relations among white men operating within the industry and the apartheid armed forces.

Although the NKPA primarily affected the guarding sector, other parts of the industry, such as the armed response sector, also grew owing to the increasing political pressure on state law enforcement. The armed response sector emerged through two types of companies. The first were the 'techies' in the late 1970s; these were companies that installed alarms for commercial businesses. The 'one-man shows', which primarily emerged in the mid-1980s, were the second type. Similar to contemporary 'bush companies', the second type largely comprised ex-policemen or ex-SADF soldiers who served a handful of clients using their own vehicles and firearms.

Although the growth of the armed response sector was not directly supported by legislation, it was promoted by police officers on the same premise: it released police officers from particular tasks and allowed them to concentrate on the job of maintaining racial segregation, one of the main aims of the South African Police (SAP). The 'old boys' network' was thus also very prominent in the armed response sector. Taken together, the National Key Point Act, the Security Officers Act, the evolution of the armed response sector and the 'old boys' network' show how the private security industry came to play a complementary role in apartheid policing (Shaw 2002: 111). The industry was regarded as the 'major "hidden" supplement to the state police' (Brogden and Shearing 1993: 71). Although profit-making was the prime motivation for private security companies, many chose to identify with the discourse of state sovereignty as opposed to framing themselves in market-based terms (Singh 2008: 44).

When the ANC assumed power in 1994, the security sector required large-scale reform. The new state police, the South African Police Services (SAPS), was formed through the amalgamation of eleven different police forces and the new government focused on restoring relationships with citizens, particularly non-white communities, which was encapsulated in the mantra of democratic and community policing. As the transformation of the SAP into the SAPS primarily revolved around improving legitimacy and accountability, tackling crime was not seen as the core aim (Cawthra 2003; Shaw 2002). Yet as crime rates continued to rise after 1994, anti-government sentiment intensified, as Shaw argues:

> For a period of time, however, government response was partly to deny crime was a problem and partly to respond in an *ad hoc* fashion as representations were made to it on particular issues. The result was a real frustration with government's inability either to concede openly that crime was a problem and then show the clear will and intention to do something about it. (2002: 34)

This neglect was one of the main reasons for the exponential boom of the private security industry in the late 1980s and early 1990s. As influx controls broke down in the late 1980s and crime started entering the white suburbs, many whites became fearful for their future; from their point of view, a change in government entailed a loss of economic privilege, a decline in political power and a reduction in social status. Many demanded immediate protection and private security companies readily provided this (ibid.).

Private security was increasingly seen as indispensable for the white minority, who were the main users of such services (ibid.). This was especially true for the armed response sector, which experienced a rapid growth during this period, as one white company owner explained: 'Armed reaction really grew then, and it was just on the back of fear [...] And electronic security, armed reaction, realized a growth – I don't think this country will ever see that type of growth again.'[5]

The continuous demand for armed response, and private security in general, was matched by a growing number of suppliers, including both the police and ex-combatants, who were not merged into the new armed forces.

Since the political transition, the industry has experienced continuous growth, as can be seen in Table 5.1, which shows the number of private security companies operating in South Africa between 2001 and 2014. Although the table shows a decrease in the number of companies between 2001 and 2004, and between 2012 and 2014, this is due to mergers within the industry and does not imply a reduction in security provision. More specifically, although the number of companies decreased from 9,364 to 8,144 between 2012 and 2014, the number of active registered security officers increased from 427,174 to 487,058.

In addition to this growth, the industry has transformed from a 'Club to Business' (Singh 2008: 43). During the transition and after 1994, the private security sector was viewed with suspicion by the post-apartheid government, who saw it as part of the old order and feared that it would foster the development of private militias bent on overthrowing the ANC government (ibid.; Shaw 2002). This was particularly true for the SOA, which was seen as a

2001	5,491
2002	4,521
2003	4,271
2004	4,212
2005	4,639
2006	4,763
2007	4,898
2008	5,504
2009	6,392
2010	7,496
2011	8,826
2012	9,364
2013	9,031
2014	8,144

Table 5.1 Registered private security providers in South Africa, 2001–14

partnership between the industry and the old state that served to protect 'the economic interests of a white-dominated and controlled industry' (Minnaar 2005: 95). To further tighten control over the industry, amendments were implemented to expand the scope of the industry, resulting in the birth of the Private Security Industry Regulation Act No. 56 of 2001, monitored by the Private Security Industry Regulatory Authority (PSIRA). In addition to increasing regulation, the state also aimed to change the racial composition of the industry, as the majority of owners and managers of companies were white. Despite efforts to escape the legacies of apartheid, the industry remains racially imbalanced. The majority of management and high-paid positions are still occupied by white men who employ a predominantly non-white force of private security officers, particularly in the guarding sector (Abrahamsen and Williams 2007; Diphoorn 2015).

Twilight policing

The private security industry thus has a long history in South Africa and functions as one of the key security actors in the governance of security. The South African state is increasingly seeking partnerships with the private security industry, although partnerships are often ad hoc owing to the lack of a coherent national strategy (Diphoorn and Berg 2014).

Originally, the armed response sector focused on providing assistance to clients in the vicinity of their homes and businesses, i.e. private spaces. However, as has been shown by various other studies (Berg 2010; Singh and Kempa 2007; Rigakos 2002), the private security industry is increasingly operating in the public realm, both by operating in public spaces and increasingly performing state-like practices through mimicking the state, thereby reproducing understandings of what the state is. In the following two vignettes, I will show how this expanding role for armed response officers occurs in both private and public spaces, and how this is based on the ability to use violence, and through their efforts with other actors.

CASE STUDY 1: DISCIPLINING MAY 2010

We're in the middle of a staff meeting when we hear about an alarm notification at an important client's residence. William,[6] a white armed response officer, is ordered to attend and asks me to come with him. When we get to the premises, an Indian male is standing outside. We initially assume that nothing is wrong, but then he waves at us to come inside the house. When we enter the residence, William and the client address each other by their first names, shake hands, and engage in some banter. It is clear that they know each other. When we move into the living room, I see the client's wife holding a young boy of about two years of age, and then notice a young black girl sitting on the couch, looking down at the ground. There is an eerie vibe, and I'm confused about what is going on. The clients tell us that the girl is a maid who has been working for them for the past fortnight. Last week, there had been two occasions when the wife had suspected the maid of stealing between R20 and R50, but she wasn't sure. She discussed her suspicions with her husband, and they decided to set a trap using four R20 notes as bait. Now the money was gone, and they were confident the maid was to blame.

The client then looks at us and says, 'We asked you to come here because we want to show her [the maid] how quick you guys come here, what will happen next time. It's not about the money – it's about the trust. I want her to know what will happen next time she does this.' He then nods at William to signify that he can take over. William approaches the girl and starts talking to her in a stern tone of voice, asking her what she did. The girl's gaze is fixed on the ground, but she is clearly afraid of William. William raises his voice and commands her to look at him and explain herself. The girl says she needed the money to buy bread for her family; she admits to stealing R10, then admits to stealing R20, and then denies the theft altogether. William grows increasingly frustrated. I stand in the corner of the room, trying to remain as inconspicuous as possible, but the girl repeatedly looks at me, probably wondering who I am and what I'm doing here.

The clients then reiterates to the girl why they called the company, and William intervenes to support their claim. 'Do you know what will happen next time they call us?' he asks. 'You'll arrest me,' replies the maid. Then William smirks and says, 'No, we're not the police. We won't arrest you – we'll beat you. I don't care how old or young you are, male or female – if you steal, you must be taught a lesson.' The client nods and supports William's threat by saying, 'You know [name of the company]? Do you know what they do? They're not the police; they'll hurt you if you do this again.' Still staring at the floor, the maid murmurs that she understands.

The clients, William and I leave the living room to discuss the matter outside. The clients question whether they should give her a second chance. William strongly advises against this: 'You can't trust her. She will steal again. Better you get an older lady; they are more reliable. These young ones … they are out to steal. Next thing you know, she'll get her friends and they'll come and steal everything.' William provides numerous examples of maids who have worked alongside criminals, including one who orchestrated an armed robbery and watched as the suspect raped the woman of the house. Nevertheless, the clients say that they want to give the maid another chance, so we return to the living room and William orders the girl to return the money she took.

The wife and I head into the kitchen for a glass of water. She repeatedly emphasizes how disappointed she is, because she treats the maid with dignity and wants to help her. I ask her why she phoned the company and not the police. She explains to me that they've been clients of the company for years; they respond quickly, she tells me, and – she stresses this – she likes 'their way of operating'. She then asserts, 'I don't want the girl arrested; I want her to know that what she did was wrong. Going to jail won't teach her anything; it will just make it worse. She needs to be disciplined, and the police won't do that for you.' I find this situation incredibly sad, and I sympathize with the maid. I somehow feel that she is not the wrongdoer, and I am appalled by the clients' and William's attempts to impart moral discipline.

On our way back to the office, William explains how these clients' problem was not uncommon: maids, gardeners and other black employees often steal from their employers. When I ask him what will happen if the maid steals again, he says, 'We will eat her.' He repeats this several times. I ask him what he means exactly. 'We'll beat her,' he replies, 'give her a good hiding … she needs to be taught a lesson. Only like that will she learn. Going to prison isn't a punishment at all.' William appears to notice my disapproval. 'People like you,' he says, 'from overseas, you think it isn't right, that it's inhumane, but they [the criminals] are the inhumane ones; they're the ones who don't care and they must be punished.'

*

This case depicts a particular role that is expected of armed response officers in the private domain, whereby clients legally entitle security officers to execute their policing needs. With a few notable exceptions, such as the national key point protection officers in South Africa, security officers worldwide do not generally possess powers beyond those of ordinary citizens. This is also the case in South Africa, where the Criminal Procedure Act 51 of 1977 compels individuals in the security industry to operate within the parameters of state law. Thus, security officers may only utilize powers granted to 'private persons'. According to Singh, the rights bestowed upon citizens in South Africa are 'far-reaching' when compared to international standards since these rights were conceived during the apartheid era, when citizens were granted powers 'to defend the state against threats to its sovereignty' (Singh 2008: 50).

Despite the fact that security officers do not generally possess more legal powers than ordinary citizens, they are granted a great deal of authority through private relationships and contracts. By entering into contractual agreements with clients, private security officers have the right to search people and property, carry out various surveillance techniques, enforce sanctions, determine access, and evict individuals from private premises (Stenning 2000). By restricting the access of particular individuals into certain spaces, security officers are exercising a power that lies 'beyond those universal rights all citizens possess' (Button 2003: 230). The legal powers of the private police thus stem from a 'legal relationship they have both with those who employ them (the property owners) and with those whom they police (persons using the property)' (Stenning 2000: 332).[7] Thus, when a citizen or business subscribes to an armed response company, he or she enters into a contractual agreement that bestows certain rights of access and conduct upon armed reaction officers on their premises. The legal rights of security officers are therefore fairly wide ranging, although unquestionably less so than those of the state police.

In this case study of 'disciplining', we see how the clients, through their contractual arrangement with the company that William works for, bestow certain rights and expectations onto William that move far beyond the traditional notions of 'armed response'. Armed response officers are increasingly providing all sorts of help in the private sphere that far exceeds a basic 'response', such as providing medical and technical assistance. They are often regarded as negotiators and mediators, being called upon to diffuse situations or to intervene between different parties, and intimidation is inherent in these roles. In the case of the errant maid, William was called upon to insert his symbolic authority, to use the threat of force to deter further acts of crime, to protect the interests of the clients, and to instil morality. Armed response officers refer to this as 'disciplining'.

Throughout my fieldwork in Durban, I experienced cases like this on numerous occasions: armed response officers were frequently called upon to 'discipline' staff members, and sometimes even acquaintances and siblings. I was initially surprised at the frequency at which armed response officers attended 'domestic disputes' between siblings, neighbours, tenants and housemates, as I assumed that this was the domain of the public police. Armed response officers and company managers described domestic disturbances as the most annoying and least rewarding call-outs. They were also regarded as the most risky and difficult: although armed response officers want to help clients and provide 'maximum service', they also feel constrained in addressing such disturbances and are concerned about the potential problems they may bring. Many armed response officers discussed their attempts to solve cases of domestic violence that had backfired on them, with the person (very often a woman) they intended to protect ending up pressing charges against them.

As armed response officers operate with a client mandate, they will usually side with their clients to protect their interests without investigating the situation. This was evident in a neighbourly quarrel that occurred in May 2010 while I was on day shift with Brian, an Indian armed response officer in his mid-twenties. We had been called out to a site to address a 'domestic'; when we arrived, we saw an Indian man (the client) sitting behind his gate and exchanging insults with an Indian woman standing on the road. The man explained to us that she was swearing at him, calling him all sorts of things, while the woman accused him of entering her house without permission and spreading rumours about her in the neighbourhood. Brian intervened and told the woman that there was nothing the company could do and that she must go to the police to resolve the dispute. He kept highlighting that she was disturbing the peace in what was a quiet residential area. When we got back into the car, Brian told me that he actually sympathized with the woman and that she was probably right, because he had heard stories of this man acting up before. When I asked him why he defended the man, he said, 'He's our client and that's all that matters. It's not my job to choose sides, but to protect our clients, not just everybody.'

In cases such as this, clients and armed response officers operate as co-actors, reading from the same script and pursuing the same goal. In the episode involving the maid, we see how the clients and William worked together in identifying the maid as the target of the performance owing to her deviant behaviour. William and the clients displayed the same mentality, and William gladly acted in a way that suited the clients' needs. However, with the tenant dispute attended by Brian, we see that this is not the case and that Brian acted against what he felt was right. These domestic disputes highlight how armed response officers are employed to impose and maintain a certain moral order and the prominent role that clients play in determining what the moral order is, who belongs to that order, and how 'outsiders' must be treated. In the case of the maid, stealing from clients was considered a crime, yet using physical means to punish her was regarded as necessary. Although William did not use physical force on this occasion, I witnessed other cases where armed response officers were expected to use force in order to convey moral teachings.

The state police are often referred to as the 'thin blue line' that serves as a moral buffer between social order and chaos. Violence perpetuated by criminals is regarded as 'bad violence', while violence that counteracts this is regarded as 'good violence', since it is intended to create and maintain a 'good' social order. Defining and preserving this distinction is increasingly the role of the private police; they have come to be involved in 'moral social ordering' (Berg 2010: 297). This is primarily due to a public perception that public institutions are failing to 'punish' and 'discipline' those committing 'bad violence'. And by defining what is permitted (and what is not) and assuming the role of the 'punisher', armed response officers are increasingly resembling vigilantes in terms of their behaviour (Jensen 2007). As moral communities must be protected and order must be maintained, violence is often seen as 'a necessary and justified form of discipline, as a legitimate way to restate and internalize the core moral values of the community' (Buur 2005: 193). In the next vignette, we will clearly see how physical violence by armed response officers is used to instil order in the public domain.

CASE STUDY 2: ARRESTING SUSPECTS[8] MAY 2010

It's Friday morning and a bunch of us are standing outside the office for a cigarette break. When a call comes in about the presence of two suspects in someone's yard, the guys throw down their cigarettes, start screaming at each other to hurry up, and rush over to their vehicle. I quickly grab my vest and hop into the front seat of the car that Pravesh, an Indian armed response officer in his late thirties, is driving.

On our way over to the premises in question, we hear over the radio that the suspects have been apprehended. When we reach the site, I am asked to stay in the car, but I can see that a group of eight armed response officers are standing around two suspects lying face down on the ground with their hands cuffed. For the next few minutes, they repeatedly hit the suspects with their batons and kick them while the suspects howl with pain. A large crowd of members of the community begins to gather. The armed response officers continue going at it hard; they thump the suspects, rebuke them, and accuse them of stealing from innocent people.

The armed response officers then pick up the suspects and I finally get a full view: the two men are bleeding from various parts of their bodies and their clothes are torn. The officers dump the suspects into the back of two pick-ups, including the one I am sitting in. The beatings continue in the rear of the vehicle, which rocks from side to side with each blow. The sound of the suspects' screams and grunts is ear piercing. Pravesh then gets into the front seat and asks me whether I am all right. When I say, rather hesitantly and unconvincingly, 'yes', he replies, 'Ach, all that violence ...' interrupted by a smirk, 'but I told you we were tough and know how to hit.'

Everyone then gets back into their vehicles and we drive approximately a hundred metres farther up the road. The suspects are taken out of the car and thrown onto the ground. I am told that I can get out of the car. For the next twenty minutes or so, the armed response officers continue to interrogate the suspects, knocking them about in a playful manner. Two officers cock their firearms, point them at the suspects and then threaten to shoot them, which is met with laughter from the other officers. The armed response officers tease and provoke one another, some using this as an opportunity to show off their fighting skills.

To cope with the situation, I purposely focus on other events happening around me. I start questioning community members about their feelings and opinions, but few seem to share my sense of disapproval and disgust. One elderly man, who has been at the scene since the beginning, explains how often the local residences have been burgled. He points to several houses that have been robbed over the last few months and to a spot (where the suspects were apprehended) where two hijackings have taken place in the last year. He then says, 'The guys deserve it – it's good that they're hitting them, they deserve it.' Other community members voice similar statements, such as 'We need these guys to stop the animals from killing us' and 'We're constantly under attack; these men need to teach them a lesson, to stop them from destroying our communities'. At one point, two bystanders even ask to join in the interrogation, but the armed response officers do not allow this.

When the police arrive, my first thought is that they will condemn the actions of the armed response officers, particularly their use of violence, and arrest some or all of them. However, nothing of the sort happens: the two police officers – an Indian male and a black female – make a few cursory inquiries and then simply place the two suspects in the back of their vehicle and prepare to head back to the police station. The two armed response officers who first apprehended the suspects are asked to come to the station to make a statement, but no further action is taken.

A week or so later, I run into the male police officer and ask him about this incident. Rather than condemning what the armed response officers did, particularly their treatment of the suspects, he actually praises it. He recognizes that 'such cases can be problematic', but he maintains that there is a 'need for it'.

In this incident, we see how armed response officers used violence to apprehend and interrogate two suspects in the open streets, i.e. public spaces. The use of violence was crucial for them to obtain and maintain legitimacy and authority; it was used to display power and to underscore their leading role. Violence is thus very often a demonstration of power, particularly when performed in public spaces (Goldstein 2004).

Armed response officers habitually use coercion and violence to apprehend, intimidate and search suspects. During their training, security officers are taught how to search individuals without the use of force, yet in practice more coercive methods are used to apprehend suspects, such that they are increasingly employing a 'detection and punishment mentality' (Berg 2010: 295). Besides physical violence, I witnessed various other forms of coercion, such as the use of pepper spray and making suspects sit or stand in very uncomfortable positions. Swearing at suspects, calling them names and making threats were also common. Armed response officers frequently made statements such as 'If you don't stop, we'll come back next time', 'Next time I won't be so polite', and 'Next time there will be more of us'. They regularly lectured suspects as a form of 'moral disciplining', admonishing them at great length for their immorality and wrongdoings. This highlights that their approach is not necessarily just about the use of violence, but also about projecting the ability to do use it. This is primarily acquired through cultivating what Martin (2013) refers to as 'force capital', which is the 'ability to deploy or threaten to deploy force across space' (ibid.: 153). Force capital includes both physical resources, such as personnel and weaponry, and non-physical resources, such as training and reputation, and is employed directly, such as through the use of physical force, and indirectly, such as through intimidation. As with the state police, the entire appearance of armed response officers is intended to convey a willingness and ability to employ coercive tools.

However, to assume that all of the armed response officers involved in the above-mentioned case were 'trigger-happy' and prone to violence would be too simple. Although some appeared to derive enjoyment from the performance, we must recognize that their use of violence was also steered by other factors and participants. In this performance, community members tolerated, encouraged and even praised the use of physical violence and thereby configured the performance. In this case (and numerous others), physical violence was accepted and legitimized by the community members as well as by the police officers who appeared later. Other actors, particularly clients, thereby shape the use of violence. In the previous example, we also saw how a client signed up with a company based on its reputation for fighting and disciplining 'wrongdoers'. Echoing the findings of Sharp and Wilson (2000: 125), clients sometimes viewed the criminal past of company employees as a 'positive advantage'. Many companies are well aware of this and emphasize their violent capabilities accordingly, as one owner cited: 'When we hear something has happened, I want as many of our vehicles as possible to go there. This is for safety reasons, so that the guys can help each other out, but it's also to show force to the community: we come as a group, a force to be reckoned with.'[9]

The expanding role of armed response officers therefore also represents an increasing use of punitive behaviour; twilight policing is based on both the ability to use, and the actual use of, violence. Furthermore, punitive behaviour cannot be reduced to trigger-happiness, but must instead be understood in relation to the parts played by other participants in either encouraging or tolerating the use of violence.

Concluding remarks

These two case studies from my ethnographic fieldwork demonstrate how armed response officers, a specific type of private security officer, play a dominant role in providing security in Durban, South Africa. Despite the rather limited legal tools available for security officers, particularly in relation to the state police, security officers are granted a great deal of authority and legitimacy. In the first case, we see how William, an armed response officer, was expected to project his ability to use violence as a form of crime prevention within the private sphere. This was done through 'disciplining' and demarcating a particular moral order. In the second case, we see how a group of armed response officers 'disciplined' two suspects in the public space and how this was encouraged and/or tolerated by the state police.

Although performed in different spheres, these two cases bear several similarities that outline various elements of twilight policing. The first is the punitive nature of the policing practices and the centrality of violence, both the capability for and the actual use of violence. And as mentioned in the introduction, private security companies may be regarded as less threatening than private military companies, but this chapter has shown the opposite, namely that they operate as 'active influencers' by greatly impacting local dynamics of security, understandings and enactments of violence, and social inequalities.

The second is the disciplinary nature, i.e. the use of violence to instil a particular type of moral order. This is interconnected with the exclusionary nature of their policing practices: as I discuss elsewhere (Diphoorn 2016), such practices are based on defending 'insiders' from socially constructed 'outsiders'. This process of defining the dangerous 'Other' that must be kept outside such borders, both physical and social, remains highly racialized in post-apartheid South Africa (Diphoorn 2015). The third issue is the key role of other actors, particularly clients, in shaping the performance of twilight policing. In both cases, we clearly see how clients tolerated and/or determined the nature of the practices, and how police officers also often sanctioned such behaviour, as is especially highlighted in the second case.

This further underlines the need to analyse such performances of security and policing in general through the conceptual lens of the 'security assemblage'. As highlighted by Abrahamsen and Williams in this volume, the framework of the 'global assemblage' provides numerous advantages when studying contemporary security practices. Firstly, the assemblage framework allows us to analyse how particular performances of security (as discussed in this chapter) emerge through the actions of numerous and different actors. Rather than looking at what one security actor does, such as a police officer or a security officer, we can examine the various means by which the efforts of various, and often diverse, actors come together and result in multifaceted forms of collaboration or competition. It is also for this reason that twilight policing is conceptualized as a 'joint performance': it is shaped by the perceptions and actions of various (security) providers. Secondly, by examining how security operates in such a multidimensional way, we can move beyond often used binaries, such as public versus private, and look more at the numerous interconnections and entanglements between various security providers, the spaces they operate in, and the beneficiaries of their actions.

Thirdly, owing to the encompassing nature of the assemblage framework, and thus the holistic approach to understanding the everyday impact of various security practices, researchers can draw from their empirically grounded fieldwork to show the various ways in which security unfolds and is given meaning. In this chapter it has also been my intent to show the benefits of ethnographic fieldwork to understanding security and the type of detailed data that can be gathered through various methods associated with ethnography, such as participant observation. Through acquiring thick description, we can further understand how on-the-ground performances of security and violence shape local realities and how they are interconnected with national, transnational and global processes and dynamics. The assemblage framework thus provides a multi-scalar approach to security that moves beyond the ideal of the Weberian state, allows us to think beyond binaries that continue to dominate much thinking about security, and understand how various actors co-produce security performances.

Notes

1 The two are often interrelated, and for the purpose of this chapter, and in alignment with the Montreux Document, the label 'PMSC/PSC' industry will be used throughout to include the various types of companies operating in the industry at large. The Montreux Document defines private military and security companies as 'private business entities that provide military and/or security services, irrespective of how they describe themselves. Military and security services include, in particular, armed guarding and protection of persons and objects, maintenance and operation of weapons systems, prisoner detention and advice to or training of local forces and security personnel.;

2 For further discussion on my methodology, see Diphoorn (2013).

3 This figure includes only the 'active' registered private security officers, which is to say security officers who are actively employed in the industry. PSIRA also maintains a database of 'inactive' registered security officers – that is, security officers who are registered with PSIRA but are not currently employed in

the industry. In 2014, there were 1,381,340 inactive security officers compared to 487,058 active security officers (amounting to a total of 1,868,398) registered security officers. I retrieved PSIRA's annual reports from the website www.psira.co.za.

4 Interview, 28 August 2010.

5 Interview, 22 April 2010.

6 All the names used in this chapter are pseudonyms.

7 In South Africa, this falls under Section 42(3) of the Criminal Procedure Act 51 of 1977, which states that '"the owner, lawful occupier or person in charge of land" may arrest a person believed to have committed any offence or who is in the process of committing an offence' (Berg 2003: 193).

8 Elsewhere (Diphoorn 2013) I also discuss this case and I specifically delve into the emotionality of participation as a heuristic device in understanding the dialectic between emotion and method.

9 Interview, 24 April 2009.

Bibliography

Abrahamsen, R. & M. C. Williams (2007) 'Securing the city: private security companies and non-state authority in global governance', *International Relations*, 21(2): 237–53.

— (2011) *Security beyond the State: Private Security in International Politics*, Cambridge: Cambridge University Press.

Altbeker, A. (2007) *A Country at War with Itself. South Africa's Crisis of Crime*, Jeppestown: Jonathan Ball.

Berg, J. (2003) 'The private security industry in South Africa: a review of applicable legislation', *South African Journal of Criminal Justice*, 16: 178–96.

— (2010) 'Seeing like private security: evolving mentalities of public space protection in South Africa', *Criminology and Criminal Justice*, 10(3): 287–301.

Brogden, M. and C. Shearing (1993) *Policing for a New South Africa*, London: Routledge.

Button, M. (2003) 'Private security and the policing of quasi-public space', *International Journal of the Sociology of Law*, 31(3): 227–37.

— (2007) *Security Officers and Policing. Powers, Culture and Control in the Governance of Private Space*, Aldershot: Ashgate.

Buur, L. (2005) 'The sovereign outsourced: local justice and violence in Port Elizabeth', in T. B. Hansen and F. Stepputat (eds), *Sovereign Bodies. Citizens, Migrants, and States in the Postcolonial World*, Princeton, NJ: Princeton University Press, pp. 192–217.

Cawthra, G. (2003) 'Security transformation in post-apartheid South Africa', in G. Cawthra and R. Luckham (eds), *Governing Insecurity. Democratic Control of Military and Security Establishments in Transitional Democracies*, London and New York: Zed Books, pp. 31–56.

De Waard, J. (1999) 'The private security industry in international perspective', *European Journal on Criminal Policy and Research*, 7: 143–74.

Diphoorn, T. (2013) 'The emotionality of participation: various modes of participation in ethnographic fieldwork on private policing in Durban, South Africa', *Journal of Contemporary Ethnography*, 42(2): 201–25.

— (2015) 'The "Bravo Mike Syndrome": private security culture and racial profiling in South Africa', *Policing and Society*, doi: 10.1080/10439463.2015.1089869.

— (2016) *Twilight Policing. Private Security and Violence in Urban South Africa*, Berkeley: University of California Press.

Diphoorn, T. and J. Berg (2014) 'Typologies of partnering policing: case studies from urban South Africa', *Policing and Society*, 24(4): 425–42.

Foaleng, M. H. (2007) 'Private military and security companies and the nexus between natural resources and civil wars in Africa', in S.

Gumedze (ed.), *Private Security in Africa. Manifestation, Challenges and Regulation*, ISS Monograph Series no. 139. Pretoria: Institute for Security Studies, pp. 39–56.

Goldstein, D. M. (2004) *The Spectacular City. Violence and Performance in Urban Bolivia*, Durham, NC: Duke University Press.

Grant, E. (1989) 'Private policing', *Acta Juridica*, 92: 92–117.

Gumedze, S. (ed.) (2007) *Private Security in Africa. Manifestation, Challenges and Regulation*, Pretoria: Institute for Security Studies (ISS).

Irish, J. (1999) *Policing for Profit: The Future of South Africa's Private Security Industry*, Pretoria: Institute for Security Studies (ISS).

Jensen, S. (2007) 'Policing Nkomazi: crime, masculinity and generational conflicts', in D. Pratten and A. Sen (eds), *Global Vigilantes*, London: Hurst and Co., pp. 47–68.

Jones, T. and T. Newburn (eds) (2006) *Plural Policing. A Comparative Perspective*, London: Routledge.

Kynoch, G. (2005) 'Crime, conflict and politics in transition-era South Africa', *African Affairs*, 104(416): 493–514.

Martin, J. (2013) 'Informal security nodes and force capital', *Policing and Society*, 23(2): 145–63.

Minnaar, A. (2005) 'Private–public partnerships: private security, crime prevention and policing in South Africa', *Acta Criminologica*, 18(9): 85–114.

PSIRA (2013/14). *Annual Report 2013–2014*, Private Security Industry Regulatory Authority, www.psira.co.za/psira/images/Documents/Publications/Annual_Reports/annual_report_2013_2014.pdf.

Rigakos, G. S. (2002) *The New Parapolice. Risk Markets and Commodified Social Control*, Toronto: University of Toronto Press.

Sharp, D. and D. Wilson (2000) 'Household security: private policing and vigilantism in Doncaster', *The Howard Journal*, 39(2): 113–31.

Shaw, M. (2002) *Crime and Policing in Post-Apartheid South Africa. Transforming under Fire*, Indianapolis: Indiana University Press.

Singer, P. W. (2003) *Corporate Warriors. The Rise of the Privatized Military Industry*, Ithaca, NY: Cornell University Press.

Singh, A. M. (2008) *Policing and Crime Control in Post-Apartheid South Africa*, Aldershot: Ashgate.

Singh, A. M. and M. Kempa (2007) 'Reflections on the study of private policing cultures: early leads and key themes', in M. O'Neill, M. Marks and A. M. Singh (eds), *Police Occupational Culture: New Debates and Directions*, Oxford, Amsterdam and San Diego: Elsevier, pp. 297–320.

Small, M. (2006) 'Privatisation of security and military functions and the demise of the modern nation-state in Africa', Occasional Paper Series, *ACCORD*, 1(2): 3–104.

Stenning, P. C. (2000) 'Powers and accountability of private police', *European Journal on Criminal Policy and Research*, 8(3): 325–52.

6 | Security Sector Reform as Trojan Horse? The new security assemblages of privatized military training in Liberia

Marcus Mohlin

Security Sector Reform (SSR) is a concept frequently used to denote the benign provision of assistance from state to state, primarily given to countries transitioning from a conflict or a post-conflict phase, to aid them in their transformation into stable and sustainable states.[1] SSR is admittedly quite a wide concept embracing all sorts of activities and shared practices, involving reform of both the judicial and military sectors, including police and intelligence organizations as well as the military. While states may be expected to be the primary implementers of such reform, private security providers and companies that specialize in military training have also been active in many major SSR programmes, most notably in Afghanistan and Iraq, but also in Africa. In Liberia, a large SSR programme was launched in the early 2000s aiming at a reform of the Armed Forces of Liberia (AFL). Because the programme was US sponsored it was initially seen as an effort at 'muscling out everybody else' and thought to contribute to an isolation of Liberia from other countries in the region (Malan 2008: 23). Some even argued that the programme did not 'sufficiently take into account the regional realities and security situation; and that it was only concerned with American interests' (ibid.: 23). This could of course be taken as an indication that SSR programmes are not necessarily as benign as they seem and that they are occasionally used as mere Trojan Horses for ulterior motives. But these two competing explanations are too shallow, and it is here suggested that we are better off viewing SSR as a field of practice underpinning the emergence of new security assemblages in which the stakes and interests of many actors collide and interact.

This chapter draws on the insights provided by Rita Abrahamsen and Michael Williams regarding global security assemblages to highlight the SSR programme in Liberia (Abrahamsen and Williams 2009: 1–17). An assemblage is here considered to be a complex web of actors and interests who both cooperate and compete that taken together as a contingent whole 'produce new institutions, practices, and forms of security governance' (ibid.: 3). The ambition of this chapter is to increase our understanding of the nature of existing networks and the different relationships of power that permeated the programme in Liberia during the crucial and formative years from 2004 to 2009 by reconstructing the positions and struggles that occurred between the actors involved (Bueger and Gadinger 2014: 81).

Since many private military security companies (PMSCs) depend on the laws and regulations of their respective home country to be able to provide services of a particular military character to foreign governments, the relationship between them is closer to that of a client–patron type. One major feature of this relationship is that the business opportunities of several companies, especially American, depend on matters and decisions pertaining directly to foreign policy and national security. The result is that many PMSCs and their contracts with foreign governments become mere tools of national security and foreign policy, and hence are closely nested with the work of its sponsoring state. For instance, in 2000 MPRI, an American PMSC, negotiated a contract with Equatorial Guinea to support the creation of a national security strategy and the formation of a coastal defence force. At first, and because the project seemed to go against US national security interests, the US Department of State delayed approval for almost two years before finally allowing MPRI to sign the contract (Brown 2000, quoted in Singer 2003: 132). Similarly, when the US government was notified that former CEO and founder of Blackwater Erik Prince had allegedly started a new company, R2, to provide military services to Abu Dhabi, it started an investigation into the matter to find out whether it was undermining national policy or not (Drummond 2011).[2]

Evidently, many, especially American, PMSCs are extensively regulated and it is not possible for them to provide military services on the international market unchecked. Since PMSCs need government approval before embarking on any international adventures they must be regarded as intrinsic parts of the same field of practice as the state. Consequentially, the neoliberal proliferation of privatized entities active in SSR programmes can not only be seen as an increase in autonomously operating private companies, but shows them to be key elements of complex networks in which the state and private actors co-work in multifaceted ways. The nexus constituting this particular type of security field has been described by Abrahamsen and Williams as a global security assemblage (Abrahamsen and Williams 2009: 1–17).

While Abrahamsen and Williams focus on global security assemblages in terms of institutions, practices and forms of security governance more generally (ibid.: 1–17), this chapter explores a specific nexus of security assemblages. Consequently, I will here address the multiplicity of actors and interests, and how they came together in Liberia under the rubric of SSR to make up a new, and very powerful, contingent whole. The case is focused around the reform programme that was executed by American military contractors DynCorp and PAE in Liberia in the early 2000s, from the 2004 to 2009. The chapter will highlight (1) the relations between the PMSCs and local power brokers – in essence the Liberian bureaucracy, (2) some discernible characteristics of PMSCs operating in fragile situations where the state is under construction, and (3) how the presence of PMSCs affects the construction of national security forces and how all of these actors become intrinsic parts of security assemblages.

It will be shown that the SSR programme provided by the American companies was not necessarily concerned with the needs of Liberia only, but also clearly connected to strategic goals held by the US government. The case study will also reveal Nigeria and other countries as parts of this assemblage. In short, this chapter views military assistance, and the contracting of such services, as a practice that reproduces and reinforces external influence over recipient states. The security assemblage constituted in and through the practice in question reflects shifting forms of distributions of capital and power between the recipient and the sender (cf. Abrahamsen and Williams 2011: 311), and it will become evident how this practice of outsourcing military training is an example of how new geographies of power are formed and how the global can be found in the local.

American strategic imperatives for engagement in Liberia

While US–Liberian relations are long standing, the American attitude towards the country over the past two centuries can at best be described as ambivalent and very much dependent on the strategic significance given to Liberia (Ellis 1999: 42). During the Second World War, for instance, the US military used airports and harbours in Liberia as links on their way across the South Atlantic to the European and North African theatre of operations (Hyman 2003: 14; Hull, quoted in ibid.: 17; Herring 2008: 561, 16–17). The partnership lasted during the first decades of the Cold War and, because of the global rivalry, stretching well into Africa, between the United States and the Soviet Union, Liberia received substantial amounts of military assistance. At the height of the conflict the United States built several sophisticated intelligence installations, harbours and airfields in the region.

In the early 1970s, under the new Liberian president, William R. Tolbert, the states of affair changed and Liberia 'moved away from a 100% pro-American line in foreign affairs' (Ellis 1999: 50–54, 62; see also Hyman 2003: 21). After the military coup in Liberia in 1980 the United States was invited again and immediately sent several military training teams to provide highly qualified assistance to the Liberian military.[3] In exchange, the USA could once again use Liberia as their main platform for intelligence activities in West Africa.

With the end of the Cold War, Africa as a whole was strategically downgraded, and over the following years the USA closed several diplomatic missions around the world and cut down on all sorts of assistance programmes (Thomson 2004: 160). The civil war that raged across Liberia therefore occurred in a period of American strategic disconnect from international commitment, leading many US decision-makers to fail to notice the opportunity to reinforce US impact in West Africa. Because of this, Liberia was left open for other actors, who used the opportunity to expand their roles in Liberian politics (Cohen 2000: 145–51). As a consequence, the United States was 'relegated to a secondary role' without much influence left there (ibid.: 151).

Military assistance as a bundle of practices

During the Accra peace accords in 2003, the Liberian interim government requested US assistance in restructuring and reorganizing a new military – the AFL – to replace the existing war structures. Even though the USA had strategic interests in establishing a presence in Liberia, it was somewhat reluctant to accept. The reason was not only that it was occupied fighting two concurrent wars in Iraq and Afghanistan that drew heavily on military assets,[4] but also because a US military presence in Africa would inevitably be met with suspicion. In general, US policy-makers felt that there was a dominant and 'widespread skepticism of US actions' in many parts of the world (Lake and Whitman 2006: 61). This perceived increase in mistrust is perhaps unsurprising, and can be illustrated by the establishment of AFRICOM in 2008, considered a way for the USA to militarize Africa, to destabilize the continent in the long run and to put US partners in Africa at risk. Arguments were raised that AFRICOM would grow to operate 'a couple of dozen military bases on the continent by 2012' (Barnett 2007). It was even suggested that 'the consolidation and expansion of U.S. military power on the African continent is misguided and [that it would] lead to disastrous outcomes' (Pajido and Woods 2007). It is not unrealistic to assume that similar fears had already been engendered in 2003 and that they had an inhibitory effect on decision-makers as regards overt American military support to Liberia.

In spite of that initial reluctance, the task to train the AFL still seems to have been appealing to many US policy-makers, especially since it would have meant that the USA would be able to reclaim leverage in a region that was of growing significance. Therefore, the US State Department seems suddenly to have determined that Liberia constituted a strategic interest and that the USA needed to meet the request from the interim government acting during the peace accords. To that effect, in February 2005 an SSR programme built around two commercial military contractors, DynCorp International and PAE, was devised at the Bureau of African Affairs at US Department of State.[5]

Devising an SSR programme that was both in accordance with the request of the government of Liberia and reflected the spirit of the Accra Peace Agreement must have been a complex undertaking (Liberian Comprehensive Peace Agreement 2003, henceforth Accra 2003). The complexity lay not only in the fact that the SSR programme was aimed at restructuring the entire AFL and creating a completely new command structure, rather than simply providing tactical military training (Accra 2003, Part Four, Article VII, para. 1b); the programme would also have to include a refurbishment of some material facilities such as housing and classrooms and headquarter buildings. To meet these goals, the US Department of State set up a programme that at first consisted of two separate parts: the first entailed the restructuring of the AFL by creating a completely new army, while the other was focused on building new military camps. Initially the training was contracted out to DynCorp while PAE was tasked with restoring and rebuilding camps and training facilities. Over time the complexity increased when it was realized that someone would also have to provide mentoring to the newly educated officers and the leadership of the new AFL. This was, however, yet to be discovered.

Interestingly, the size of the AFL that was supposed to be recruited was never outlined in the Accra peace accords, nor was it specified by the US Department of State in the first tender for the contract. Instead, it was decided in the Bureau of African Affairs at the US Department of State, together with the DynCorp initial programme team. The main driver of the force size seems to have been financial restraints (McFate 2010: 64; also McFate 2008). Because of this main driver, officials within the Bureau of African Affairs could decide the size of the new AFL by arguing that the Liberian government would 'not be able to sustain anything larger than an army of some 2,000 men',[6] even though this stands in sharp contrast to a 2007 RAND report, based on an independent military strategic assessment, suggesting that Liberia needed a force of close to four thousand soldiers (Gompert et al. 2007: 31, Fig. 4.2).

The fact that such reasoning decided the size of the future force is not necessarily surprising given the fact that the entire SSR programme was funded by the US State Department. The effort of setting up a new AFL is estimated to have cost somewhere in the vicinity of $240.56 million through the end of fiscal year 2009. At this time, the major part of the training had been completed. The question of funding illustrates an area of contestation between some of the actors. The lion's share of the funding went into restoration and maintenance of the two AFL bases, Camp Sandee Ware and Barclay Training Centre (BTC) (Cook 2010: 22), while only some $5 million went into actual military training of the AFL.[7] One result of the competition over funding was that an important part of the planned reform package for the Liberian Ministry of Defence was terminated, leaving many of the civil servants inadequately trained (ibid.: 22–3, 77).[8] Another consequence was that all human rights training that the US State Department had requested be part of the training curriculum was terminated.[9]

Building the Liberian army

The contract finally awarded to DynCorp towards the end of 2004 was very vague and short, about one page long, and really only had one nucleus sentence: 'recruit and train a 2,000 man army'.[10] There was not much more regarding details, except for the explicit guidance that the training should include classes on civics and human rights.[11] Because of the vagueness in the initial contract, DynCorp received additional task orders to specify further projects and special undertakings, for instance to demobilize the Liberian soldiers that had fought in the war. The training programme finally proposed by DynCorp, and accepted by the State Department, comprised a long period of recruitment and vetting of potential soldiers. This was to be followed by a twenty-two-week training cycle with four distinct parts: the first two consisting of a total of twelve weeks of basic military training, while the third and fourth focused on different types of leadership training. After having been accepted for training, each recruit underwent a total of eight weeks' initial entry training (IET) followed by four weeks of advanced infantry training (AIT). Soldiers selected for training as non-commissioned officers and officers then went on to a six-week basic non-commissioned course (BNOC), after which officers' candidate school (OCS) followed for those few who had shown leadership skills. All training was focused on the lowest possible tactical level – fire teams, squads and platoons – and concerned only the most basic infantry tasks. Usually, the first part of any generic military training is about mental and physical hardship, but for the training of the AFL the US government had also specified a comprehensive package of civics and human rights to be included in the curriculum. The idea seems to have been for DynCorp to foster a sort of citizen soldier and to inculcate democratic values in the new AFL. In their proposal, DynCorp therefore increased IET to comprise eleven weeks.[12] However, owing to financial restraints and a lack of funding, this was scaled back to eight weeks with human rights and rule-of-law training being eliminated from the process.[13]

Cooperation and competition

The least familiar part of the Liberian SSR programme is the involvement of American defence contractor PAE. That their contract is not more frequently discussed is an interesting fact in itself as it evolved over time to become what must probably be regarded as the more important and influential part of the two commercial contracts.[14] Initially it was concerned with camp construction and maintenance only, but after a while came to include specialized and advanced training and mentoring of AFL officers and soldiers (Malan 2008: 29). Basically, the second part of the contract involved two parts: the first was a sort of on-the-job training of the soldiers recently graduated from initial and advanced training. After having been transferred to the AFL, all soldiers received additional training depending on their position within the organization. The training was focused on the creation of functioning infantry platoons and companies with the purpose of establishing coherent combat units out of what had up until that moment been nothing but a large cohort of individual soldiers. The second part was more aimed at training the leadership and was executed through the provision of American advisers and mentors to Liberian officers and officials on every level within the entire AFL, from the Ministry of Defence all the way down to Brigade and Battalion HQs.[15] The exact extent to which this mentoring was carried out is not known,[16] and it has not been possible to verify in detail what the mentoring looked like and how it was conducted. There are, however, indications that the PAE part of the training started quite late, around November 2007, and that it was more limited in scope and complexity than what is suggested by the task order.

What can be said, though, is that the training by PAE differed from that of DynCorp in three important aspects: the first is that PAE training was executed inside the confines of the AFL, as opposed to the DynCorp training that had taken place outside the actual AFL chain of command and on special bases; the second was that it focused on developing specific military skills and was aimed at creating functioning units rather than training individual soldiers; and the third was that the PAE training was intended to be more long-term. By providing training that focused on military occupational speciality skills,[17] the idea seems to have been to assign each and every soldier to a specific slot in the AFL hierarchy, thus creating a fighting organization out of what was, prior to that, an incoherent mass of individual soldiers.

Contracting as security assemblage

By contracting out military assistance from state level, via PMSCs, and into another foreign government, the PAE especially became embedded in the entire AFL hierarchy, from the Liberian Ministry of Defence all the way down to the staff of individual units. The distinctions between private and public actors, national and international, and between the global and the local became blurred as citizens of many countries as well as a diverse range of interests were represented in, and nested into, every level within the entire Liberian military structure. The width of all these diverse strategic interests, and the power that followed, which permeated this nexus, reflects new practices at operation in the international security field. The reach of these types of new security assemblages imply that actors and influence become nested not only militarily, but also politically (see Abrahamsen and Williams, this volume).

The process in which foreign citizens and military officers took leading roles in the development of the different military strategies illustrates 'the dual process of state disassembly and (global) reassembly' of the state of Liberia (Abrahamsen and Williams 2009: 3–4). While the US State Department was the financial sponsor and the two PMSCs were the implementers, Liberian officials lacked control of the events and did not execute ownership of the training process. It was almost as if the security of Liberia was restructured and subordinated to become a part of foreign security goals and structures. Thus, the Liberian Ministry of Defence and its armed forces became partly disassembled from the other parts of the Liberian government and instead became vertically linked to another complex of actors: the United States Department of State and PMSCs. Furthermore, it can be argued that this network was also organized around regional actors. Several West African states (including Nigeria, Sierra Leone, Ghana and Benin) provided officers to the AFL and held important positions in the organization.[18] The most striking example is the Command-Officer-in-Charge (COIC); a position equivalent to a chief of defence and held by a general from Nigeria.[19] The presence of these ECOWAS officers serving in various positions in the AFL underscores how complex the Liberian security network became, and it is an illustration of what can be considered a rearticulation of the state of Liberia. However, and even though it can be argued that the Liberian Ministry of Defence became 'assembled' in a fundamentally new way where the public and the private, the global, the regional and the local were locally interweaved, it does not necessarily mean that Liberia was simply weakened. Instead, the presence of such complicated networks signals new modes of global governance.

While senior US officials usually claim that the military assistance provided to Liberia was intended to build the basis for a strong and resilient military force, there is a distinct tension between the training actually provided and the perceived military needs of Liberia.[20] According to the Liberian National Security Strategy (NSSRL), the threats facing Liberia were mainly internal: new rebellions and civil strife. The country could also be affected by instability in neighbouring countries, either indirectly by streams of refugees and displaced persons, or directly by criminals and armed gangs crossing into the country, some of whom were thought to be able to ignite new rebellions (Liberian MoD 2008a). From a Liberian perspective, the requirement was to have a strong military that had the capacity to face these very threats. However, given the discrepancy between the military training that was provided by the contractors and the perceived military needs identified by Liberian officials, the contractor-led training package resulted in what was considered by some as a total absence of the qualified citizen army Liberia so desperately needed.[21]

An interesting remark that reflects the discrepancy between the training provided and competing ideas as to what Liberia actually needed was made by US Marine Corps Colonel Craig Bailey, seconded to the Liberian Ministry of National Defence.[22] While writing the Liberian National Ministry Strategy (NMS) Colonel Bailey suggested that a force that was to meet the demands required almost five thousand soldiers (Liberian MoD 2008b). Similarly, the NMS stated that the Liberian military ought in fact to be organized 'around a 4,900-man armed force [that was] predicated on the need of the AFL to possess certain functions, capabilities, and attributes. These functions, capabilities, and attributes [were] designed to support national military objectives, which in turn [were] designated to meet the threat to national and AFL centers of gravity.'[23] Some even argued that the Liberian army required 5,000–6,000 soldiers to be of any use in the country.[24] These numbers are significantly larger than the 2,186-soldier army that the Bureau of African Affairs at the Department of State had decided should be trained through its commercialized SSR programme and the difference clearly signals a competition between the different actors, and their different interests.

Conclusions

This chapter has addressed the complexities of the SSR programme that was executed by American defence contractors DynCorp and PAE and several West African nations in Liberia in the early 2000s. It has highlighted the relations that existed between a variety of actors and local power brokers, some characteristics of PMSCs that operate in fragile situations where major SSR programmes are implemented, and the impact that such companies have on the construction of national security forces and how these become intrinsic parts of security assemblages.

The main theme that pervades this chapter is that the security assemblages and the associated SSR practices and activities that constitute the emergence of new 'institutions, practices and forms of security governance' in the shape of SSR programmes are very powerful (Abrahamsen and Williams 2009: 3). The control and authority which the US State Department had over DynCorp and PAE, and the impact these PMSCs' training had on the AFL, went far beyond the Liberian state and its sovereignty. More precisely, the American state-sponsored training programme and all the associated actors, including a wide array of advisers and foreign officers, participated in a rearticulation not only of the traditional notion of public and private, but also the relationship between the global, the regional and the local. By contracting out military assistance to the Liberian state, the USA could operate both politically and militarily and establish its presence in ways that blurred the distinctions between what was previously known as public and private, as well as between overt and covert actions.[25] This practice of contracting out military assistance while at the same time inviting other actors such as ECOWAS resulted in Liberian local security needs becoming nested into, even overshadowed by, regional and global security concerns, thus in effect changing the dynamics of Liberian authority over its sovereignty.

A final remark to be made is that military training sites, such as those seen in Liberia, are temporal and spatial areas where contesting norms, values and interests meet, collide and interact. In that process, new security practices emerge and old ones are reshaped and reconfigured. This clearly reflect the tendency that modern SSR programmes do not necessarily strengthen states, which is often said to be at the core of them, but instead bring forth and enhance existing 'relationships between security and the sovereign state, structures of political power and authority, and the operations of global [symbolic as well as material] capital' (ibid.: 3; my emphasis in brackets). SSR programmes must therefore be seen as having an assembled character whereby different actors are both enmeshed and interweaved, and they can no longer only be seen as benign to the reform process of which they are said to be integral parts.

Acknowledgement

This chapter is adapted from the doctoral dissertation entitled 'The strategic use of military contractors: American commercial military service providers in Bosnia and Liberia: 1995–2009' (Helsinki: National Defence University, March 2012).

Notes

1 unssr.unlb.org/SSR/Definitions.aspx, accessed on 25 August 2016.

2 Some argue that Erik Prince was in fact not involved in the company at all and a R2 representative has actually denied his involvement; see Mazzetti and Hager (2011).

3 Interview with Lieutenant General (retd) Henry S. Dubar, 7 October 2008.

4 Interview with Mike Bittrick, 15 December 2008.

5 Interviews with Bittrick and Colonel Al Rumphrey.

6 Interview with Susan McCarty, 15 December 2008. Compare, for instance, with Olson and Gregorian (2007: 33).

7 Interview with Bittrick, 15 December 2008.

8 Interviews with Magnus Jörgel, 3–10 October 2008 and 4–11 February 2009.

9 Interview with Jeff Rodriguez of DynCorp, 7 February 2009, Barclay Training Centre, Monrovia, Liberia.

10 Interviews with Bittrick and Christine Cissa and Mike Hicks of DynCorp, December 2008.

11 Interviews with Bittrick and Rumphrey; see also McFate (2010).

12 Ibid.

13 Interview with Rodriguez; International Crisis Group (2009: 12).

14 At a late stage in my research PAE opted out from being interviewed. Therefore, facts about their contract to provide mentoring to the AFL originate from secondary sources only. Some data has been developed but only time will tell what the exact role of PAE was.

15 Interview with Rumphrey, 10 February 2009.

16 Several countries (Nigeria, Sierra Leone, Ghana and Benin) provide officers to the AFL. Cf. 'Seconded ECOWAS soldiers contributing to the Armed Forces of Liberia', *Armed Forces Today*, (3)1: 43, 11 February 2009. The most striking example is the Command-Officer-in-Charge (COIC), a position held by a general from Nigeria (July 2007 to 2014, the late Major General Suraj Alao Abdurrahman).

Only a few demobilized former AFL officers have been vetted and reactivated as officers in the new AFL. One such example was Lieutenant Colonel Aaron Torma Johnson, retired in 2005 by the NTGL/Government of Liberia, but reinstated in active service in 2008 by the president to serve as a senior officer in the AFL. He was the Deputy Command-Officer-in-Charge (DCOIC) for the AFL and the chief of staff of 23rd Infantry Brigade. 'PROFILES: Lt Col Aaron Torma Johnson Deputy COIC, AFL', *The AFL Guardian*, 1(7): 6, November 2008. See also 'Seven reinstated AFL officers off for training', *Armed Forces Today*, (2)1: 45, 11 February 2008.

17 For a list of all US Army MOS, which inspired the training, see army.com/info/mos/all, accessed 25 August 2016.

18 'Seconded ECOWAS soldiers contributing to the Armed Forces of Liberia', *Armed Forces Today*, (3)1: 43, 11 February 2009.

19 From July 2007 to 2014, the late Major General Suraj Alao Abdurrahman.

20 Historically, the Liberian military has adopted oppressive rather than protective roles as regards the Liberian people. Therefore, it is not inconceivable that there is an international interest in maintaining a weak and disorganized army in Liberia in order to prevent it from yet again becoming an instrument of oppression (Utas 2009; International Crisis Group 2009: 17–18).

21 Interview with Lieutenant General (retd) Henry S. Dubar, 7 October 2008.

22 Email from Colonel Craig N. Bailey, USMC, 15 October 2010; also interview with Colonel Perry Buxo, US Army, and Lieutenant Colonel Andy Hart, UK Army, 8 October 2008, Barclay Training Centre, Monrovia, Liberia.

23 Ibid., and Liberian MoD (2008b).

24 Interview with Dubar, 7 October 2008.

25 The same thing was true in the mid-1990s when MPRI trained the Bosnian military; see Mohlin (2014).

List of respondents

Bailey, Craig N. (email, 15 October 2010), USMC colonel, during 2008 adviser to the AFL.

Bittrick, Michael J. (15 December 2008), Washington DC. Former US Air Force Intelligence Officer. At the time of the interview, Deputy Director for Regional and Security Affairs at the Bureau of African Affairs (AF/RSA) at the US Department of State.

Buxo, Perry (8 October 2008), Barclay Training Centre, Monrovia, Liberia. US Army colonel. At the time of the interview an adviser to the AFL.

Cissa, Christine (18 December 2008), Falls Church, Virginia, USA. Contract manager at DynCorp.

Cohen, Herman J. (17 December 2008, and successive emails and letters), Washington DC. US ambassador to Senegal and Gambia 1977–80, Assistant Secretary of State for African Affairs 1989–93.

Dubar, Henry S. (7 October 2008), Monrovia, Liberia. Lieutenant general and former chief-of-staff of the Armed Forces of Liberia (1980–90). At the time of the interview he was the senior military adviser to the Liberian minister of defence.

Gompert, David (email,1 April 2009), with RAND Corporation.

Hart, Andy (8 October 2008), Barclay Training Centre, Monrovia, Liberia. UK Army lieutenant colonel. At the time of the interview an adviser to the AFL. Hicks, Mike (18 December 2008), Falls Church, Virginia, USA. Former US Army lieutenant colonel. At the time of the interview an employee of DynCorp.

Jörgel, Magnus (several conversations, 3–10 October 2008; 2–11 February 2009), Monrovia, Liberia. Former Swedish Army lieutenant colonel. At the time of the interviews he was the senior adviser to the Liberian minister of defence Brownie Samukai on SSR issues.

McCarty, Susan (15 December 2008), Washington, DC. Bureau of African Affairs at the US Department of State.

Rodriguez, Jeff (7 February 2009), Barclay Training Centre, Monrovia, Liberia. Rodriguez was at the time DynCorp programme manager in Liberia

Rumphrey, Al (10 February 2009), Monrovia, Liberia. US Army colonel. At the time of the interview he led the Office for Defense Cooperation (ODC) at the embassy in Monrovia.

Bibliography

Abrahamsen, R. and M. Williams (2009) 'Security beyond the state: global security assemblages in international

politics', *International Political Sociology*, 3(1): 1–17.
— (2011) 'Privatization in practice: power and capital in the field of global security', in E. Adler and V. Pouliot (eds), *International Practices*, Cambridge: Cambridge University Press, ch. 12.
Barnett, T. (2007) 'The Americans have landed', *Esquire*, 7 June, www.esquire.com/news-politics/a3083/africacommando707/, accessed 11 February 2016.
Brown, J. (2000) 'The rise of the private-sector military', *Christian Science Monitor*, 7 July.
Bueger, C. and F. Gadinger (2014) *International Practice Theory: New Perspectives*, Basingstoke: Palgrave Macmillan.
Cohen, H. (2000) *Intervening in Africa: Superpower Peacemaking in a Troubled Continent*, New York: St Martin's Press.
Cook, N. (2010) *Liberia's Post-War Development: Key Issues and U.S. Assistance*, Washington, DC: Congressional Research Services.
Drummond, J. (2011) 'US studies legality of American-led private army', *Financial Times*, 15 May, www.ft.com/cms/s/0/4144461c-7f20-11e0-b239-00144feabdc0.html#axzz3p6ucregB, accessed 22 October 2015.
Ellis, S. (1999) *The Mask of Anarchy*, London: Hurst & Co.
Gompert, D. C., O. Oliker, B. Stearns, K. Crane and J. Riley (2007) *Making Liberia Safe: Transformation of the National Security Sector*, Santa Monica, CA: RAND Corporation, www.rand.org/pubs/monographs/MG529, accessed 11 February 2016.
Herring, G. (2008) *From Colony to Superpower: U.S. Foreign Relations Since 1776* (Oxford History of the United States), New York: Oxford University Press.
Hyman, L. (2003) *United States Policy towards Liberia 1822 to 2003: Unintended Consequences?*, Cherry Hill: Africana Homestead Legacy Publishers.
International Crisis Group (2009) 'Liberia: uneven progress in Security Sector Reform', Africa Report no. 148, Brussels: International Crisis Group.
Lake, A. and C. Whitman (2006) *More than Humanitarianism: A Strategic Approach towards Africa*, New York: Council on Foreign Relations.
Liberian Comprehensive Peace Agreement (2003) *Comprehensive Peace Agreement between the Government of Liberia and the Liberians United for Reconciliation and Democracy (LURD) and the Movement for Democracy in Liberia (MODEL) and Political Parties*, Accra, 18 August.
Liberian MoD (2008a) *National Security Strategy of the Republic of Liberia (NSSRL)*, Monrovia: Liberian MoD.
— (2008b) *National Military Strategy: AFL, Efficient, Affordable, Accountable (NMS)*, Monrovia: Liberian MoD.
Malan, M. (2008) *Security Sector Reform in Liberia: Mixed results from humble beginnings*, Carlisle: Strategic Studies Institute.
Mazzetti, M. and E. Hager (2011) 'Head of private military firm denies affiliation with ex-Blackwater chief', *New York Times*, 6 June.
McFate, S. (2008) 'Lessons learned from Liberia: Security Sector Reform in a failed state', *RUSI Journal*, 153(1).
— (2010) 'I built an African army', *Foreign Policy*, 7 January.
Mohlin, M. (2012) 'The strategic use of military contractors: an American commercial military service providers in Bosnia and Liberia: 1995–2009', PhD dissertation, Helsinki: National Defence University.
— (2014) 'Shadow wars: private military companies as strategic tools', *St Antony's International Review*, themed issue on 'Private military and security companies', February.
Olson, L. and H. Gregorian (2007) *Side by Side or Together? Working for security, development & peace in Afghanistan and Liberia*, Centre for Military and

Strategic Studies at the University of Calgary.
Pajibo, E. and E. Woods (2007) 'AFRICOM: wrong for Africa, disastrous for Liberia', *Foreign Policy in Focus*, 26 July, www.fpif.org/articles/africom_wrong_for_liberia_disastrous_for_africa, accessed 11 February 2016.
Singer, P. W. (2003) *Corporate Warriors: The Rise of the Privatized Military Industry*, Ithaca, NY: Cornell University Press.
Thomson, A. (2004) *An Introduction to African Politics*, London: Routledge.
Utas, M. (2009) 'Malignant organisms: continuities of state-run violence in rural Liberia', in B. Kapferer and B. E. Bertelsen (eds), *Crisis of the State: War and social upheaval*, Oxford: Berghahn Books, pp. 256–91.

7 | Political becoming and non-state emergence in Kenya's security sector: Mungiki as security operator

Jacob Rasmussen

Global security assemblage and ethnographies of non-state security

Over the last decades, Kenya has gone through a series of political upheavals and societal changes. In addition to these internal developments, changing international security interests in the eastern African region and shifting global dynamics in the security sector have transformed the security landscape of Kenya dramatically. This chapter investigates how the reconfiguration of the security sector in Kenya has provided opportunities for new and alternative actors and how it has produced new alliances within the sector. Investigating the security sector at a time of transformation and change, the chapter reveals how the new opportunities and alliances are unstable and in a constant process of emergence, which presents the different actors a space for political influence and political becoming. The chapter focuses on the Mungiki movement and its involvement in the social and political upheavals in Kenya as an example of how non-state actors can find their way into the security sector and how they use security as a tool for organizational institutionalization and political becoming. Mungiki was one of the main perpetrators in the 2007/08 post-electoral violence, at the same time that the organization has been systematically persecuted by state security agents. This presents Mungiki as an intriguing case for investigating how the politics of security plays out.

The chapter draws on long-term ethnographic fieldwork on the Mungiki movement and shows how the everyday considerations and experiences of non-state actors assists us in understanding security as a process of emergence; hence it supplements more mainstream studies of security that tend to focus on the role of the state and formal institutions. Despite the local focus of the chapter, the global dynamics in the security sector and their influence on security politics and practices in Kenya frame the analyses of Mungiki as security provider. Rita Abrahamsen's and Michael Williams' global security assemblage theory elaborates how different actors interact and compete in a transformed security sector; hence it provides an analytical framework for unpacking the complex transformations within the Kenyan security sector (see Abrahamsen and Williams 2010: 90).

It is argued that ethnographies of non-state actors in relation to global security assemblages add insights well beyond the global by inserting understandings of everyday processes of emergence and becoming usually left out of the more generalized analyses of the workings of security politics. The predominant statist perspective of much of the private security literature overlooks the non-state perspective, though some of the drivers and expressions tend to be similar. Therefore, using Mungiki to show how localized expressions of security emerge as part of the global security assemblages, the chapter adds nuances to how apparently marginal events and actors are nevertheless at the centre of how power is produced and problematized (see Roitman 2005: 419).

Rita Abrahamsen and Michael Williams define global security assemblages as 'complex, multi-sited institutional orders where a range of different security agents interact, cooperate, and compete to produce new practices and structures of security governance' (Abrahamsen and Williams 2010: 95). Abrahamsen and Williams build on Saskia Sassen's argument on global assemblage theory, which posits that the state is no longer the primary focus for organizing governance (this also applies to the security sector); rather, the analytical attention is directed towards new actors, new relations and new roles (Sassen 2006; Abrahamsen and Williams 2010: 89). Hence, this chapter investigates how a new actor like Mungiki establishes and maintains its relations to the state while carving out a new role for itself in the security sector and in Kenyan society in general.

Abrahamsen and Williams argue that the transformation of global structures happens in three phases: first, a process of disassembly where public functions are outsourced or taken up by private actors; second, a development phase where the private actors or non-state actors acquire new capacities that enable them to operate at the global level; and the last phase involves the process of reassembly in which the new actors become part of global assemblages embedded in national settings, yet operate on a global scale (ibid.: 91).

Their focus is on the role of private security companies within the security sector. However, rather than writing off the role of the state as diminishing, as much globalization theory has tended to do, Abrahamsen and Williams argue that the state is not per se losing its power or authority owing to such transformations of the security sector; instead the state plays a key role in enabling new actors and new relations to emerge (ibid.: 91; cf. Sassen 2006). Furthermore, the incorporation of new actors in the new security assemblages produces new practices and structures of security governance owing to the constant interaction, cooperation and competition amongst actors (Abrahamsen and Williams 2010: 95). The global in this regard is constituted by the disassembly of public functions, thereby changing the role of the state without necessarily diminishing its authority; the state now enables alliances between new and old actors connected to global systems. The state has encouraged private security companies to operate within state structures which have enabled them to build their capacity; a similar observation can be made in regard to non-state security actors like Mungiki. Therefore, looking at the changed role of the state and its changing relations to new security actors also provides the opportunity to look at non-state actors like Mungiki within the framework of the global security assemblage.

Before going into the ethnographic accounts of Mungiki's security engagements, it is necessary to gain an understanding of how the Kenyan security sector has transformed over time and what role the state has played through these transformations. Following the analytical overview of fragmentation within the security sector in Kenya the chapter builds up to the ethnographically informed section on Mungiki. The analysis of Mungiki through the lens of global security assemblages is focused on Mungiki's relation to the Kenyan state and politics, justice and authority, as well as how the movement has been able to find its way into the security sector. In conclusion, it is argued that Mungiki is both part of the wider security sector and subjected to the security practices of the state, and shows how this ambiguous position of Mungiki in Kenyan society carves out a peculiar space for political becoming.

Framing security reform and the disassembly of the security sector in Kenya

The fall of President Moi's oppressive regime and the change to multiparty democracy in 1992 formally initiated a change that had been brewing at the grassroots level and in civil society circles up through the 1980s; though it took another ten years before the long-serving KANU party was replaced by NARC (National Rainbow Coalition). In addition to these democratic tendencies, which at the surface level promised oversight and a changed role for the police, the 2007 elections erupted into violent clashes driven by political and ethnic clashes following allegations of electoral fraud. These violent clashes initiated a range of transformative processes including investigative commissions, juridical and police reforms, and a constitutional referendum in 2010, as well as interventions by the International Criminal Court (ICC) and UN special rapporteurs. The commissions and tribunals were to analyse the roots of the conflict and, in turn, provide for future reconciliation and resilience in the fact of conflict. As such, the post-electoral violence (PEV) became the catalyst for actually initiating security reforms and for commissions to look into past atrocities, such as the Truth, Justice and Reconciliation Commission (TJRC), alongside ongoing police reforms. The flawed elections fuelled a political crisis shaped in part by an upsurge in youth militarization in which the Mungiki movement has been placed at the centre on the one hand and, on the other, of particular interest to Al-Shabaab.

In the same period, Kenya has become a target of international terrorism, noted in the 1998 bombings of the US embassy in Nairobi, the 2013 Westgate shopping mall attack, and the 2015 Garissa University College attacks, all of which have attracted global attention. Partly as a consequence of these attacks in Kenya, and as a consequence of neighbouring countries hosting training grounds for international terrorist groupings, Kenya has become an important ally for Western-led anti-terror initiatives. Furthermore, for the first time as an independent nation, in 2011 Kenya undertook offensive military interventions in a foreign state through its attacks on the Al-Shabaab militia in Somalia.

Taken together, these developments have seen the security dynamics of Kenya drastically reconfigured. Internal political and ethnic conflicts, external military engagements, large-scale corruption of public funds, and political wrangles regarding how best to avoid the challenges of the International Criminal Court (ICC) have influenced how various arms of the Kenyan police and military relate to one another and to the wider public. In addition, private security operators and non-state security actors alike are tangled up in struggles about how to define, provide and govern security in Kenya. In the following I trace the political development of security in Kenya by showing how security politics in Kenya in different ways have been centred on maintaining political power, pointing in turn to the close links between security forces and domestic political interests.

Securing the one-party state At independence in 1963, Kenyan's common goal of overcoming colonialism through national unity was achieved. Soon after, opposition to the ruling Kenya African National Union (KANU) party arose. In an attempt to prolong the unity of independence and to strengthen its grip on power, KANU co-opted and crushed the opposition and effectively became synonymous with the Kenyan state. It was a challenge to avoid divisions among the more than forty different ethnic groupings while simultaneously retaining the power of the state. KANU refined the colonial 'ideology of order' by building up an increasingly repressive regime, where order was a tool with which the ruling elite repressed political opposition, dissidents and people who insisted on accountability, and in general kept the governed in place (Odhiambo 1987: 189–91). What was left of the Mau Mau rebellions from the 1950s anti-colonial fight for land and freedom was crushed. Rather than as a defensive bulwark against foreign threats, President Jomo Kenyatta structured the military forces to consolidate state power by centralizing the control of the military and further enhancing the ethnic dimension of the military left by the colonial regime to ensure it suited the interests of the political elite (Katumanga 2013: 137). The paramilitary police structures of the General Service Unit (GSU) and the Administration Police (AP) were placed directly under presidential command to counter internal threat from factions within the military (ibid.: 138–9).

In repressing early opposition, the regime also dismissed alternative ideas of decentralizing power, most notably the notion of majimboism (regionalism).

On another level, the Kikuyu elite tried to conceal and silence internal divisions within the Kikuyu community (the largest of Kenya's forty-two ethnic groups, composing close to 20 per cent of the population) to keep grip on power (Lonsdale 2002). Further, a series of (alleged) state-sanctioned killings of opposition figures took place: opposition politicians such as Pio Gamma Pinto and Tom Mboya were killed in the 1960s, J. M. Kariuki in 1975, and Minister of Foreign Affairs Robert Ouko in 1990 (Cohen and Odhiambo 2004: 4–6). Coupled with large-scale corruption scandals, these killings remain at the core of what civil society has dubbed Kenya's culture of impunity, which continued in the post-electoral violence of 2008, the extrajudicial killings of Mungiki members from 2007 to 2009, and in the recent killings of Muslims preachers (KNCHR 2008; Alston 2009; Al Jazeera 2014).

At the death of the first independent president, the Kikuyu Jomo Kenyatta in 1978, Daniel Arap Moi from the smaller tribe the Kalenjin assumed the presidency. Following a failed coup against him in 1982, Moi turned Kenya into a de facto one-party state, as well as initiating an ethnic change of guard within central security units like the GSU and the Special Branch (Katumanga 2013: 140). Moi was president for twenty-four years and, even after caving in to the popular pressure for multiparty elections in 1992, managed to use oppressive mechanisms and divisive political strategies to remain in power for two consecutive multiparty elections. During the struggle for multiparty democracy in the early 1990s Moi's regime revived the idea of majimboism but with an outspoken ethnic dimensions intended to create divisions – the regime successfully played on inherent tensions between the regions and the nation (see Anderson 2010: 23). Moi deployed the secret intelligence service – Special Branch (known for its widespread use of torture) – to clamp down on opposition leaders, intellectuals and the general citizenry (Katumanga 2013: 140).

Democratization and increased security fragmentation

Democratization in 1992 increased the contestation over the presidency as politicians were now guaranteed only five years in power during which they could extract wealth from the state (Branch 2011). The increased competition led to fragmentation of the political elite (Branch and Cheeseman 2008; Kagwanja and Southall 2010: 3).

The ethnic clashes surrounding the elections in the 1990s were in some ways opportune for Moi's regime as they demonstrated the 'dangers' of political pluralism and legitimized enduring state oppression. Through the 1990s, the use of youth gangs as political and ethnic militias to create political disorder became a widespread instrument in the quest to maintain power (Kagwanja 2001; Katumanga 2005). Despite the employment of youth militias to commit and take the blame for the extralegal violence of the state (Kagwanja 2001), the president retained strong control over the police and the military, which since independence have seen a continuous creation of special units loyal to the needs of shifting presidents (Musila 2012: 159–60; Katumanga 2013). However, with the informalization of political violence and security, the state's monopoly on the legitimate use of violence has been eroded (Branch and Cheeseman 2008; Kagwanja and Southall 2010; Mueller 2008).

Owing in part to the economic crisis in the 1980s and political developments in the 1990s, Kenya suffered from a reputation for violence and crime (Gimode 2001; Katumanga 2005; UN Habitat 2002). The scarce police presence in many areas reduced residents' faith in the police as an institution and their legitimacy as providers of security. Furthermore, many Nairobi residents perceived the police as part of the criminal problem as much as they saw them as the solution to it (Gimode 2001: 321–2; Katumanga 2005; Abrahamsen and Williams 2010: 202–4). Similar patterns describe the relation between the state and residents of the northern territories and large parts of the Kenyan coast. Inspired by community policing projects from the USA and South Africa, Kenya decided to introduce community policing initiatives in Nairobi to improve the level of security and restore faith in the police through closer relations with communities (Brogden 2005; Ruteere and Pommerolle 2003). The community policing pilot projects sought to build trust in the police and fight crime at the same time, but they failed as they were neither implemented nor assessed properly (Brogden 2005: 77–8). As many of the areas had established traditions of running their own security initiatives, community policing initiatives were to some extent perceived as legitimizing vigilantism, which over the years helped to establish local youth gangs as quasi-legitimate security providers (see Ruteere and Pommerolle 2003). However, the police have continually resolved to respond robustly and, in so doing, have continued to neglect underlying factors when responding to crime and violence in the poor neighbourhoods of Kenya's urban centres (Ruteere et al. 2013).

This community policing initiative reflects a wider problem of not only a lack of trust in the police but also a general experience of a security shortage whereby state security forces have been used for regime consolidation rather than for providing individual or public security (Ngunyi and Katumanga 2012: 31–2), a tendency that has seen a growth in private security provision at all levels of Kenyan society (Abrahamsen and Williams 2010: 198). Nairobi has been labelled as a city under siege, owing not only to the crime rate but also to the fractured and competing security operators, and there seems to be little coordination between the police, private security companies and non-state actors, resulting in uneven access to security provision and a blurring of lines between different actors (Colona and Jaffe 2016).

Besides these domestic developments, the 1990s also witnessed an expansion of military forces intended to build the capacity to engage in military operations outside Kenya while still having the capacity to tackle internal threats to order (Katumanga 2013). Conflicts in Somalia, northern Uganda, Rwanda and Sudan had spillover effects on Kenya in terms of refugees and the arms trade, which forced Kenya to deal with the security threats from its neighbours (Murunga 2005: 144–5). The conflicts also introduced further Western and international aid and security presence in Kenya's border regions, and Kenya's international role in regional and international security conflicts was further enhanced by the 1998 terrorist attack on the US embassy in Nairobi. Suddenly Kenya was a key player in regional stabilization in terms of managing development aid and refugee support. It also become a central actor in the war on terror, which influenced sharing of security and intelligence reports as well as a foreign military presence in the form of training and support to the Kenyan military. The recent focus on piracy off the coast of Somalia has encouraged Kenya to address maritime security to protect both national and international threats to market and trade interests, which has resulted in international development support of the Kenyan marine. As with the war on terror, Kenya was also under pressure from the international community to play a central judicial role in battling piracy (Taussig-Rubbo 2011). However, Kenya declined to take on the role of supporting international justice at a time when their current president (Uhuru Kenyatta) and vice-president (William Ruto) had pending cases at the ICC. Furthermore, Kenya's military engagements against Al-Shabaab in Somalia since November 2011 have also marked a shift in how Kenya approaches external security threats and how they are linked to international security politics (Olsen 2014; Anderson and McKnight 2015).

Securitization of Africa

One of the central global influences on the disassembly of the Kenyan security sector is the merger of security and development (Abrahamsen 2005; Collier and Ong 2005: 18; Duffield 2001). Abrahamsen criticizes Western foreign politics for increasingly being based on an understanding of Africa as a danger and a threat to the international community, what she calls the securitization of Africa (Abrahamsen 2005: 56). Abrahamsen refers to the Copenhagen School of security studies and their theoretical understanding of how particular speech-acts allow and legitimize a security intervention or a securitization move (cf. Buzan et al. 1998). However, she argues that the discourse on the securitization of Africa is more than merely a linguistic act, and that it has real and practical implications on the ground when the international focus on the continent shifts from development to becoming primarily organized around security (Abrahamsen 2005: 68).

This tendency is especially prevalent in the global war on terror, and in eastern Africa this process has been accentuated following terrorist attacks in Kenya on both Western and Kenyan targets. The politics Abrahamsen criticizes builds on the increased merging of security and development in politics and practice (cf. Duffield 2001; Buur et al. 2007). One of the key claims of the security–development nexus is that poverty acts as a catalyst for particular violent threats such as terrorism, meaning that a securitizing of poverty is not only necessary but in itself justifies a security intervention. Similar discourses and actual interventions have been applied by the Kenyan state to Mungiki and more recently to Al-Shabaab, manifesting themselves as extrajudicial killings by secret police squads (Rasmussen 2010; KNCHR 2008; Al Jazeera 2014). Following this logic, for the state to provide more viable solutions to the poor and marginalized population it needs to secure them first, and herein lies the ambiguity that securing the poor means providing security for them and making sure that they don't present a security threat to the wider society. In the case of Mungiki, the state has used secret death squads to 'free' Kenya from what it presents as a violent and brutal menace, similar to the rhetoric that has been used in the militant clampdown on so-called radical Muslim clerics associated with Al Shabaab mobilization. Ironically, both Mungiki and the Muslim clerics claim legitimacy by representing the interests of the poor and marginalized citizenry. Secret death squads have been a way for the state to deal with political and security threats, yet they threaten to undermine the legitimacy of the state's security interventions while adding to an increasing militarization of society.

The above outline of the main transformations of the Kenyan security sector has shown how the Kenyan state since independence has been an important co-producer of ethnic politics as well as continuously fragmenting the security landscape. The state's history of oppression and accumulation of personal wealth has effectively created a culture of impunity where the key objective has been preserving state power in the hands of the elite. Chief Justice Willy Mutunga has called the current Kenyan state of affairs a 'bandit economy' where political leaders control criminal cartels that extort the citizens, who live in fear of violent repercussions if they speak out against them (Lindijer 2016). These politics have simultaneously undermined the state's ability to legitimately keep order and provide security and eroded its monopoly on the legitimate use of violence. The internal focus on keeping power has influenced how security is practised and performed by a variety of actors and has coincided with a global attention to security matters that increasingly affect Kenya. These developments have created room for a variety of national and international security actors (both formal and informal) to enter the scene of security politics and security provision in Kenya.

The above provides an understanding of some of the broader political dynamics underlying Kenya's political crisis and the changing processes of disassembly of the security sector. The Mungiki movement is situated amidst these political processes and practices characterized by exclusion, corruption, oppression, violence, impunity and exception to the rule, all of which are central grievances for Mungiki against the Kenyan state. All are central aspects of how security manifests itself in practice and influence how Mungiki and other security actors have to negotiate and navigate their role in Kenyan security politics. In the following, I briefly introduce the Mungiki movement to situate it against this understanding of the broader dynamics of Kenyan security politics as it is currently being reassembled.

Mungiki as a vehicle for social and political becoming

Since its formation in Central Province in the early 1990s, Mungiki has been labelled as a youth gang, a political militia, a vigilante group, a millenarian movement, a traditionalist sect, a grassroots organization and a political party (Servant 2007; Anderson 2002; Kagwanja 2005; Kilonzo 2008; Wamue 2001; Gecaga 2007). The movement has been engaged in activities that justify the use of each of the categories to describe particular aspects of the movement at given times. The simultaneity of these activities points to the dynamic and transformational potential of Mungiki and emphasizes its continuous but changing relation to the state and to the society it operates in.

In the Kikuyu language *Mungiki* means multitude, masses or people. As such, the emic term for the movement has its own descriptive value in defining the movement as indeterminable. Mungiki often try to capitalize on this indeterminacy both in terms of the strength of their numbers and in terms of their actual practices (Rasmussen 2013). On one hand, Mungiki's ability to gather huge crowds at political and religious rallies testifies to their ability to show numerical strength, yet their actual support base is indeterminate. On the other hand, as their involvement in the PEV and their control of local security exemplify, their ability to constantly establish uncertainty about their actions and intentions (whether peaceful or violent) reveals the indeterminacy in character. Mungiki continuously downplay their violent engagements, yet there is always a latent potentiality for violence, which lives through narratives of their brutal killings and through the secret ritual oaths performed at initiation into the movement. As such, Mungiki embodies a certain level of political agency through its name; they appear to have the potential to form a mass movement of disenfranchised youth who can potentially make a democratic difference through their sheer numbers, and they appear to have the ability to influence politics through the potential threat of masses of violent youth running amok.

Mungiki's main recruitment base is amongst poor and disenfranchised Kikuyu youth – to begin with in poor rural areas and later in Nairobi's informal settlements. The poor youth is often seen as a challenge to Kenyan society, owing due to their numbers and partly because they face unemployment and limited access to political participation, hence providing for a potential conflictual relation to society. When youths are mobilized into Mungiki they become political and they become ambiguously positioned in relation to the wider set of security practices; first, Mungiki is an officially illegal movement, which makes the members potential subjects of the state's violent actions as exemplified by extrajudicial killings. That is in itself political. Second, Mungiki cells operate as security providers on a local level as they have provided their violent services to the Kikuyu political elite on a number of occasions. This places Mungiki as an alternative to state security provision, yet at the same time as a subcontractor of state-sanctioned security and violence. On the one hand Mungiki fills a gap in poor urban areas left by state security operators, and on the other hand they perform violent acts outsourced by the state. Finally, the fact that some Mungiki members were amongst the ICC witnesses against Uhuru Kenyatta has added a political dimension to the membership of Mungiki, as they could potentially influence presidential politics and notions of justice and national authority.

The localized and everyday perspective of non-state actors like Mungiki challenges the framework of global security assemblage theory as it reveals the friction between the state and non-state actors like Mungiki as the lines separating the public from the private are transformed. At the same time, it reveals how the global assemblage is defined as much by the exclusions it produces (see Collier and Ong 2005: 12). Whereas Abrahamsen and Williams in their work on the global security assemblages focus on private security companies in part using Nairobi as a case example (Abrahamsen and Williams 2010: 172), Mungiki provides insights into how the poor residents of Nairobi outside the walled neighbourhoods guarded by private security companies seek security and protection. Abrahamsen and Williams argue that cities are the sites of struggle over security, and cities are the sites where new forms of security governance transgress the boundaries between public and private, and where the global and the local emerge (ibid.: 174–5). Mungiki, in this view, displays how localized expressions of security emerge as part of the global security assemblages while their seemingly local engagements nevertheless influence how power is produced and problematized.

Becoming a member of Mungiki is a highly ritualized process, and it means becoming a member of a moral and religious community. New members must undergo baptism and take an oath of unity at their initiation into the movement; it marks the formal process of becoming a member of Mungiki and it is an important way of investing the members with the power of Mungiki's knowledge, history and traditions, which are to a large extent a reinvention of Mau Mau rituals and practices. After initiation, members are placed in local cells named after the traditional Kikuyu warrior bands that were also the inspiration for the organization of Mau Mau. The religious aspects of Mungiki are often presented as demonic and uncivilized practices (cf. Kilonzo 2008; Knighton 2009), which has the effect of reducing the movement's multiplicity to a singular identity. Stressing the production of identity in Mungiki's heterogeneity allows for violent engagements to be part of what makes up Mungiki while nevertheless allowing these engagements to take a political character (Frederiksen 2010).

Mungiki organize themselves along the lines of the old Mau Mau warrior bands, and in doing so they reinvent themselves as revolutionaries in the present and invest in themselves the powers of the past. By linking their identity to the Mau Mau movement, Mungiki establishes a common place in Kenyan history for the members that provides an ideological point of reference and a position in society as marginalized and largely unrecognized. The importance of such identity politics and their influence on political becoming and violent actions is often overlooked through the lens of global assemblage theory. While the analytical inclusion of identity politics positions the movement within a broader history of order and security in Kenya as global security assemblage theory also would, it adds an everyday perspective of emergence to the motives and understanding of Mungiki's normative positioning vis-à-vis the Kenyan state.

Focusing on the relational aspects between Mungiki and the state allows us to move analytically beyond the violent engagements as purely criminal and illegal and instead to understand them as tantamount to the politics of security. Through the lens of security, we can see how Mungiki's relation to the Kenyan state is constantly shifting, and it reveals how authority is renegotiated and how the state enables militarized youth groupings as proxies for violent actions yet simultaneously tries to control or even dismantle them.

Investigating Mungiki and their security engagements through the lens of global security assemblage theory places the movement within a broader analytical frame than usually applied to them, as it positions them analytically on an equal footing with formal institutions like the police and the military. In so doing we can focus on the relational aspect between Mungiki and the state without solely focusing on antagonism or conflict, but also on what that relation reveals about how security is produced and negotiated by a variety of different actors inside Kenya. Furthermore, it moves beyond the instrumentalist approaches often used to describe Mungiki's relation to the state, where Mungiki is seen mainly as young guns for hire to politicians.

Emphasizing the constantly shifting relations between Mungiki and the Kenyan state presents Mungiki with some agency and hence as an emergent political actor. Furthermore, including the ethnographic perspective of a non-state actor like Mungiki adds an everyday perspective not prioritized to the same extent in Abrahamsen and Williams' macro-level political analyses of various security actors and how they are connected to each other and to global flows. In some ways, the ethnographic perspective might come at the cost of a wider generalizability and larger-scale political analysis, but it contributes an understanding of and a view on the everyday and mundane and its role in the production of the global assemblages (see Collier and Ong 2005: 17). It means that the global aspect of the assemblages presents itself in a less explicit way; rather than seen as a direct global connection the analysis of the global in Mungiki's changing role in the Kenyan security sector manifests itself in the key determinants that produce exclusion inherent in the assemblages in which Mungiki is enmeshed.

The emergence of militarized youth groups

Mungiki has been one of the most influential non-state actors in the political changes in Kenya for the last two decades. Mungiki has played a central role in Kenyan popular politics as a Kikuyu cultural and religious revivalist movement claiming to fight poverty and inequality, while also being one of the main protagonists in the 2007/08 post-election violence and pro-constitution human-rights-friendly activism in the 2010 constitutional referendum. Furthermore, Mungiki's involvement in more mundane activities such as security and transport provision, garbage collection and criminal extortion has placed the movement and its members at the centre of poor Kenyans' everyday concerns regarding security. The poor people are often marginalized from both private and state security provision; hence alternative modes of security organization have emerged (Anderson 2002; Ruteere 2011).

Despite its religious and cultural roots, Mungiki is often associated with the widespread emergence of youth gangs in the 1990s, which is popularly perceived as a response to difficult socio-economic circumstances, increased urban growth, insecurity and the absence of the state in many poor areas of urban Kenya (Anderson 2002; Katumanga 2005; Ruteere et al. 2013). The Mungiki movement is widely believed to be among the most violent and influential of these gangs (Anderson 2002; Branch and Cheeseman 2008; Mueller 2008; Maupeu 2008: 224; Kagwanja and Southall 2010). Emerging largely as a response to the absence of the state in poor neighbourhoods, after democratization in 1992 the youth gangs were increasingly mobilized for political purposes by the state and sometimes rewarded with almost unconditional and unsanctioned control over local areas (Katumanga 2005; Mueller 2008). This also characterizes Mungiki's rise to fame as fierce security providers in Nairobi's Eastlands (Maupeu 2008). Politicians showed little interest in and capability for demobilizing the youth militias (Branch and Cheeseman 2008: 14–16; Mueller 2008: 189–93; Kagwanja and Southall 2010: 12–14). Certain levels of disorder were deemed increasingly opportune for politicians as the militias could be mobilized to fragment the opposition, while also serving as a tool for elite corruption, and lastly, in case of public outcry, the violent behaviour of the militias would justify strong responses against them to show leadership (Branch 2011).

However, prior to the elections of 2002 and following a particularly violent clash between Mungiki and a group known as 'the Taliban' most of the militias (including Mungiki) were banned (Anderson 2002). Despite the ban, many of the youth militias didn't dissolve; instead they became semi-autonomous units that would act with impunity as guns for hire for the highest bidder. They were left to pursue their own interests, which were not limited to criminal behaviour and economic survival but included security and other order-making functions; and some activities became increasingly politicized (ibid.; Branch and Cheeseman 2008). Mungiki were probably the most multifaceted and best organized of the groups banned in 2002, as they were founded on a different basis to most of the other gangs they were associated with. Mungiki and these other groups operate at the margins of the state's core areas of security seeking further influence and inclusion, yet, depending on the political situation, the state seems to allow them in while simultaneously treating them as a general threat to national and local security. Since the 2002 elections, the state has persecuted Mungiki with varying intensity by setting up secret police death squads to systematically kill members of the movement in an extrajudicial manner (Ruteere 2008; Alston 2009). This is partly seen as settling political scores, as Mungiki publicly supported the opposing presidential candidate in 2002, and partly seen as an attempt to deliver the public from the militia menace.

Mungiki's everyday performances of security, development and violence

Mungiki has been active in general security provision in Kikuyu-dominated poor neighbourhoods where they work as night guards at marketplaces and parking lots. Koigi, a local Mungiki cell leader from Nairobi's Eastlands, narrates how he was part of a week-long battle with Masai morans in the Kayole neighbourhood over the right to provide security. According to Koigi, Mungiki forcefully chased the Masai away by showing up in large numbers and beating them up. After days of violence the Masai gave up the territory and Mungiki took over local order-making and security functions. Koigi works as a night guard looking after the parked *matatus* (informal public transport), but as a cell leader he also plays a role in deciding whether or not to clamp down on local crime. He reveals how he has violently disciplined the local youth, who, in turn, have gone on to become new Mungiki recruits. In some areas these undertakings have had overlaps with community policing initiatives (Ruteere and Pommerolle 2003; Rasmussen 2010), with the difference that Mungiki don't have any formal working relation with the police. According to Koigi and his friends in the local Mungiki cell, they provide security for the local vendors while the police are demanding bribes.

Visits to the dump site next to the quarry in Kayole with Koigi and his friends reveal how city council garbage trucks pay 'commission' to Mungiki, members of whom have taken charge of garbage collection, and its sorting at the dump site. This business provides a solid income to the movement and jobs to the members, yet local residents have little choice but to accept Mungiki's garbage services. Similar situations prevail within certain parts of the *matatu* sector (Rasmussen 2012), and the movement has expanded its service provision to include control of water distribution in some slum areas, as well as the production and retailing of counterfeit music and film at marketplaces.

Mungiki's ad hoc security provision has helped the movement expand its operational sphere in search of market shares for the movement's members, and this process raises questions concerning the meaning of 'private security'. Mungiki's fees can be viewed as either taxation or extortion, and this ambiguity has been raising concerns about the legitimacy of Mungiki's security operations. Whichever way one looks at it, the movement's expanded security operations (whether forced or not) have contributed towards their political authority and power as well as playing a central role in institutionalizing the movement in Kenya.

An illustrative example of how the state has enabled Mungiki in their security efforts is Mungiki's capture of lucrative routes in the *matatu* industry in Nairobi and central Kenya. Many of the movement's members are recruited from the *matatu* sector, which has become a central source of income for the movement and its individual members. Mungiki made advances in the sector around the time of the 2002 elections. The *matatu* sector had for years been unregulated, and many passengers considered it unsafe as it was infested with crime and violence. In order to control and profit from the routes, security had to be improved en route, at the staging points, and at the adjacent marketplaces. Mungiki and other non-state groups started building their capacities in this field and slowly began capitalizing on this. In this period, Mungiki were in competition with a number of other youth groups of varying organizational size and structure, all of whom were operating on the margins of the law, but in areas where the state had limited presence. In return for Mungiki's official support to high-ranking politicians, Mungiki were allowed to take over routes from other vigilante groups without police interference (Katumanga 2005; Anderson 2002; Kagwanja 2005).

Ethnographic insights into the everyday operations in the *matatu* sector reveal how Mungiki's criminal activities (such as extortion and violence) are perceived as similar to those of the state (Rasmussen 2012). Mungiki members working in the *matatu* sector accuse the police of systematic bribery, illegal arrests and fabricated charges against them. In the members' view, the state's allegedly corrupt and violent practices legitimize Mungiki's illegal activities, as Mungiki in their own view are not only formally marginalized but also marginalized in the informal sector. While Mungiki's engagement in the *matatu* sector provides jobs and the possibility of individual economic growth for members, the movement reinforces its political potentialthrough the collective, and through the collection and redistribution of fees. Through the individual contributions to the collective, Mungiki claims to show how the individual is part of bringing about a collective change the state is not able or is unwilling to do.

The global dimension appears to be at some distance from the everyday perspective of such seemingly marginalized individual members of an illegal organization like Mungiki. Despite their exclusion from the formalized politics of security, Mungiki constantly transgress into the areas under the control of formal security operators. Mungiki's ongoing struggles to carve out a space for themselves at the local and national levels is a constant battle for inclusion or connection, as the assemblage of security politics in Kenya is not only about formation but as much about exclusion (see Collier and Ong 2005).

Mungiki and the International Criminal Court (ICC)

As previously alluded to, Mungiki members were listed among the key witnesses at the ICC trial against six prominent Kenyans accused of instigating the 2008 PEV, among them the current president Uhuru Kenyatta and his vice-president William Ruto. In the 2013 presidential elections, Kenyatta and Ruto formed what became known as the 'alliance of the accused' and managed to win the election on a dominant narrative of international vilification of the ethnic identities of Kikuyu and Luo represented by the core electorate of the two candidates (Lynch 2014). As such, the ICC intervention that sought to allocate responsibility for the violence and brutality of the previous election was successfully turned on its head and became an issue of international violation of Kenyan sovereignty. The international interventions pushing for redress for the PEV victims, and for police, military and judicial reforms, saw Mungiki placed in opposition to Uhuru Kenyatta, who had allegedly mobilized their violent services in 2008. The ongoing reforms of public security institutions and the increased focus on private security at all levels of Kenyan society opened up new spaces for non-state actors like Mungiki to become involved in security. The inherent tensions within the security sector in the years between the 2008 PEV and the 2013 elections not only produced instability and partiality, they allowed for the emergence of new alliances influenced by the global forces enhancing the disassembly of the Kenyan security sector (see Collier and Ong 2005: 12). The intervention by the ICC invited Mungiki to position themselves against their alleged former patron Uhuru Kenyatta and potentially gain influence in national politics and issues of impunity and justice.

Sociologist Saskia Sassen has argued that the ICC belongs to a specific category of specialized and normative global assemblages composed of territory, authority and rights that increasingly seem to escape the grip of national institutional frames (Sassen 2008: 62–3). Being situated above and beyond the nation-state, such institutions challenge the complex interdependency between rights and obligation, and between power and the law, because they can intervene in and judge on internal matters from outside (ibid.). The ICC is the first global public court with universal jurisdiction among its signatory member states (ibid.: 62). The ICC and similar institutions coexist with nation-states, meaning that the global is to be found inside the nation-state and in compliance with national law and order, yet at the same time they produce contestations and advocate a partial denationalization of authority (ibid.).[1] Examples of such contestations could be the UN special rapporteurs challenging the existing culture of impunity, or Kenyan members of parliament trying to mobilize support in the African Union (AU) for a collective withdrawal of the Rome Statute (including the ICC). Hence, such institutions have the potential to unsettle existing norms within the nation-state. Given that the ICC accused a number of influential political figures and officials within the Kenyan security sector following the PEV while partly building the case on Mungiki members' testimonies, the interference of such specialized global assemblages as the ICC further influenced the relation between Mungiki and the Kenyan state.

The ICC accused the current Kenyan president Uhuru Kenyatta of having allegedly bought the violent support of Mungiki to commit retaliation attacks against Kalenjin and the Luo people during the post-election violence in 2008 (ICC 2015). The case against Uhuru Kenyatta has now fallen apart and the charges have been dropped. Allegedly, Mungiki received a large sum of money for these violent services, hinting at an economic and pragmatic logic to Mungiki's involvement in the PEV violence. The insufficient evidence against Uhuru Kenyatta leaves open the question of who was behind mobilizing Mungiki, but according to official reports investigating the PEV, high-ranking politicians and officials within the security forces assisted armed Mungiki members' movement through military roadblocks to undertake the attacks (TJRC 2013; CIPEV 2008). Besides the financial aspects, there is an ethnic dimension whereby Mungiki protected the interests of poor Kikuyus who were persecuted by Kalenjin attacks. However, a further motive that seems to be as interesting is the possibility that the Mungiki used the violence to tarnish the reputation of the political elite who bought their services, hence seeking political influence based on their previous violent behaviour. Ultimately, the credibility and legitimacy of the Mungiki witnesses and their testimonies were brought into question, and this uncertainty was a central factor in the ICC case falling apart (ICC 2015). At the determination of the case, the ICC accused the Kenyan government of withholding central documents and intimidating witnesses (ibid.).

There seem to have been economic, political and security justifications behind Mungiki's violent engagements in the PEV, which brought the country to a standstill. Regardless of who assisted Mungiki, the PEV reveals how involved the Mungiki was in the fragmentation of security provision as the movement provided local security services while furthering its political interests through threats to national security and stability. Simultaneously, some state actors used Mungiki as a proxy for the state to do its dirty work both at the level of everyday local security provision and in terms of settling political and ethnic scores during the heightened national conflicts.

The examples of Mungiki's security engagements show how the movement constantly transgresses the boundary between the formal and the informal and thereby attains the power to make things work. As such, Mungiki's security provision in many ways seems to be driven by their market interests and as such mirrors how the state's security services have been employed for internal political and economic interests, as much as for securing the nation and its citizens (see Ngunyi and Katumanga 2012). This points to the argument made in the introduction that the disassembly of the security sector opens new spaces for alternative actors, even if the space was not filled by state agents in the first place.

Mungiki's control of the *matatu* industry, the violent activities, the extortion and the security provision, in addition to its engagement in the PEV, have not only placed Mungiki firmly within the wider fragmentation of the Kenyan security sector, they have also positioned Mungiki as a security threat, which was only accentuated by the possibility of Mungiki providing central witnesses to the ICC. As such, Mungiki became something that needed to be securitized (see Buzan et al. 1998). Besides police persecution for illegal activities, members of the movement have, as previously mentioned, been targeted by extrajudicial practices of the state. Over the years several hundred Mungiki members have disappeared and been killed (Alston 2009; KNCHR 2008). These extrajudicial killings and the violent persecution of Mungiki members were, according to the ICC prosecutor Fatou Bensouda, part of covering up the traces of the political orchestration of the PEV and to intimidate Mungiki members and dissuade them from testifying at the ICC trial (ICC 2015: 44).

The aftermath of the PEV, especially the ICC intervention, not only influenced the campaigns and results of the 2013 presidential elections (Mueller 2014), it also impacted on the security sector and the ongoing assemblage processes. Not only were the Kenyan government involved in tackling external security threats like offshore piracy and Al-Shabaab-led terrorism, the ICC intervention challenged the authority of the Kenyan state through its supranational and universal jurisdiction (see Sassen 2008: 62). At a time of general debate about justice and security, the ICC intervention was used by politicians to centre political debate on the protection of national sovereignty rather than on providing justice for the victims of the PEV (Mueller 2014). The disassembly of the security sector in itself doesn't mean a threat to the authority of the state. Yet the emergence of non-state actors like Mungiki as security actors combined with the intervention of a supranational global institution like the ICC was suddenly perceived as a challenge to the authority of the state. Owing to its association with the PEV, the current regime has struggled to acquire legitimacy for their general security practices as they have constantly been caught between expectations of providing security for the people while sidelining the legal principles protecting citizens' rights. The alleged political mobilization of Mungiki during the PEV serves as a reminder of how the state outsourced its violence, only to later violently persecute Mungiki in order to cover its tracks. The ICC case threatened to bring that into the open, and to legally persecute the ruling elite for the dubious security practices.

Conclusion

As the Kenyan police and military are perceived as much a security hazard as a guarantor of security, the majority of Nairobians have come to rely on some form of private security regardless of social status (Abrahamsen and Williams 2010: 197–9). Non-state and non-corporate organizations like Mungiki present themselves as alternative security providers in poor locations, though embody the same ambiguity as public and private security providers do, namely that of being providers of both security and insecurity.

This chapter has traced how Mungiki entered the limelight of violent youth politics in Kenya from a political perspective with regard to how the state has been implicated in outsourcing the use of violence, which has created room and potential for alternative actors to take part in the reconfiguration of the security landscape in Kenya. The global influences informing the securitization of Kenya, and Africa in general, put pressure on the Kenyan state to engage in international security alliances. Simultaneously, they demanded certain codes of conduct and allegiance to human rights. It is here that we see non-state actors like Mungiki emerge as security operators with political agency. The uneven and unequal distribution of state-sanctioned security and private-company-led security provision leaves a security gap in the poor areas, which is not fulfilled through development engagements. Hence, actors like Mungiki emerge to capitalize not only on the state's inability or unwillingness to provide security in these areas, but also draw attention to the state's inability to properly securitize these areas. Non-state actors like Mungiki appear more flexible than the state in terms of continually transgressing the division between a developmental discourse, with the aim of providing development through security, and the state's unequal delivery and rights negligence in the security sector. Despite their flexibility, Mungiki can't combine the two as they constantly fall into the role of being something that needs to be securitized.

The general restructuring of the security landscape has not only seen a reconfiguration of the lines between the public and the private, but the way security and order are maintained has also been transformed (see Abrahamsen and Williams 2009: 3). Local forms of security are expressed differently across social and geographical settings, and Mungiki's security interventions in Nairobi and central Kenya reveal how poverty and ethnicity inform these expressions. Such normatively varied and unequal distribution of security highlights some of the exclusive consequences of the global security assemblage as they manifest themselves at a local level in Kenya.

Mungiki emerged in Kenya as a response to political oppression and a lack of cultural recognition, through tapping into generational grievances concerning access to education, employment and political participation. However, the institutionalization of Mungiki in Kenya must partly be seen as an effect of the general restructuring of the security landscape, as Mungiki's entanglement in various forms of security provision provided them with a platform for strengthening their influence on local service provision and national politics.

The case of Mungiki exemplifies some of the ways in which the authority of the state is performed anew through the increased fragmentation of security provision and the gradual dissolution of the state's monopoly on the use of violence. At the same time it reveals how the state nevertheless functions as a key actor in facilitating the continuous reconfiguration of security (see Abrahamsen and Williams 2009, 2011).

Despite the state persecution of Mungiki, the movement has managed to survive for more than two decades by continually moving in and out of positions where their security engagements can be seen as political. Simultaneously, these strategic adaptations have allowed Mungiki to actually become political in arenas beyond the security sector – for example, in relation to human rights issues or as part of a general political mobilization of disenfranchised youth.

Mungiki's involvement in the PEV shows how violent politics feeds into other forms of politics and political becoming. The intervention of the ICC in an attempt to provide justice to the victims of PEV and Mungiki's involvement in the case underscore the complexity of security politics, but also of the global assemblage of normative agendas concerning justice and its relation to state authority. As such, the analytical perspective on a non-state actor like Mungiki in an exceptional case like the Kenyan one allows us to see how organizations that appears excluded and marginal to global flows and discourses still provide important insights into the workings and process of the global security assemblage.

The presentation of Mungiki as both providers of local security, as a liability to national and local security, and as victims of the Kenyan state's excessive security undertakings adds further complexity to our understanding of the local implications of security reconfigurations, especially in situations where security actors are employed in struggles over political power and economic gains. As such, the global security assemblage has local consequences that go well beyond the security sector as it influences how supposedly marginal non-state actors like Mungiki carve out discrete spaces for political becoming through their everyday security activities.

Acknowledgements

I would like to thank the editor Paul Higate for his thorough review comments and patience, and my colleagues Laust Schouenborg, Lars Buur and Johan Fisher for giving valuable and insightful comments to early drafts of this chapter.

Note

1 The ICC and similar institutions might project a global image, but the normative baggage they are founded on is based on Northern/Western values. As such, they are not objective or neutral; at least, that is what Kenyan opponents of the ICC intervention argue when labelling the ICC as a neocolonial invention.

Bibliography

Abrahamsen, R. (2005) 'Blair's Africa: the politics of securitization and fear', *Alternatives: Global, Local, Political*, 30(1): 55–80.

Abrahamsen, R. and M. C. Williams (2009). 'Security beyond the state: private security in international politics', *International Political Sociology*, 3: 1–17.

— (2010) *Security beyond the State: Private security in international politics*, Cambridge: Cambridge University Press.

Al Jazeera (2014) *Inside Kenya's Death Squads*, Investigative documentary by Kris Jepson.

Alston, P. (2009) *UN Special Rapporteur on Extrajudicial, Arbitrary or Summary Executions Mission to Kenya 16–25 February 2009*, UN Office of the High Commissioner for Human Rights, 25 February, url: 10.6.2010, www. ohchr.org/EN/NewsEvents/Pages/DisplayNews.aspx?NewsID=8673&LangID=E.

Anderson, D. (2002) 'Vigilantes, violence and the politics of public order in Kenya', *African Affairs*, 101(405): 531–55.

— (2010) 'Majimboism: the troubled history of an idea', in D. Branch, N. Cheeseman and L. Gardner (eds), *Our Turn to Eat. Politics in Kenya since 1950*, Münster: Lit Verlag, pp. 23–51.

Anderson, D. and J. McKnight (2015) 'Kenya at war: Al-Shabaab and its enemies in Eastern Africa', *African Affairs*, 114(454): 1–27.

Branch, D. (2011) *Kenya. Between Hope and Despair, 1963–2011*, New Haven, CT: Yale University Press

Branch, D. and N. Cheeseman (2008) 'Democratization, sequencing, and state failure in Africa: lessons from Kenya', *African Affairs*, 108(1): 1–26.

Brogden, M. (2005) '"Horses for courses" and "thin blue lines": community policing in transitional society', *Police Quarterly*, 8(1): 64–98.

Buur, L., S. Jensen and F. Stepputat (eds) (2007) *The Security Development Nexus: Expressions of sovereignty and securitization in Southern Africa*, Uppsala/Cape Town: Nordic Africa Institute/HSRC Press.

Buzan, B., O. Wæver and J. de Wilde (1998) *Security – a New Framework for Analysis*, Boulder, CO, and London: Lynne Rienner.

CIPEV (2008) *Report of the Commission of Inquiry into Post Election Violence*, Nairobi: Government of Kenya, www.kenyalaw.org/Downloads/Reports/Commission_of_Inquiry_into_Post_Election_Violence.pdf.

Cohen, D. W. and A. Odhiambo (2004) *The Risks of Knowledge. Investigations into the Death of Hon. Minister John Robert Ouku in Kenya, 1990*, Athens: Ohio University Press

Colona, F. and R. Jaffe (2016) 'Hybrid governance arrangements', *European Journal of Development Research*, 28(2): 175–83.

Collier, S. and A. Ong (2005) 'Global assemblages, anthropological problems', in S. Collier and A. Ong (eds), *Global Assemblages. Technology, politics, and ethics as anthropological problems*, Oxford: Blackwell.

Duffield, M. (2001) *Global Governance and the New Wars: The merging of development and security*, London: Zed Books.

Frederiksen, B. F. (2010) 'Mungiki, vernacular organization and political society in Kenya', *Development and Change*, 41(6): 1065–89.

Gecaga, M. G. (2007) 'Religious movements and democratisation in Kenya: between the sacred and the profane', in G. Murunga and S. Nasong'o (eds), *Kenya. The Struggle for Democracy*, London: Zed Books, pp. 58–89.

Gimode, E. A. (2001) 'An anatomy of violent crime and insecurity in Kenya: the case of Nairobi 1985–1999', *Africa Development*, 26(1/2): 295–335.

ICC (2015) *Public Redacted Version of 'Second Updated Prosecution Pre-trial Brief, 26 August 2013, ICC-01/09-02/11-796-Conf-AnxA*, 19 January.

Kagwanja, P. M. (2001) 'Politics of marionettes: extra-legal violence and the 1997 elections in Kenya', in M. Rutten, A. Mazrui and F. Grignon (eds), *Out for the Count. Democracy in Kenya*, Kampala: Fountain Publishers, pp. 72–100.

— (2005) 'Power to Uhuru. Youth identity and generational politics in Kenya's 2002 elections', *African Affairs*, 105(418): 51–75.

Kagwanja, P. M. and R. Southall (2010) 'Kenya's uncertain democracy: the electoral crisis of 2008', *Journal of Contemporary African Studies*, 27(3): 259–77.

Katumanga, M. (2005) 'A city under siege: banditry and modes of accumulation in Nairobi, 1991–2004', *Review of African Political Economy*, 106: 505–20.

— (2013) 'Morphing mirror images of military culture and the emerging nation state insecurities', in F. Vrey, A. Esterhuyse and T. Mandrup (eds), *On Military Culture: Theory, practice and African armed forces*, Cape Town: UCT Press.

Kilonzo, S. M. (2008) 'Terror, religion or socialism?: the faces of Mungiki sect in the Kenyan public space', CODESRIA conference paper, presented Yaoundé, Cameroon, December.

KNCHR (Kenya National Commission on Human Rights) (2008) *The Cry of Blood. Report on Extrajudicial Execution and Disappearances*, Nairobi: Kenya National Commission on Human Rights.

Knighton, B. (2009) 'Mũingiki "madness": the counter-story to Gitarĩ's modernization by mainstream churches', in B. Knighton (ed.), *Religion and Politics in Kenya: Essays in honour of a meddlesome priest*, New York: Palgrave Macmillan, pp. 223–50.

Lindijer, K. (2016) 'Kenya has become a "bandit economy", says Chief Justice Willy Mutunga', africanarguments.org/2016/01/11/kenya-has-become-a-bandit-economy-says-chief-justice-willy-mutunga/.

Lonsdale, J. (2002) 'Contests of time: Kikuyu historiography, old and new', in A. Harneit-Sievers (ed.), *A Place in the World: New Local Historiographies from Africa and South Asia*, Leiden: Brill, pp. 201–54.

Lynch, G. (2014) 'Electing the alliance of the accused: the success of the jubilee alliance in Kenya's Rift Valley', *Journal of Eastern African Studies*, 8(1): 93–114.

Maupeu, H. (2008) 'Revisiting post-election violence', in J. Lafargue (ed.), *The General Elections in Kenya 2007, Les Cahiers d'Afrique de l'est*, 38, Nairobi: IFRA.

Mueller, S. D. (2008) 'The political economy of Kenya's crisis', *Journal of Eastern African Studies*, 2(2): 185–210.

— (2014) 'Kenya and the International Criminal Court (ICC): politics, the election and the law', *Journal of Eastern African Studies*, 8(1): 25–42.

Murunga, G. (2005) 'Conflict in Somalia and crime in Kenya: understanding the trans-territoriality of crime', *African and Asian Studies*, 4(1-2): 137–62.

Musila, G. (2009) 'Phallocracies and gynocratic transgressions: gender, state power and Kenyan public life', *Africa Insight*, 39(4): 39–57.

— (2012) 'Violent masculinities and the phallocratic aesthetics of power in Kenya', in S. O. Opondo and M. Shapiro (eds), *The New Violent Cartography: Geo-Analysis after the Aesthetic Turn*, Abingdon: Routledge, pp. 151–70.

Ngunyi, M. and M. Katumanga (2012) *From Monopoly to Oligopoly of Violence. Exploration of a Four-Point Hypothesis Regarding Organised and Organic Militia in Kenya*, Nairobi: UNDP and TCH.

Odhiambo, A. (1987) *Democracy and the Ideology of Order in Kenya*, Praeger.

Olsen, G. R. (2014) 'Fighting terrorism in Africa by proxy: the USA and the European Union in Somalia and Mali', *European Security*, 23(3): 290–306.

Rasmussen, J. (2010) 'Mungiki as youth movement: revolution, gender and generational politics in Nairobi, Kenya', *Young – Nordic Journal of Youth Research*, 18(3): 301–19.

— (2012) 'Inside the system, outside the law: operating the matatu sector in Nairobi', *Urban Forum*, 23(4): 415–32.

— (2013) 'Kenya: Mungiki regroup pre-election in search of political influence', africanarguments.org/2013/02/01/kenya-mungiki-regroup-pre-election-in-search-of-political-influence-%E2%80%93-by-jacob-rasmussen/.

— (2016) 'Sacrificial temporality: Mungiki's ritualised mobilisation', in S. Jensen and H. Vigh (eds), *Beyond Radicalisation*, Copenhagen: Museum Tusculanum.

Roitman, J. (2005) 'The garrison-entrepôt: a mode of governing in the Chad Basin', in S. Collier and A. Ong (eds), *Global Assemblages. Technology, politics, and ethics as anthropological problems*, Oxford: Blackwell.

Ruteere, M. (2008) *Dilemmas of Crime, Human Rights and the Politics of Mungiki Violence in Kenya*, Nairobi: Kenya Human Rights Institute.

— (2011) 'More than political tools: the police and post-election violence in Kenya', *African Security Review*, 20(4): 11–20.

Ruteere, M. and M. Pommerolle (2003) 'Democratizing security or decentralizing repression? The ambiguities of community policing in Kenya', *African Affairs*, 102(409): 587–604.

Ruteere, M., P. Mutahi, B. Mitchell and J. Lind (2013) *Missing the Point: Violence Reduction and Policy Misadventures in Nairobi's Poor Neighbourhoods*, Evidence Report no. 39, Sussex: Institute of Development Studies (IDS).

Sassen, S. (2006) *Territory, Authority and Rights: From Medieval to Global Assemblages*, Princeton, NJ: Princeton University Press.

— (2008) 'Neither global nor national: novel assemblages of territory, authority and rights', *Ethics and Global Politics*, 1(1/2): 61–79.

Servant, J. (2007) 'Kikuyus muscle in on security & politics: Kenya's righteous youth militia', *Review of African Political Economy*, 34(113): 521–6.

Taussig-Rubbo, M. (2011) 'Pirate trials, the International Criminal Court, and mob justice: reflections on postcolonial sovereignty in Kenya', Humanity: An International Journal of Human Rights, Humanitarianism, and Development, 2(1): 51–74.

TJRC (2013) *Final Report of the Kenyan Truth, Justice and Reconciliation Commission*, Nairobi: TJRC.

UN Habitat (2002) 'Crime in Nairobi: results of a city-wide victim survey', Safer Cities Series, Nairobi: UN.

Wamue, G. (2001) 'Revisiting our indigenous shrines through Mungiki', *African Affairs*, 100(400): 453–67.

8 | *Parapluies politiques*: the everyday politics of private security in the Democratic Republic of Congo

Peer Schouten

This chapter explores the politics of everyday private security provision in the Democratic Republic of Congo. It first provides an overview of the private security sector in the DRC, to then provide a discussion of the rise of the sector, and subsequently situate it within the broader politics of everyday security provision by picking out and articulating some of the threads that make up the intricate fabric of Congo's security multiverse. It puts forward the premise that private security provision is a specific instantiation of a broader web of productive entanglements between state and society in the Democratic Republic of Congo. In this web of associations, the very notions of public and private become subverted and tangled in a complex choreography of security actors at the centre of Congo's specific patterns of order-making and accumulation. In order to advance this premise, the exploration of private security provision in the DRC must be premised on, and articulated within, the broader everyday politics of security provision in the country. While for semantic reasons alone private security provision might be considered in opposition to public security, as we will see, this a priori is partially substituted for its opposite in the everyday politics of security provision in the Congo.

In making this argument, the purchase of the assemblage approach resides in its emphasis on association over institution and on fluid relations over fixed binaries in the composition of social worlds. Indeed, in Congo, a context where state institutions do not afford a generalized level of security, being (dis) connected in the right way to the right people assumes central importance. It is always a hot topic of conversation what new alliances have formed between big men, who has been able to enrol a powerful figure behind his hopeful scheme, and, more darkly, which new violent plots unfold along fractured but temporarily coinciding interests. After decades of state failure, Congolese have become masters in the art of association – as one interlocutor in Bunia put it aptly, 'here, you don't need technical know-how, you need technical know-*who*'.[1] This chapter explores how private security operates as an extension of this logic. In this context, binaries such as public and private cannot be the starting points of a study of everyday security provision but should rather be taken as the ongoing outcome of novel associations and alliances between localized sets of actors, interests and contextual constraints. As we will see, the spread of private security companies in Congo over the last two decades has resulted in a landscape that cannot be reduced to either violent capitalism or state failure. Rather, private security companies help reinvent longer-standing inequalities and forms of association and exclusion in the DRC's particular brand of political economy. This chapter should be read as an attempt to unearth some of the entanglements between everyday security provision and the ongoing formation of this political economy in the places where private security companies thrive.

The Congolese private security sector at large

Private security companies are formally registered corporations that, in the DRC, provide a host of services, ranging from static guarding to risk assessment and from cash-in-transit to bodyguard services. As will be expanded upon below, private security companies – henceforth PSCs – first made their appearance in the DRC in the 1990s, when Mobutu's power started to crumble as a result of waning support from Western political elites (see Reno 2006). Now there are currently around one hundred PSCs (locally called *sociétés de gardiennage*) in the DRC, employing over thirty thousand security personnel, active everywhere from Kinshasa to the copper belt in Katanga and the volatile parts of eastern Congo.[2] Manned security, or 'static guarding' through the physical presence of human guards, is by far the most important service offered, to the extent that security consultancy, electronic security and cash-in-transit are negligible (constituting together only about 5 per cent of total activities).[3] This 5 per cent includes military advisory and training services, a range of high-value contracts for the US Department of Defense, working to implement SSR and anti-LRA operations with the armed forces (FARDC).[4] Employment in the (US$60 million)[5] sector is growing at an estimated rate of 5 per cent, or by 1,500 guards, annually.[6] Concomitantly, despite ongoing consolidation in the sector through merger and acquisition, the number of PSCs has risen from thirty-five to forty-five in 2007 (De Goede 2008: 43) to around seventy in 2009 (Kasongo 2009) and to over one hundred in 2012. As in other African countries, the private security sector is dominated by a number of larger firms, often with expatriate management and/or ownership, existing side by side with a large number of smaller, national – and often only partly formalized – security companies.

Table 8.1 below – the result of over sixty interviews conducted inside and outside Congo – presents a comprehensive overview of the contemporary private security sector in Congo. As the table reveals, two companies (G4S and Delta Protection) together make up 33 per cent of the Congolese private security sector, while ten large companies make up roughly 70 per cent of the market. It is important to note that this table provides a snapshot for 2013, and that numbers of guards per company shift constantly as major clients change contracts.

The table also indicates PSC coverage – a not unimportant issue given the sheer size of the DRC. Reflecting the fact that Congo has no national transport grid, private security companies often limit their services to either the western (mainly Kinshasa, Boma and Matadi) or the eastern part of the country. A Belgian director of the private security company ASCO, which is active only in Kinshasa and Bas-Congo, explains: 'given that the context is so different in Kinshasa from the eastern Congo, any organization needs two country managers: one for the west, and one for the east, which is commercially and politically oriented not towards Kinshasa, but much more towards its eastern neighbours.'[7] As a result, in eastern Congo, a different range of PSCs dominates the market to those active in Kinshasa: for instance, the Kenyan PSCs KK Security and Warrior Security and the Ugandan Top SIG, reflecting regional cultural, economic and geopolitical influence spheres, next to a number of local PSCs.

Company name	Employees	Approximate market share (in static security)	First active in Congo	Relations to state security	Deployment
ASCO	900	3%	2000	PNC	Countrywide
Bras Security	2,000	7%		PNC/ANR	Katanga
Delta Protection	5,000	17%	2000	PIR	Countrywide
Graben Security	1,200	4%	2003	PNC	Eastern Congo
GSA	950	4%	2008	OPJ	Countrywide
G4S	5,000	17%	2001	PNC	Countrywide
HDW	900	3%	1994	PNC	Kivus
Magenya Protection	1,500	5%	1993	PNC	Kinshasa
New Escokin	1,500	5%	1987	PNC	Kinshasa
Top SIG	820	3%	2009	PNC/ FARDC	Eastern Congo
Total	19,770	68%			

Table 8.1 Overview of the private security sector in the DRC in 2013

Notes: ANR = Agence Nationale de Renseignements; OPJ = Officier de Police Justicière; PIR = Police d'Intervention Rapide; PNC = Police Nationale Congolaise
Source: Data compiled by author (originally appears in Schouten 2014: 123)

The predominance of manned guarding in private security services means that PSC guards – clad in uniforms that sometimes seem to mimic those of the Congolese police, sometimes of the army, or even the UN – are located at the gates of the compounds that punctuate the Congolese landscape. They are organized in teams that have a site supervisor – for larger clients – or a supervisor for a certain part of town. As PSCs are by law not allowed to carry firearms in the DRC, armed police are hired to back up the security arrangements with coercive power. Most PSCs also sport a rapid intervention team: a jeep with military-style open-air seats mounted on the back, on which a number of extra guards and armed police are transported in case of alarm. In non-urban settings, PSCs and Congolese police-for-hire usually accompany corporate vehicles moving between offices and operational sites. As a rule, management is expatriate, both reflecting ownership structures and because white staff are considered more 'representative' towards potential clients. Part of the service seems to consist of informal risk analysis by PSC management for their clients, and the larger PSCs also provide an evacuation service for when 'things go wrong'.[8]

The trajectory and topography of Congo's private security companies

As flagged above, in the vast country that Congo is – the size of western Europe – private security clusters predominantly around the geographical margins of the country: in Kinshasa in the west, and along the eastern borders of the country. Private security managers estimate that over 30 per cent of all private security guards are found in Kinshasa alone; if one adds the thousands of guards in Lubumbashi and Goma, over half of all Congolese private security guards are accounted for. The rest of the country is nearly completely devoid of private security companies. So how can we make sense of this landscape? As suggested by the global security assemblage approach, the significance of the private security companies is hardly graspable if we take private security companies as discrete actors. Rather, studies of private security assemblages in other contexts draw attention to the ways in which the spatial articulation of private security companies intersects with the spatial organization of *other* governance processes (see the chapter by Abrahamsen and Williams in this volume). This means investigating the specific sites and spheres of activity around which private security assemblages are constructed. Who are the main clients driving demand? What exactly is being secured? If theory is always for someone, for some purpose (Cox 1981), this arguably holds even more for security arrangements.

Most of the studies on private security companies in sub-Saharan Africa focus on specific classes of actor that deploy private security. They thus implicitly posit that functional differences between types of actor in Africa can explain the prevalence of private security companies. A dominant suggestion is that the sites in Africa where private security companies concentrate are the locations where global capital 'touches down' (Abrahamsen and Williams 2011: 122); the individual nodes in this landscape of private security are the 'pockets of productivity' (Leonard 2008) or, as Hönke puts it, 'transnationalised bubbles of governance' (2010: 126): sites that contrast with the surrounding landscape by constituting concentrations of international economic activity. It seems that from Nairobi to Cape Town and from Freetown to Lagos, PSCs concentrate geographically in African capitals and around enclaves constituted by international organizations or industrial operations (often mineral extraction) owned and run by foreign corporations. A host of studies focuses exclusively on the latter, conveying the impression that the topography of private security companies concentrates predominantly around transnational extractive enclaves (Appel 2012; Ferguson 2005; Hönke 2013).

The emergence of private security in the DRC (1990–97): securing international business

On the surface, this argument seems to hold in the case of Congo. Indeed, the only previous study that provides an empirical mapping of the private security sector in the DRC confirms this: according to De Goede, private security companies concentrate around the mining sector because 'it is the most important industrial sector in the country' (De Goede 2008: 37). The reason why private security companies predominantly figure around mining and other transnational businesses in Congo can be traced back to the emergence of the private security sector, roughly corresponding to the collapse of the Zairean state in the 1990s.

In short, private security initially concentrated explicitly around the small groups of expats remaining during Mobutu's demise – largely diplomats and mining entrepreneurs – who deployed PSCs to increase physical security faced with increasingly unreliable Zairean security forces. Interviews with those involved in setting up Congo's first private security company indicate that the expat community – limited as it was by the 1990s – felt increasingly unsure about Mobutu's capacity and willingness to guarantee their security, which he had hitherto done by deploying special FAZ (Forces Armées Zairoises) forces around expat premises. During the pillages of 1991 and 1993, military and civilians alike looted Kinshasa and other big towns, leaving much infrastructure destroyed in their wake. From guards of the established order and the role of foreigners therein, the Zairean security forces turned into the largest threat to that order, and foreigners and their assets were ready targets for looting and destruction. Because there were few expats left when the Zairean state collapsed, there was only a very restricted market for private security companies, concentrated mainly around the remaining critical sources of revenue for the flailing Mobutu regime: the copper mines of Katanga and the diamond mines in Kasai.

The first private security company in Congo (then Zaire) was started by Belgian entrepreneur Philippe de Moerloose in 1984. DSA (Defence Systems Africa) started out by offering guarding services to select embassies and diplomatic residences in Kinshasa, and after 1991 also to other companies related to De Moerloose's business empire, famous for the fortunes made with Demimpex, his car exporter (De Goede 2008: 44; cf. Halloy 2007). The second PSC was Escokin (Entreprise de Service et de Commerce de Kinshasa), which started in 1987 as the internal logistics and security department for Mobil Oil, and would only gradually provide guarding (and other producer services) to further clients such as General Motors, Chevron and other American corporations then still active in Zaire. DSA and Escokin would remain the only two formal private security companies until, in 1992, the DSL (Defense Systems Limited) was introduced to Zaire by an American called Jonathan Garrett.[9] DSL initially provided security to the operations of the diamond giant De Beers around Mbuji-Maji and to the American embassy through a subsidiary (USDS, US Defense Systems), later providing security for a broader section of expatriate-run businesses.[10]

To illustrate with gold mining in Province Orientale, there are over a thousand private security guards active in the province, most of which are indeed concentrated around industrial mining companies. As of 2013, there is not a single extractive industry company in that province that does not make use of private security.

Consolidation of the private security sector (1998–2003): securing the 'international community'

The picture that arises from the emergence of the private security sector in Zaire confirms the emphasis in the literature on transnational corporations – and particularly mining – as constituting the core of the topography of private security in sub-Saharan Africa. Given Congo's history of violence, it is seductive to slip into imagining private security as the result of state failure or somehow part of a particularly violent brand of extractive capitalism in Congo (e.g. Small 2006). It is, however, important to emphasize that the workings of global capital are not sufficient to explain the topography of private security companies in the DRC. On the contrary, demand for private security services has mostly come from actors that explicitly define themselves both as non-profit and as involved in state reconstruction. Next to mining, private security companies also concentrate around international actors that define themselves explicitly as non-profit: the NGOs and IOs that engage in disaster relief, humanitarian aid and other development activities associated with peacekeeping and state-building.

The addition of humanitarian actors to the topography of private security can be situated in the consolidation of the private security sector that roughly corresponds with the onset of the second Congo War, or, more specifically, with the formulation in 1997, by the L. D. Kabila regime, of the first regulatory disposition specifically targeting private security services since 1965.[11] This formed the legal framework that would compound the surge in private security companies with the arrival of MONUC (Mission de l'Organisation des Nations Unies en République Démocratique du Congo) in 1999 (Kasongo 2009: 9–11).

Yet the use of private security by MONUC doesn't stand alone. Literature on humanitarian security notes an increasing reliance by aid organizations on private security companies (Cockayne 2006; Pingeot 2012; Stoddard et al. 2009). From the early 1990s, the UN had steadily outsourced more and more tasks to private security companies.[12] Throughout the 1990s, the UN had increasing difficulties staffing its ambitious missions, both in financial terms and in terms of human resources (Pingeot 2012: 22). This was due in part to a loss of interest in missions and a concomitant military downsizing after the end of the Cold War, which, in turn, also led to a surge in the availability of military trained personnel (Lock 1999). When MONUC was launched in 1999 after the Lusaka agreement, the UN would, in Congo, too, from the very start secure its premises and staff ('force protection') through a combination of MONUC Police (sourced from UN peacekeepers) on the one hand, and PSCs supported by armed Congolese National Police (PNC) on the other.[13] By securing the complex and costly infrastructure that the UN often had to build from scratch in Congo, this security apparatus greatly facilitated the UN's work. Serving as a model for not only UN agencies but also the many NGOs and other humanitarian organizations making use of the same infrastructures on the ground, the UN's choice to work with PSCs would have a significant impact on the way aid would secure itself in Congo, and, subsequently, entrench security disparities between expats and local populations (Koddenbrock and Schouten 2014). In Goma, North Kivu, approximately 80 per cent of the roughly two thousand guards working for nine PSCs[14] are deployed around the international development community, with most of the rest working for the few industrial mining corporations surviving and a small number for other businesses – the omnipresent mobile phone antennas and beer depots.

The Second Congo War thus meant the initial onset of a pattern that would subsequently stabilize into the contemporary characteristics of Congo's private security sector, namely its concentration around foreign aid on the one hand and foreign mining on the other. What is particularly striking is that the humanitarian community in Congo deploys the same security strategy of militarized compounds, and often makes use of the services of the same private security companies, as mining companies. To underscore that it is more than a coincidence that both types of international actor deploy private security companies for their operations in Congo, we can point at the observation by Avant and Haufler, who note a broader convergence in the way that multinational corporations and aid organizations similarly secure their operations 'abroad'. As they put it: 'Although we agree that their missions and motivations are distinct, we are struck by intriguing similarities in their trajectories over the past 20 years in their overseas operations' (2012: 255–6; cf. Branovic 2011: 29). This seeming convergence overlaps with yet another: private security companies in the DRC, as elsewhere in sub-Saharan Africa, concentrate mainly around the few spaces dense with functioning infrastructure – the technical backbone crucial for the operations of transnational actors (Schouten 2014).

So what is the significance of the rise of the private security sector for the everyday politics of security provision in the DRC? In order to explore this question, this chapter deploys some of the insights from the security assemblage approach (see the chapter by Abrahamsen and Williams in this volume) to show how everyday private security provision resembles, differs from or tangles with the state security sector in the country. Essentially, the security assemblage approach rejects a priori assumptions based on institutional affiliation and foregrounds the multiplicity of actors that tangle in any specific security arrangement. Deploying this sensibility will also call into question the utility of the notions of public and private to qualify everyday security arrangements and practices in Congo. Following John Dewey's suggestion that 'the public' is an effect rather than a pre-existent reality to be called upon (1927), this chapter shows how the 'quality' of security as either public or private is rather the unintended outcome of schemes geared to secure ulterior objectives.

The two logics of everyday public security

Part of what makes Congo a failed state in the eyes of many is that the institutions that are *de jure* mandated to provide public security often *de facto* dramatically fall short of this legal ambition, because many of its agents seem to obey different logics altogether in deploying their coercive prerogatives. At the risk of brutal simplification, I suggest that for purposes of the present discussion these ulterior logics that pervade everyday security provision can be grouped under two distinct headers, even if in practice they might be instantiated simultaneously.

The first logic is private accumulation. Whether the reason is low – or even unpaid – salaries, simple greed, a heritage from long periods of conflict (Garrett et al. 2009) or the presence of some sort of broader and more ephemeral set of social norms (see Eriksson Baaz and Verweijen 2014), many of those who are supposed to provide public security are consistently involved in a form of privatized entrepreneurship. This goes for the Congolese armed forces (FARDC), the police (PNC) as well as for the ubiquitous intelligence agency (ANR).

These public security agents in Congo invert the imperative to 'make things public' and instead deploy their office to make things – and especially valuable things – private. One of the rare studies published on the topic, Eriksson Baaz and Olsson (2011), debunks the myth that predation is disorganized and ad hoc; evoking an image powerfully captured by Bayart et al. (1999), they show how, in the case of the PNC, extortion is highly organized and rents flow up structurally along command chains that seem to function best as hierarchies of predation. Most encounters with a representative of any of these institutions are accompanied by a demand for money, and many of them are part of broader parasitic schemes – with local civil authorities – which wrest resources from the 'productive' economy (cf. MacGaffey 1987; Emizet 1998). While the threat of coercion might not be manifest in any of these exchanges most of the time, it looms over all encounters with security agents all of the time.

The second logic that pervades the everyday provision of security is repression. If public security is often construed as ideally being about the security of all within a given national territory, in the DRC those in offices concerned by law with guaranteeing this hypothetical common security are often used to ends best characterized as 'regime security' instead (Reno 1998). Whether the hangover of colonial mistrust of its subject population, a legacy of Mobutu's famed paranoia, or explicable with reference to some other cause, any action that is considered to impinge on what is construed as the interest of the regime – and this is itself an aleatory notion, malleable like wax in the hands of individual local representatives of the state – is liable to be responded to with threats, arrests or worse. While repression manifests itself in punctual eruptions of violence (breaking up demonstrations), the atmosphere of potential threat to state security looms over many an encounter with state security agents – particularly so in zones of special government interest such as important urban hubs or mining concessions that generate high rents.

While separable analytically, the logics of private accumulation and repression, conveniently, seem mutually reinforcing and often both haunt encounters with state security agents. A vocal civil society member, an artisanal miner operating in an industrial concession, or a successful entrepreneur might be arrested by a local security agent on some vague charge related to the security of the state, only to be released for as much money as possible. People will speculate long after about what logic prevailed in any such incident: intimidation or extortion.

What both logics share is first that they both act out in 'public space': the 'stuff' on which repression acts is most often public manifestations of discontent with the regime, and private accumulation often targets circulation of economic activities in 'public' spaces such as roads and marketplaces. Just as parasites need their host body, the political economy of state security in Congo is dependent on an outside; its spectre of repression is contingent on imminent threats; its predation on 'productive' activities needs to stop short of extinguishing it (see Serres 1982). What they both also share is that they radically subvert the notion of 'public' both in relation to security and in relation to space, to the point where one wonders how useful the term 'public' is at all in Congo save to denote a (radical? subversive? but at least emancipative) ambition (see Englebert 2002). Anything is either suspect or a potential source of income, or both.

Because the logics of repression and private accumulation pervade what could otherwise be considered 'public' space, it disappears; or, as Filip Reyntjens (2005) puts it – insisting on holding on to the notion – public space is privatized and criminalized in Congo. Just to illustrate, one of the minute ways in which this happens is that security agents suck things out of the public sphere and 'make public matters private': one will be accompanied by an ANR agent away from the street, out of view, and any issue – failing to present some document which isn't even issued by government; the quantity of valuable product not declared, etc. – will be settled outside of public space, as a private affair. In the transaction, the settled event itself becomes criminal; who was a victim before is now complicit in the perpetuation of the skewed logics underpinning everyday public security provision in the DRC (see Eriksson Baaz and Verweijen 2014). While the ambition of many in Europe is to make their concerns public, it is no wonder that Congolese prefer to keep things private, perhaps as a response to living with decades of this (see Emizet 1998) – having one's interests circulate in public space, after all, entails a big risk. All this doesn't mean public security doesn't exist in the Democratic Republic of Congo; it rather means that public security provision is simply not the only thing happening. For instance, if public security might be the stated rationale for deploying an army unit at a particular road junction, whether public security is indeed served is something to be re-evaluated at each and every encounter with passers-by. The difference between public security and insecurity might reside somewhere in the fine balance between levying too much or just acceptable amounts of illegal taxes, and the kind of threats used to levy them (see Newbury 1984).

Everyday geographies of complicity

Yet to so oppose the state to society would also be to conjure up a fiction. As Migdal (2001) and Evans (1995) have forcefully argued, any clear opposition of the two rests on a combination of distortion and abstraction. In Congo, *private* affairs also work through associations with state security agents, to the extent that it might be said that any entrepreneurial enterprise that 'gets big' will irrevocably (be forced to) have what, following Congolese, I call a *parapluie politique* – 'political umbrella' – casting a fickle shadow of state endorsement and state security over its operations (see Utas 2011). The most obvious of the ways in which this sort of 'public–private partnership *avant la lettre*' manifests itself is that big entrepreneurs have shadowy associations with powerful political players or high-ranking security agents (associations that, paradoxically, need to be made partially public to have the deterrent effect they're meant to have). According to an old pattern (Tull 2003), this concerns a monetized 'direct line' between client and patron that guarantees security in case of any issue. In Goma, the gossip is ubiquitous around which of the city's big entrepreneurs has ties to which political or military figures in a specific new deal; in the absence of newspapers, these rumours themselves might approximate the notion of 'public' closest (see De Boeck 2014). As a result, any encounter or contest between 'big men' will always be informed by their associations with respective politico-military hierarchies, or, to state it differently, there is no civil society; civil society is always polluted by the web of associations across the civil–military divide, which means that even encounters between civilians can, in fact, either be considered partially militarized or, conversely, quickly escalate. The associations between entrepreneur and umbrella are so blurred that in many cases it's not clear whether the political/security agent is strategized by the entrepreneur or whether, conversely, the entrepreneur is just a front for the operations of the political/security agent; in this game, the line between bribery and extortion is reinvented on a daily basis; as a result, the question whether it is 'the private' or entrepreneur which steers security geographies or 'coercion' or the soldier that shapes commercial activities is always an empirical one – and a slippery one at that, as it will often itself prove the outcome of individual struggles.

Congolese have developed a special term for the skill to navigate everyday geographies of extortion and bribery, calling the capacity to get by despite – or thanks to? – this organized anarchy *débrouillardise*, 'getting by' (see De Villers et al. 2002). This 'getting by' conjures up a vague modicum of complicity, necessary to stumble through the fog of uncertainty that constitutes the landscape of security agents and public authority more broadly. As our interlocutor from the introduction put it, one needs 'technical know-who' to navigate this landscape. An example of this relation of complicity is an association of drivers that might collect an envelope among its members and offer it to a high-ranking police chief, to be temporarily relieved of roadside taxes at the checkpoints under his command. These hierarchies of complicity might also shift over time; the security agent in question not only benefits from producing illegality in monetary terms, but has also gained the sovereign power of being able to denounce and disallow the activities that he endorses for a fee (see Verweijen 2013). While *débrouillardise* literally means 'un-fogging', it operates best within the fog, leaving intact a veil of opacity, an operating space of options where illicit transactions and successful modus operandi are kept in the dark, away from potential scrutiny.

Of security mimicry and membership[15]

Another way in which private affairs work through their entanglement with state security agents is through arrangements in which Congo's state security forces are hired for dedicated – private – security services. As already hinted at above, in urban areas – most notably Kinshasa, Goma and Lubumbashi – this privatization of public security is institutionalized through the guarding service of the Congolese police (PNC). If we just take Kinshasa, in the year 2000 this service consisted of 150 policemen; a year later it grew to 500 men, and became institutionalized in a separate *batallion de garde* with a separate camp (Camp Mobutu). In 2001, guarding services of the PNC had already expanded so much that the battalion had grown into a *brigade de garde* of 2,000 policemen.[16] The growth of this branch of the police largely followed the proliferation of private security companies in the same period. As in the DRC private security guards are, by law, not allowed to bear arms, many private security companies have a number of dedicated police agents integrated into their patrol teams – thus folding the monopoly on force into their reach – and advise clients to add a police agent to the handful of private guards that make up the guarding team for any compound.

While initially driven by large international actors – mining companies, embassies, UN agencies – smaller NGOs and large hotels have followed their example and have also started to resort to such private security measures. For instance, many of the humanitarian organizations mimic the high military standards set by MONUSCO and UN agencies, leading to a homogenization of the outward appearance of the humanitarian presence in Goma. This involves barbed-wiring of compound walls and double entry gates, often with a security checkpoint. While many of the fortified aid compounds mainly cluster in one *quartier* (Himbi), humanitarian space nevertheless comprises an archipelago of compounds dotting the urban landscape of Goma (cf. Koddenbrock and Schouten 2014; Büscher and Vlassenroot 2010). Second, the centrality of security measures to interveners leads to increased mimicking of these measures by Congolese entrepreneurs, who wish to attract expats and their money to their hotels, restaurants and landholdings by building watchtowers and high fences around them. Wealthy hotels and bars now frequently also hire PSC guards and police agents, and build watchtowers and barbed-wired fences, in order to pass the UNDSS (United Nations Department of Safety and Security) vetting and become entangled in the intervention assemblage, and wealthy Congolese by preference 'hang out' and organize their meetings in similar settings as a way of affirming prestige. To differentiate themselves in the jungle of fly-by-night private security companies, some private security companies pride themselves on having 'special ties' to particular influential PNC figures to facilitate *efficient* protection for their clients. For instance, Delta Protection has French management composed of former French police, which was involved in training their 'own' section of the nascent PNC, the PIR (Police d'Intervention Rapide), which is arguably more disciplined and better equipped than other branches of the PNC. As historical ties remain, Delta now has a privileged relationship with the PIR, offering their services as a unique selling point in private security contracts.

If private security companies mainly concentrate around the archipelago of infrastructures managed by mining companies and large aid agencies (Schouten 2014), the drive for membership in the prestigious and exclusive community of those who can afford private security has now trickled down to small shopkeepers and bars; and in large urban centres, private security guards flanked by a police agent are a ubiquitous sight at the entrance of all kinds of establishments. In today's Kinshasa, there are over eight thousand PNC guards in three *brigades de garde*, each headed by a separate general, while North Kivu, for instance, is home to a *batallion de garde* of approximately five hundred PNC agents. In sum, then, the rampant profusion of private security guards across urban landscapes has perhaps less to do with a quality of insecurity than with fashions and patterns of imitation reminiscent more of Bourdieu's conception of social competition over cultural capital. Nevertheless, the contradictory effect is that police agents, who could be said to literally embody the public, in effect are involved in the production of private space.

One unintended side effect of the proliferation of privately secured spaces which fold, via the 'private' police, the state monopoly of force into their set-up is paradoxically a contribution to some sort of contamination of the surrounding – criminalized – public space with a simmering public security. Indeed, parts of upscale neighbourhoods in Kinshasa (Gombe) and Goma (Himbi) are now home to chains of privately secured compounds where guards and police agents on private payrolls keep an eye on the road, as well. The agents on the payroll of private security companies are monitored better, and are at a higher risk of being fired. As a result of the far-reaching privatization of security in these areas, circulating at night has become more secure in these selected spaces – even for those who don't pay.

This pattern of order-making, in which the proliferation of spaces of private security leads to a contamination of Congo's polluted public space with actual public security, would not surprise some arch-liberal historians of state formation. The spectre of public goods as a side effect, an unintended outcome, of the pursuit of private wealth runs deep through classical political philosophy, dating back at least as far as John Locke, whose historical account of state formation in America takes government to be the natural consequence of the private ambitions of settlers.

Security as mediated (dis)connection

However, to equate the privatization of security in Congo with some sort of pattern of liberal proto-state formation would be to misread a subtle and partial side effect for a much larger and contradictory set of associations. First and foremost, the privatization of security in Congo leads to (yet another) fracturing of space between the expatriate and the local, between concentrated capital and infrastructure and its absences, between what in colonial times were called *l'Afrique utile* and *l'Afrique inutile* (Schouten 2014). This becomes evident if we leave Congo's main urban hubs and look at the articulation of private security in the remote mining regions of the east, where the *brigade de garde* does not formally exist. There, the intertwining of public and private security around internationalized infrastructures takes a different shape. From fieldwork and interviews in Province Orientale, it seems there is a structural tendency for mining corporations to maintain a few dozen armed police just outside the main corporate premises.[17] As Table 8.2 shows, both PSC and PNC form an intricate part of the way in which industrial mining operations are organized in the DRC, with each mining company involving a security apparatus composed of dozens of PSC guards supported by armed police agents at a rate of at least ten to one. Field research indicated that, additionally, some mining corporations have reached a – financially mediated – 'agreement' with the Congolese armed forces (FARDC) to deploy on strategic locations around the private infrastructural network that mining corporations operate and maintain.

Mining company	Location of main base camp	PSC name	PSC number	PNC	FARDC
Anglo Kilo Gold	Mongbwalu (Ituri)	G4S (Group 4 Securicor)	100	28	–
Kibali Gold	Durba (Haut Uele)	Universal Security	154	30	50
Kilo Gold	Adumbi (Mambasa)	CSS (Congo Solution Security)	80	8–10	–
Loncor Resources	Yindi (Mambasa)	First Security	100	12	–
Mineral Invest	Wanga (Haut Uele)	–	–	3	2

Table 8.2 Overview of security arrangements for mining companies in Province Orientale

Source: Data compiled by author (originally appears in Schouten 2014: 123)

This kind of security public–private partnership was most institutionalized in the case of Kibali Goldmines in Haut Uele, where until 2013 FARDC were stationed around mining infrastructures – both machinery and road networks – throughout the concession, and were integrated into the paramilitary hierarchy of an Israeli-run private security firm called CSM (Congo Service & Maintenance) that secured Kibali's operations (Matthysen et al. 2012: 36). While this particular arrangement has ended and many of the soldiers are out of view in the concession, Kibali Goldmines still has a dedicated FARDC base just next to its enclosure. But the point is a different one: just as the balance between buying protection and being forced to pay is a thin one for Congolese entrepreneurs, so reports circulated that, actually, the mining company had been forced into an uncomfortable straitjacket by its security subcontractor – forced to purchase all subcontracting from CSM and gradually losing control over large parts of operations. And, more broadly, this example shows that rather than standing opposed to the logic that drives complicity between Congolese entrepreneurs and their 'political umbrellas', the link between private security companies and expatriate-run enterprises is also meant to provide security through connections to power that operate in the background. This becomes evident if we follow the connections behind their local manifestation as security apparatus represented mainly by badly paid, uniformed, Congolese guards. While most international actors operating regionally as a rule employ transnational private security companies, expecting to retain a distance from local conflict networks, the private security companies that are most effective in volatile environments in Congo are thoroughly entangled with local conflict networks.

As an example, the Israeli PSC and logistics company discussed above was able to 'facilitate' the Kibali mine's gold-mining operations in the north-east of Congo because of direct ties to the high military strata around President Kabila. While the set-up is now different, the mining company still sucks up security and public authority in and around its concession, indirectly wielding vast repression through local police agents and soldiers (Pax and CERN 2015). And while the mining company officially defers in conflict situations to 'the appropriate national authorities', just to be sure they also work through traditional authorities to achieve their goals. The mining company put a local chief who doubles as a *député national* on its payroll to intervene in conflicts with factions of the local population opposed to the mine.[18] More broadly, in Kinshasa and Goma it is common knowledge among security experts which of the national or local private security companies are owned by which army or police general, meaning that many security personnel will be soldiers without uniform. According to the director of a private security company who worked for DSL at the time, a crucial part of the kind of services DSL offered concerned advice and mediation between clients (mostly extractive industries) and host-state security forces. As an example, the private security company Top SIG supplies security to Heineken's full subsidiary Bralima, Soco Oil and other corporate clients operating in the most volatile zones of eastern Congo. It is able to deflect problems for its clients by being entangled in regional conflict networks, in part by having Congolese armed forces on the payroll, hiring different commanders of the Congolese armed forces in civilian garb, and by the fact that it is a subsidiary of the Ugandan Saracen, a South African mercenary network tied to Salim Saleh, a general involved in mineral smuggling and half-brother of President Museveni (Kinsey 2006: 29), who has been accused repeatedly by the UN of illicit weapons-for-mineral trade through the UPDF (Uganda People's Defence Force) in the DRC. A manager of one of the PSCs mentioned explains it as follows:

> Our clients don't trust police and FARDC. But they need to be connected, both to community (for reliable information) and to armed forces (for intervention). Because they are operating in a *zone rouge*, mining clients also need connections to FARDC – it depends on *relations*: to be able to make a client's life easy, you need to have good relations.[19]

Observations from another national PSC manager confirm that their unique selling point is their ability to manage relations with unpredictable local authorities.

> If you work in an environment such as this, you can sign your contracts, *être en ordre avec les autorités*, but then you need to go to the terrain. And there, you find perhaps rebels, perhaps FARDC people who aren't being paid by the authorities, local chiefs, same story. So if you want to work there, you have no choice: you need to be in order with these people. Need to find out what their needs are, and how to negotiate these. You need protection. So that is what we can do. We can manage, create a good climate. Why choose us? We know all officials, and we have all the logistical means.[20]

As this PSC manager explained, by being associated with military hierarchies or the conflict actors that pose the most significant threat, the PSC can pre-empt and settle security issues before they reach the gates of the compound – without the client formally knowing.[21] The advantage for international clients is that they can *claim* to be disconnected as a legal entity from local conflict networks in volatile environments, but in practice *effective* disconnection and security are possible only by being associated with conflict networks in the right way – through powerful local intermediaries.[22] The goal of the private security managers is to become the exclusive intermediary and therefore obligatory passage point for their international clients; the central spokesperson on the dangers of operating in eastern Congo, able to keep international clients behind their walls while they act on behalf of the company in relation to local authorities, whether administrative, traditional or illicit. For international actors, this means they can choose to work with international PSCs (with the benefit of adherence to global standards) and national ones (with the benefit of embeddedness and smoothened political connections). By being related to the 'right' general, clients are shielded from *other* predatory state representatives.

The informal ties of private security companies are part of a broader repertoire of 'risk management' strategies that allow international actors to maximize leverage and profitability stemming from the high risks involved in operating in Congo, while minimizing accountability. All such strategies crucially hinge on the importance of being connected to the right people in the right way, while avoiding the wrong kind of connections. The second factor has to do with the subcontracting of logistical chains by Western actors. As indicated, international actors control transnational logistical chains through networks of subcontractors. In many cases in Congo – particularly for companies relying on 'market access' and thus nationwide distribution chains for profits – these networks of subcontracting mean that, ultimately, local entrepreneurs are responsible for high-risk logistical operations in volatile environments. This means they bear the brunt both of material damages inherent in navigating regions where transport infrastructure is most notable for its absence, and of navigating the choreography of checkpoints where different security networks engage in often illicit taxation.

The advantages for multinationals of this strategy of governing by 'discharge' (see Hönke 2010) are threefold. First, they retain private control over the whole logistical chain. Second, by outsourcing to local contractors, they can 'squeeze contracts', as one corporate manager active in eastern Congo put it, meaning they can maximize profit for services that don't conform to international labour standards. Third, through subcontracting, they diffuse accountability for engagements that their activities entail with conflict actors. As an example, I found that Heineken's national subsidiary Bralima paid logistics subcontractors money that subcontractors need to pay at checkpoints of the rebel movement M23, thus contributing to the sustaining of human rights abuses in eastern Congo (Miklian and Schouten 2013). As another example, many NGOs and humanitarian organizations in Goma, eastern Congo, hire extensive premises behind thick barbed-wired compound walls from local businessmen and women in order to disentangle themselves from local security threats. Yet it is common knowledge in Goma that many of the premises concerned in prime locations are the property of regional warlords, often investments to launder money gained through illicit mineral exports (Schouten 2011).

While private security companies offer security by forming an entanglement with political power, conversely formal privatization is also a way for Congolese political elites to actually increase their control over pivotal spheres of activities and strategic resources by privatizing economic activities *away* from political contenders (see Hönke 2010: 117; Hibou 2004: 5). Because the regime in Kinshasa and regional civil and military authorities depend on revenues from such extraverted 'pockets of productivity' (Leonard 2008), the formal (and informal) presence of the DRC state is concentrated in and around the topography of critical infrastructures (Schouten 2014). As an extension of the way politico-military power in Congo connects to business, this means that Congolese government officials attempt to maximize participation in revenue-sharing from infrastructural nodes' productivity through personal relationships, thereby becoming obligatory passage points for the functioning of transnationalized business (Kuditshini 2008; cf. Nest 2002). NGO and mining operations not only bring important resources directly to central government (Vlassenroot and Raeymaekers 2009); by laying out infrastructure and constituting a demand for expanded security, they might also extend political and economic control over territories where the government hitherto had only a weak presence. In that sense, business and humanitarian spaces are also government spaces, infrastructurally extending the hand of the state. Private security companies do not necessarily weaken, but rather reconfigure, state power, reinforcing regime interests in those infrastructural spaces where privately secured international investments circulate. As such, private security companies are part and parcel of the contemporary reinvention of the spatial model of 'archipelago state formation', which in Congo strongly echoes the selective spatial manifestation of colonial power.

Conclusions

This chapter has outlined some of the politics at play in everyday patterns of private security provision in the Democratic Republic of Congo. In outlining some of the differences, overlaps and tensions between de facto modes of public and private security provision, it hoped to illustrate a number of points that can be summarized as follows. First, the private security sector in Congo is thoroughly Congolese. While it might be fruitful to apply some analytical insights emanating from other contexts to the private security sector in Congo (see, for instance, Schouten 2011 and 2014), crucial aspects of the politics of security will then always elude the observer. I have discussed how private security assemblages in Congo reflect two broader Congolese logics of everyday security provision. First, private security provision is as much an extension of the logic of the 'political umbrella' that is both a predator of, and exceeds, the private security sector as it is a service of static guarding. Second, and by extension, private security is also an instantiation of the logic, dominant in the Congo, of security as 'being (dis)connected' in the right way. It is here in particular that an assemblage approach – foregrounding the quality of connection over institutional affiliation – has most purchase. Private security companies can only 'secure' if they are plugged into broader everyday geographies of complicity that make up the ever-shifting fabric of Congolese social worlds. The quality of these connections and their implication for the balance between public and private is difficult to generalize, as it is rather the outcome of everyday (re)negotiations between stakeholders. Third, in assessing the role of private security in the overall landscape of security provision, public and private needs to be taken as endogenous to everyday security practices; as we have seen, public security might result as the unintended outcome, as a side effect, of efforts to attain ulterior goals. An example of this, the proliferation of *private* security arrangements in Congo might, counter-intuitively, have led to a surge in public security in some places. Finally, while this chapter has attempted to outline some of the insidious ways in which predation pervades everyday security provision, I have hoped to underscore that predation, repression and private security are all contingent on the existence and reproduction of an 'outside', whether in terms of productive economies on which to piggyback or criminalized public spaces from which to establish distance. In articulating these points, I have hoped to contribute to ongoing debates on the politics of security provision and the distribution of public authority more broadly by stressing the contingency of notions that are normally taken as universal a prioris in everyday practice.

Notes

1 Interview in Bunia, 2014.

2 Estimates vary, however, according to measurement methods, reaching as low as 17,500; yet such measurements seem to correspond exactly to the number of larger – 'above board' – PSCs.

3 Interview, G4S.

4 De Goede chooses to exclude more military-oriented security services in her overview of the Congolese private security sector, and did not find such security services in 2007 (De Goede 2008: 36).

5 2011 estimate by DRC PSC management triangulated with other PSCs.

6 Interview, G4S Kin. This correlates well with an extrapolation of current figures back into history: De Goede estimated the total PSC population in the DRC at 25,000 in 2007 (2008: 42).

7 Interview, PSC manager, Kinshasa, 2012. This holds not only for PSCs; most large institutional entities – corporations, embassies, NGOs – have dedicated managers for the east.

8 Source: interviews with PSC management, Kinshasa and Kigali.

9 DSL was founded in 1981 by Alistair Morrison, a former SAS officer (Vines 1999: 134). As such, it was one of the earliest transnational private security companies in the world. DSL was the second PSC founded by former British Special Forces, after ControlRisks, which had been founded around 1975. During its early years, it was deployed to protect oil installations across the African continent and, for instance, also guarded diamond companies during Angola's civil war.

10 Interview, ASCO.

11 *l'Arrêté ministériel 006/97 du 9 juillet 1997*, followed by *l'Arrêté ministériel 008/98 du 31 mars 1998*.

12 Among one of the first such contracts, it hired DSL in the former Yugoslavia as early as 1992, for a range of services that would employ, at its height, 430 DSL staff in 1995 (Østensen 2011: 16–17; Vines 1999: 134).

13 Interview with UNDSS, 2011.

14 Whereas Büscher and Vlassenroot found only four PSCs in Goma (KK Security, Delta Protection, Graben Security and Intersec) in 2008 (2010: 267), this number has doubled in less than two years (in late 2010, these were complemented by HDW, Magenya, Royal Sec, Star Sec, Top Sec and G4S). Source: survey conducted in Goma, November/December 2010.

15 Being obviously borrowed from the title of Ferguson (2002).

16 Interview, *brigade de garde* commander, Kinshasa, September 2011.

17 A review of sources indicates the same holds for the MIBA diamond mines, where a security apparatus consisting of 300 armed police and 1,000 industrial guards was managed and surveilled by OSS's approximately thirty to sixty all-expat employees and the ANR (Congolese secret service) (Amnesty International 2002a, 2002b: 8). According to reports, the ruthless approach of OSS – and the significant difference made by their introduction of security technologies such as body scanners (De Goede 2008: 49) – did manage to reduce losses substantially (Renauld 2005: 14), re-establishing not only a certain – albeit controversial – distance between the informal and transnational formal mining economies, but also a flow of mineral revenues to the Kabila regime.

18 Interviews in Watsa, December 2014.

19 Interview, Top SIG, Kinshasa, 2012.

20 Interview, CSS Beni, 2011.

21 Interview, Goma, September 2012.

22 Interview, Top SIG, Kinshasa, September 2012. In a similar instance, G4S was accused of using US money to pay Afghan warlords to provide security for US military operations (see Tiron 2010).

Bibliography

Abrahamsen, R. and A. Leander (2016) *Routledge Handbook of Private Security Studies*, London: Routledge.

Abrahamsen, R. and M. C. Williams (2008) 'Public/private, global/local: the changing contours of Africa's security governance', *Review of African Political Economy*, 35: 539–53.

— (2011) *Security beyond the State: Private Security in International Politics*, Cambridge: Cambridge University Press.

Amnesty International (2002a) 'Diamonds cost lives', *The Wire*, 32.

— (2002b) *Making a Killing: The diamond trade in government-controlled DRC*, London: Amnesty International.

Appel, H. (2012) 'Offshore work: oil, modularity, and the how of capitalism in Equatorial Guinea', *American Ethnologist*, 39: 692–709.

Avant, D. and V. Haufler (2012) 'Transnational organisations and security', *Global Crime*, 13: 254–75.

Bayart, J.-F., S. Ellis and B. Hibou (1999) *The Criminalization of the State in Africa*, London/Bloomington: International African Institute in association with J. Currey/Indiana University Press.

Branovic, Z. (2011) *The Privatisation of Security in Failing States: A Quantitative Assessment*, Geneva: DCAF.

Büscher, K. and K. Vlassenroot (2010) 'Humanitarian presence and urban development: new opportunities and contrasts in Goma, DRC', *Disasters*, 34: S256–S273.

Cockayne, J. (2006) *Commercial Security in the Humanitarian Space*, New York: International Peace Academy and UN DPKO.

Cox, R. W. (1981) 'Social forces, states and world orders: beyond international relations theory', *Millennium – Journal of International Studies*, 10: 126–55.

De Boeck, F. (2014) 'The making of publics in Kinshasa', Paper presented at the Religion and Migration Initiative conference, Wits University.

De Goede, M. J. (2008) 'Private and public security in post-war Democratic Republic of Congo', in S. Gumedze (ed.), *The Private Security Sector in Africa*, Country Series, Pretoria:

Institute for Security Studies, pp. 35–68.
De Villers, G., B. Jewsiewicki, L. Monnier et al. (2002) 'Manières de vivre: économie de la "débrouille" dans les villes du Congo/Zaïre', *Cahiers africains* [Africa Studies], 49, Tervuren/Paris: CEDAF/L'Harmattan.
Dewey, J. (1927) *The Public and Its Problems*, New York: Henry Holt.
Emizet, K. N. F. (1998) 'Confronting leaders at the apex of the state: the growth of the unofficial economy in Congo', *African Studies Review*, 41: 99–137.
Englebert, P. (2002) 'A research note on Congo's nationalist paradox', *Review of African Political Economy*, 29: 591–4.
Eriksson Baaz, M. and O. Olsson (2011) 'Feeding the horse: unofficial economic activities within the police force in the Democratic Republic of the Congo', *African Security*, 4: 223–41.
Eriksson Baaz, M. and J. Verweijen (2014) 'Arbiters with guns: the ambiguity of military involvement in civilian disputes in the DR Congo', *Third World Quarterly*, 35: 803–20.
Evans, P. (1995) *Embedded Autonomy: States and industrial transformation*, Princeton, NJ: Princeton University Press.
Ferguson, J. (2002) 'Of mimicry and membership: Africans and the "New World Society"', *Cultural Anthropology*, 17: 551–69.
— (2005) 'Seeing like an oil company: space, security, and global capital in neoliberal Africa', *American Anthropologist*, 107: 377–82.
Garrett, N., S. Sergiou and K. Vlassenroot (2009) 'Negotiated peace for extortion: the case of Walikale territory in eastern DR Congo', *Journal of Eastern African Studies*, 3: 1–21.
Halloy, V. (2007) 'Le Belge aux 320 millions de chiffre d'affaires', *Focus*, Antwerp, pp. 52–4.
Hibou, B. (2004) *Privatizing the State*, New York: Columbia University Press.
Hönke, J. (2010) 'New political topographies. Mining companies and indirect discharge in Southern Katanga (DRC)', *Politique Africaine*, 120: 105–28.
— (2013) *Transnational Companies and Security Governance: Hybrid practices in a postcolonial world*, London: Routledge.
Kasongo, M. (2009) *La Sécurité Privée en République démocratique du Congo*, Kinshasa: Securitas Congo.
Kinsey, C. (2006) *Corporate Soldiers and International Security: The rise of private military companies*, London: Routledge.
Koddenbrock, K. and P. Schouten (2014) 'Intervention as ontological politics: security, pathologization, and the failed state effect in Goma', in C. Bell, J. Bachmann and C. Holmqvist (eds), *The New Interventionism: Perspectives on War-Police Assemblages*, London: Routledge.
Kuditshini, J. T. (2008) 'Global governance and local government in the Congo: the role of the IMF, World Bank, the multinationals and the political elites', *International Review of Administrative Sciences*, 74: 195–216.
Leonard, D. K. (2008) 'Where are "pockets" of effective agencies likely in weak governance states and why? A propositional inventory', IDS Working Papers.
Lock, P. (1999) 'Africa, military downsizing and the growth in the security industry', in J. Cilliers, P. Mason and Institute for Security Studies (South Africa) (eds), *Peace, Profit or Plunder?: The privatisation of security in war-torn African societies*, Halfway House: Institute for Security Studies, pp. 11–36.
MacGaffey, J. (1987) *Entrepreneurs and Parasites: The struggle for indigenous capitalism in Zaire*, Cambridge and New York: Cambridge University Press.
Matthysen, K., F. Hilgert, P. Schouten et al. (2012) 'A detailed analysis of Orientale Province's gold sector', Antwerp: IPIS.
Migdal, J. S. (2001) *State in Society:*

Studying how states and societies transform and constitute one another, Cambridge: Cambridge University Press.

Miklian, J. and P. Schouten (2013) 'Fluid markets. The business of beer meets the ugliness of war', *Foreign Policy*, pp. 71–5.

Nest, M. (2002) *The Evolution of a Fragmented State: The Case of the Democratic Republic of Congo*, New York: Department of Politics, New York University.

Newbury, M. C. (1984) 'Ebutumwa Bw'Emiogo: the tyranny of cassava. A women's tax revolt in eastern Zaïre', *Revue Canadienne des Études Africaines* [Canadian Journal of African Studies], 18: 35–54.

Østensen, Å. G. (2011) *UN Use of Private Military and Security Companies: Practices and Policies*, Geneva: DCAF.

Pax and CERN (2015) *Géant minier Kibali: oter les impuretés pour que l'or soit pur*, Utrecht/Kinshasa: Pax/CERN.

Pingeot, L. (2012) *Dangerous Partnership: Private Military and Security Companies and the UN*, New York: Global Policy Forum.

Renauld, A. (2005) *République Démocratique du Congo – Ressources Naturelles et Transferts d'Armes*, Brussels: GRIP.

Reno, W. (1998) *Warlord Politics and African States*, Boulder, CO: Lynne Rienner.

— (2006) 'Congo: from state collapse to "absolutism", to state failure', *Third World Quarterly*, 27: 43–56.

Reyntjens, F. (2005) 'The privatisation and criminalisation of public space in the geopolitics of the Great Lakes region', *Journal of Modern African Studies*, 43: 587–607.

Schouten, P. (2011) 'Political topographies of private security in sub-Saharan Africa', in T. Dietz, K. Havnevik, M. Kaag et al. (eds), *African Engagements – Africa Negotiating an Emerging Multipolar World*, Leiden: Brill, pp. 56–83.

— (2014) 'Private security companies and political order in Congo: a history of extraversion', Gothenburg: School of Global Studies, University of Gothenburg.

Serres, M. (1982) *The Parasite*, Baltimore, MD: Johns Hopkins University Press.

Small, M. (2006) 'Privatisation of security and military functions and the demise of the modern nation-state in Africa', Occasional Paper Series, Durban: African Centre for the Constructive Resolution of Disputes (ACCORD), pp. 1–44.

Stoddard, A., A. Harmer and V. DiDomenico (2009) 'Private security contracting in humanitarian operations', HPG Policy Brief.

Tiron, R. (2010) 'Senate panel: U.S. money was funneled to Afghan warlords with links to violence', *The Hill*.

Tull, D. M. (2003) 'A reconfiguration of political order? The state of the state in North Kivu (DR Congo)', *African Affairs*, 102: 429–46.

Utas, M. (2011) *African Conflicts and Informal Power – Big Men and Networks*, London: Zed Books.

Verweijen, J. (2013) 'Military business and the business of the military in the Kivus', *Review of African Political Economy*, 40: 67–82.

Vines, A. (1999) 'Gurkhas and the private security business in Africa', in J. Cilliers and P. Mason (eds), *Peace, Profit or Plunder?: The privatisation of security in war-torn African societes*, Cape Town: Institute of Security Studies, pp. 123–40.

Vlassenroot, K. and T. Raeymaekers (2009) 'Kivu's intractable security conundrum', *African Affairs*, 108: 475–84.

Epilogue: African assemblages of private security

Mats Utas

When it rains the whole area goes tick-tick-tick as drops fall on the electric fences. Visitors are greeted with a sign saying 'Warning criminals you are entering a Blue Zone 24 hours dedicated patrols in operation'; we are in the thriving white ghetto Umhlanga outside Durban, South Africa, where 'blue' refers to private security rather than public. This is my first visit to South Africa and it is a very different – and to some extent disturbing– experience compared to my previous stays in West and East Africa. In Durban the airport works more smoothly than any in Sweden. Roads in Kwazulu-Natal are great. Traffic is flowing, with traffic police monitoring our movements. The scenery is fantastic, with impressive huge farms and private security. People are nice and forthcoming, yet we constantly end up talking about security. Our landlord, taxi drivers and people on the street, regardless of colour, sooner or later end up talking about security.

We walk the short distance from Umhlanga village to our house. There is a security vehicle on almost every street corner, there is a security guy on a bicycle, and every house is displaying at least one sign advertising the private security company they use. The company Blue Security is dominant in this area with individual houses using other firms. The monthly fee for security is said to be roughly equal to an average state pension. Everybody has electric fences; even a taxi driver we talk to admits having an electric fence on the walls around his house in the rather low-class area where he resides. In Umhlanga it is considered a necessity and walls are tall and impersonal, the streets something of a no-go area between the houses situated in lush grounds. Our house feels safe despite the panic button next to the bed, but the strict security focus signals dangers out there. It is quite unsettling to imagine being attacked in the street outside; you are almost certain to be on your own with few opportunities to escape. It is unlikely that anyone would open their electric gate for you if you are in need of temporary shelter. Thus, the Blue Zone contributes towards a feeling of insecurity which stands in stark contrast to its intended aim.

As Tessa Diphoorn writes in her chapter in this volume, South Africa is regarded as the 'absolute' champion of the global security industry in Africa.

Furthermore, South African security companies maintain dominant positions across the entire continent. On a map they will be dotted out across the territory, and are particularly active in capital cities and mineral-rich areas. In many places they are part of an *archipélisation* of production where new forms of indirect governance can be observed (Hönke 2010). Jana Hönke calls this 'bubbles of company governance' where bodies of security providers increasingly play governing roles in local society. As many security companies operate across the continent they connect the 'bubbles', creating an intricate web of security governance. International aid business reinforces these bubbles because of the ongoing fortification of aid compounds, as well as the increased security concerns of international NGOs and UN agencies. Mark Duffield (2012) has called this the bunkering of the aid industry, as these actors increasingly employ the same security companies, and thus strengthen the assemblages between aid and extractive industries on the continent.

In an earlier article Duffield (2002) talked about a new security terrain where networks have 'become the new morphology of social life'. A network logic 'modifies production, experience, power and culture as it expands across transborder social and political space' (ibid.: 155). Organized violence is increasingly non-territorial with initiatives venturing well beyond borders and less dependent on state sponsorship (ibid.: 158). Security, still often seen as the flip-side of violence, has transformed in the same fashion. Alex de Waal (2009) talks about an African 'political marketplace', where violence is just another commodity to be traded. 'A provincial elite group that is dissatisfied with its share of national patrimony can stake a claim to a better payout, either through the electoral process and related party-focused bargaining, or by using violence' (ibid.: 104).

This is clear in the case of northern Nigeria, where political strongmen have been highly dissatisfied with their marginal roles at the national bargaining table. As a result, they have played the violence card by informally supporting the Boko Haram militia (Alao 2013). Yet, on the other hand, this is also a question of security, as in some regions local populations see groups within the Boko Haram family not so much as a security threat, but rather as a provider of security (albeit partial and ambivalent) that these communities have previously lacked; Boko Haram is thus also a part of the marketplace for security.

The paucity of work around the nexus that links traditional security spectra of the state and private security providers with 'local', 'traditional' or 'home-grown' security actors has inspired the current volume. Contributions have revealed the immense complexity and intricacies characteristic of these configurations of actors, and it is through this approach that we have illuminated the breadth and depth of the contemporary security landscape on the continent. As Rita Abrahamsen and Michael Williams note in this volume, we do not, however, view the local and global as matters of scale. Rather, the local, national and international could be seen as reversible aspects of the same fabric in that they are shaped by myriad connections to which contributors in the current volume are acutely sensitive.

In his chapter on the Democratic Republic of Congo (DRC), Peer Schouten describes the security scene as a multiverse where private and public security are shaped in a productive entanglement. As in South Africa, security in the DRC continues to boom. Security providers tie state-governed activities,[1] the national army and militias to international companies in the extractive industries, primarily in the mining sector. Furthermore, these connections also link the international humanitarian sector and UN peacekeeping operations, which frequently outsource protection to private security providers. Private security providers often hire staff from the national police and military as one way to maintain a connection to these hierarchies. Despite the sometimes dubious activities, links to such state actors provide them with needed credibility in the national sphere. In a similar fashion, they also hire staff from local militias and rebel groups as a means to co-opt them, and because these actors are trusted or feared in the local arena. Related arrangements can be found across the continent.

In his chapter on Somalia, like Schouten, William Reno reveals how international private security providers frequently collaborate with local actors deeply entrenched in the conflict. Somewhat paradoxically, both partners provide a measure of local order, but also perpetuate violence and instability. Reno argues that, at times, a number of larger international companies replace government services with the help of local security providers. In further elaborating, he shows how 'alternative indigenous networks', including local security firms, are instrumental in both collecting knowledge and violently coercing populations on the ground. Just as in the DRC, the line between licit and illicit and between private and public remains weak to the point that it may be suggested that such differences are analytically meaningless (see, among many others discussions, Buur et al. 2007; Lund 2006; Pratten and Sen 2007; Roitman 2005). But while the DRC case highlights the importance of ties between international companies and big men within the state, Reno points out that another state, the United States, uses these security providers as proxy forces for their informal governance. In his chapter on Liberia, Marcus Mohlin asserts that the two US private military security companies active in the country's Security Sector Reform (SSR) programme act as Trojan horses. International private security providers, often with roots in the USA or England, have played a significant role in SSRs in Afghanistan and Iraq. Yet Mohlin shows that in a tiny country like Liberia they have the decisive capacity to dominate the entire security sector and, in so doing, further US political interests. Global politics plays a major role in the field of private security, with international companies arguably serving as the very bonds between internationally strong states and state governance on the ground on the African continent.

Maya Christensen's chapter in this volume reiterates the pattern of global power but reverses the flow. She shows how government soldiers and former militia and rebel soldiers from Sierra Leone get employed by private security companies in Iraq. This intricate process involves a British security company, staffed partly by British Sierra Leone veterans, government officials in Sierra Leone, and army and former rebel/militia commanders. Under the umbrella of global security, little attention is given to the fact that some of the Sierra Leonean security workers have carried out gruesome atrocities in the country's civil war. Another striking element of Christensen's observations – framed in terms of pure monetary value – is the stark divide between security staff from the North and those from the South. This is painfully observed by the Sierra Leoneans when they meet US and European security staff and compare their pay cheques and employment conditions.[2] Once again, we note the very particular ways in which novel security assemblages facilitate extreme differentials of power that perpetuate prevailing structures at the level of the everyday and the international.

As observed in the chapters above, global security assemblages not only play into global and local power regimes, but also connect with the humanitarian world (also an important regime of power). I have over the last ten years received several offers from international mining companies in Liberia and Sierra Leone to aid them in devising strategies for development projects in the areas where they operate.[3] All of these companies acknowledge a social responsibility, informed by a general understanding that the success of their business depends on fostering good relations with local communities. In a similar sense, Rita Abrahamsen and Michael Williams' chapter demonstrates the importance of Corporate Social Responsibility (CSR) for a gold-mining company in Tanzania. In part, the company is obliged to adhere to CSR – a prerequisite for almost all international companies in contemporary times – but in this instance this imperative also provides for greater security within its specific local context. In this sense aid has, as stated by Duffield, 'become a technology of security' (2002: 154). This is something that peacekeeping operations adhere to as well. For instance, both West African and UN peacekeepers in Liberia and Sierra Leone attempted to nurture good relations with local communities by helping to reconstruct their war-torn environments through quick-impact projects. Considerable resources were spent on repairing roads, rebuilding schools and community houses, though results were sometimes mixed and the attempt to effect 'force protection' through these projects often fuelled unintended consequences for peacekeepers.

A further aspect of the security assemblage Abrahamsen and Williams highlight in Tanzania turns on the salience of local security actors. Thus, after cooperation with the national police force became problematic and compromised, 'local' trust bonds with non-state security providers in the guise of a quasi-legal 'vigilante' group called Sungusungu increased. This group has over the years been used to protect, amongst other things, cattle from raids by neighbouring cattle rustlers – but also at times they have raided cattle from the very same neighbours. Abrahamsen and Williams show the efficiency of involving such groups, despite incongruities, and moreover how it is a necessity in many settings on the continent.

Peter Albrecht, in his piece on Sierra Leone, points out that 'traditional leaders' and locally organized security providers (such as Sungusungu) deal with between 80 and 90 per cent of disputes in the global South. These actors form a more widespread and encompassing security phenomenon than private and state-run security services combined. Sierra Leone is a country of 'extreme localization' (Fanthorpe 2001: 372) with regard to the distribution of authority and power in the rural areas. Albrecht's chapter emphasizes the dire need to devote more attention to this set of actors in the African security assemblage. The inspector general of the Sierra Leonean police talks about 'policing by consensus', whereby a variety of non-state actors participate alongside the national police force. This, Albrecht points out, is nothing new in the Sierra Leonean context, nor anything that came about because of the collapse of the state or the civil war, but rather 'a deep-seated hybrid order'. Within the hybridity of this security assemblage, 'traditional' secret societies also play their part. West African secret societies are a well-researched topic in cultural and social anthropology, but have received limited attention in studies of security. As Albrecht shows in his study, these organizations are not just politically and legally important, but provide a certain amount of predictability in the security sector as well. In addition to Albrecht's case, it is also important to highlight how secret societies, although at times an obstacle, can provide security to mining enterprises, plantations and NGOs in the region – at times without the knowledge of expatriate staff and managers.

If the above case is particularly instructive on rural areas, Jacob Rasmussen's chapter on Kenyan Mungiki, often described as a violent youth gang and a weird religious sect, offers an urban example of the security assemblage. In response to both internal political changes and increased regional and global insecurity, the traditional security landscape of Kenya has metamorphosed, creating space for a semi-traditional movement, with regional (rural) and ethnic roots, in the urban security landscape. Although a modern post-colonial creature, Mungiki branded itself as a successor to the Kenyan Mau Mau independence movement. On paper, Mungiki is an illegal movement, thus in this aspect differing from the Sierra Leonean secret society Poro and the Tanzanian Sungusungu. But regarded from Mungiki's position in identity politics, it is very much part of the everyday affairs of state in Kenya. The political position of Mungiki, which Rasmussen points out is in a constant process of development, also forms the basis for the movement's role in the national security assemblage. As a security outfit on the ground, Mungiki controls market areas, lorry parks and lucrative *matatu* (minibus) routes. From a security perspective, it is both an agent of fragmentation of security provision (noted during the post-election violence that occurred in the country in 2007), and a provider of local security in certain areas. Mungiki, then, caters for the security of some and the insecurity of others, and combines business, politics and protection in one.

It is also possible to look at security assemblages as partially responsible for moulding and creating moral communities. Not only do they cater for security, but they also discipline and punish communities. This is an important contribution in Tessa Diphoorn's chapter on South Africa. Steffen Jensen (2007) has pointed out that when public institutions fail to punish citizens committing crime, armed actors, including the police, start behaving like vigilante forces. In this situation Diphoorn shows how, with the blessing of police, private security providers attempt to solve domestic disputes through, in this instance, the disciplining of a domestic worker. Using coercive means, they become part of a national creation (although fractured) of moral subjects and have come to view their roles as a form of force protection.

Other dimensions of the African security assemblage

This volume provides a broad spectrum of cases of security assemblages across the African continent. A whole variety of cases overlapping, but not repeating each other, has been presented. Still there are topics that ought to get more attention, and in the rest of this epilogue I intend to raise a few thematic fields that warrant future attention.

In Somalia, in the mid-2000s, an alliance of local courts started to challenge the violent rule of warlords. In many parts of the country they re-established some form of order based on Islamic law. Jointly, they formed the Islamic Courts Union or the Sharia Court Alliance (Hansen 2013). In order to maintain security they had to rely on a new set of actors that defied the overarching logic of clans that had shaped much previous fighting. One of these groups was held together with a loose religious ideological base rather than clan logic – Al-Shabaab. During the height of the Sharia Court Alliance, Al-Shabaab functioned as a security provider to the Court Alliance, especially in Mogadishu. After Ethiopia once again sent forces to crush what they saw as the subregionally threatening Court Alliance, Al-Shabaab was pushed into another trajectory, and transformed into the militant jihadist organization we know today (ibid.). The transmutation of vigilante security providers into more blatant armed rebel groups is a not uncommon feature and stands as a security dimension on the continent worthy of further study. This is also clear for eastern DRC with regard to militias, such as the Mayi-Mayi, who initially protected local citizens, before morphing into aggressors, being remobilized into the national army, and then morphed again into a local militia (Jourdan 2011; Vlassenroot and Van Acker 2001). These patterns are also clear in my own research: the West Side Boys militia had its roots in the national army, before turning into a violent group preying on a rural population. This group was then reinstated as a proxy force to the Sierra Leonean government with the aim of crushing the RUF rebels they had previously fought alongside (Utas and Joergel 2008). After the end of the war, units of the West Side Boys were once again remobilized as a security force for the incumbent political party, prior to the 2007 elections (Christensen and Utas 2008). With these cases in mind we ought to remember that the identities of security provider and violent aggressor are constantly shifting, as are the security assemblages within which they are nested.

In war zones and post-war countries ex-combatants can function as agents of both security and insecurity. Chapters by Reno, Schouten and Christensen underscore this fluid identity that helps to explain the challenges faced by countries attempting to move beyond the civil war dynamic. In an apparently contradictory fashion, when ex-combatants are demobilized many end up working in the security sector. I have recently, for instance, together with Anders Themnér, researched former commanders in rebel movements and their roles in the aftermath of the Liberian civil war (Themnér and Utas 2016). Many commanders have become security brokers between elite (both economic and political) and former foot soldiers, and they have either on an informal basis or more formally been involved in security enterprises. Post-war security assemblages of these kinds are particularly interesting because they cater to a double need. They elicit protection from criminal and violent actors, who constitute a good proportion of former combatants, and employ such potentially criminal elements in order to make them less likely to target one's business. By employing an ex-combatant, one can make constructive use of their status as a violent and feared character with a certain measure of military discipline (the latter quality often being overlooked in the literature), while simultaneously pacifying their network. This double bind of security plays out on a larger scale as well.

The Movement for the Emancipation of the Niger Delta (MEND) was militarily active in the oil-rich Niger Delta region in Nigeria in the mid-2000s. Causing serious concern primarily for international oil companies active in the region, through kidnappings and blowing up pipelines, they forced their way into the Nigerian marketplace for security, and the realm of national politics (Ukiwo 2007; Obi 2010). When Goodluck Jonathan, a Christian southerner, inherited the presidency after the incumbent president passed away, the activities of MEND gradually ceased (already in 2009 there was an amnesty programme for the group), any remaining actions eventually being viewed as piracy, or forms of criminality other than rebellion. The MEND leader, Henry Okah, was arrested in South Africa and later charged with terrorism. Although kidnappings and bombings that could be traced to the movement continued, much was now infighting, and most MEND rebels avoided being sentenced for any kind of war crime; within the leadership of the movement some progressed in the state hierarchies, for instance in the security sector. The best known case is Government Ekpemupolo, a.k.a. Tompolo, who established a security company contracted by the Jonathan government to fight piracy in the waters of the Niger Delta he previously fought in. This transformation attracted international attention when Tompolo's company bought seven warships from the Norwegian navy (Bøås 2014). Within five years, Tompolo had transformed himself from a rebel commander responsible for kidnapping and ransoms to the owner of a security company awarded government contracts of (allegedly) hundreds of millions of US dollars. This case offers a rather extreme – though somewhat unexceptional – case of role-switching within this instance of an African security assemblage.

Executive Outcomes (EO) was a South African security outfit under the leadership of former South African Special Forces and security services. By the end of apartheid, predominantly white South African officers and soldiers left the country looking for new opportunities. Security work, aiding governments and a role in various insurgencies occupied EO. Highly trained and violence-prone, they became implicated in a number of questionable political and economic deals on the continent (Shearer 1998). They were frequently employed in proximity to exploitative industries. As South African companies have for a long time had a major share in the diamond industries, EO was often employed in diamond-rich countries. Sierra Leone was such a case. As EO first entered Sierra Leone they fostered close ties with the Branch Energy Group with large economic interests in the country (Keen 2005). The company was first hired by the Sierra Leone military government in 1995 in order to train and strategically organize the country's army in the fight against the RUF incursion that started in 1991. However, in 1998, they simply switched sides as they started training RUF soldiers in Liberia (and, later on, Liberian security forces), and re-entered Sierra Leone from that side. When EO staff, by then no longer officially part of the outfit, shifted sides in the Sierra Leone conflict, RUF was in control of diamond-rich areas and thus EO retained influence over the flow of diamonds from Sierra Leone. When the war was over EO as a company had long been dissolved, but on an individual basis former South African mercenaries were being employed as heads of security for diamond companies in the country and, at times, also as managers.

The most recent conflict in the Central African Republic (CAR) has been ongoing since 2012. It has recently transpired that the UN peacekeeping mission in the Central African Republic, MINUSCA has been renting premises from a diamond company which is on the UN Security Council's sanctions list. The company, BADICA, is on the list because they have bought diamonds, despite the international ban on diamonds from the country, and been associated with two major militias in the country, Séléka and the Anti-balaka.[4] MINUSCA has also used an aviation firm owned by the company for transportation within the country. This type of assemblage in the security/conflict sector is hopefully not that common, though I am reminded of a similar situation in Liberia between the UN and a Dutch entrepreneur who escaped to Liberia in the mid-eighties after being placed on Interpol's wanted-persons list for heroin trafficking. Guus Kouwenhoven was closely associated with Charles Taylor and aided him in exporting products such as rainforest timber despite being on the UN's sanctions list. Kouwenhoven also allegedly brokered major arms deals and aided in setting up facilities for training militias that subsequently fought in neighbouring Côte d'Ivoire. Despite this background the UN continued to rent the largest hotel in town and other premises from him. Once again we see the coupling of security and criminal interests in the international assemblages.

My knowledge of Sierra Leone is grounded in my experience of living there between 2004 and 2006. I first came to the country, however, in 1992, when the civil war was just starting. I have predominantly conducted research among ex-combatants residing in the streets in the aftermath of the civil war. The successful ones are those who graduate from living on the streets to become taxi drivers or security guards. Security is an important role for ex-combatants, as I have described above, with the most prestigious and possibly lucrative positions being those offered by an international company. Dragon – let's stick to his *nom de guerre* – in 2006 secured a job for the G4S group and one day came to my gate in his grey uniform. Subsequently, he became the personal driver for the British head of the organization. The Brit had a yacht on the shoreline of Freetown and at least once Dragon helped to load boxes from the Brit's car onto a speedboat that went out to the yacht. In 2008 the Briton and his son were arrested for trafficking cocaine as part of a larger bust of an international drug ring, shipping narcotics from Latin America through Sierra Leone en route to Europe. Dragon later told me that he suspected that the cargo he handled was drugs, but that he turned a blind eye towards it. During the same bust another of my informants, who worked as a security guard for expatriate diamond dealers (amongst others), helped two Venezuelan expatriates to escape from Freetown into hiding in a safe house on the peninsula. When the drug ring was uncovered my Ukrainian neighbours, helicopter pilots that I had not seen for two years, also went missing. The police searched the house for evidence and, according to other neighbours (I was no longer residing there), left with computers. This case is instructive as it shows assemblages between former ex-combatants, international private security companies and the global drugs trade.

Now I jump ten years farther back in time. In 1996 I was conducting fieldwork in the Ivoirian city of Danané. It was virtually a refugee camp in this period, with Liberians occupying almost every second house. Danané was at the time a solid and safe support area for Charles Taylor and his NPFL rebels. There I met Taylor's mother, and Taylor's notorious son Chuckie, currently serving a long prison term in the USA for war crimes in Liberia, and also some of Taylor's business associates. At Les Lianes, the fanciest hotel around at the time, there was a particular table where the Taylor people would gather. Arriving there one night I met a lonely Swede, a young man around my age who appeared nervous and lost. Speaking to him in our common language made him relax a bit. He started talking about his reason for coming. He was there waiting for an NPFL contact who would take him through Liberia to Sierra Leone, where he intended to strike an arms deal with the RUF rebels. Next day he was gone and I never saw him again.

And then there was Fred. In 1997/98 I conducted fieldwork in Monrovia and stayed in a small flat downtown. Next to me lived a young Liberian prostitute. She and her two friends invited me to a party with their boyfriends. They were all former Executive Outcomes contractors, two South Africans if I remember correctly, and Fred, who originated from Fiji. All three of them had left Sierra Leone, where they, as I described above, had for some time fought alongside the government against the RUF rebels. With a shift of government they were chased out of Sierra Leone and ironically ended up with a new contract given by Taylor to train RUF soldiers. That night I was standing with Fred as he was barbecuing a whole lamb. He did not give me the full story, but bits and pieces of his life. He had the saddest eyes I ever encountered. Later I met up with a Sierra Leonean soldier who had fought alongside Fred. He pointed out that during his years of fighting he had never seen a person kill with such fervour and lack of mercy as Fred.

Paul Higate opened this book by referring to the nefarious activities of Executive Outcomes in, for instance, Sierra Leone. The chapters in this volume have only touched upon such dimensions of the global security assemblage on the continent, yet such facets – detailed in the latter part of this epilogue – also form part of the security assemblages in Africa. Guus Kouwenhoven, the international criminal, became a wealthy man by renting estates to the UN peacekeeping mission, my Swedish compatriot through selling guns to the RUF, and Dragon's British boss by dealing in drugs. Criminal or not, they are all part of the African security assemblage.

Prior to closing this book, I want to tell a final story from Liberia. It is early 1998 and I am standing in the bar of a seedy downtown nightclub in Monrovia. It is early, and the place is almost empty. A middle-aged European man approaches me, stating that he is broke and wonders whether I can buy him a beer. I comply. He is Greek in origin, but has spent most of his life in southern Africa. He is in Monrovia to hustle for a job, he says. When he asks me what I am doing in Liberia I tell him that I am an anthropologist. I have to tell him what anthropology is and I explain something about understanding social structures. He then looks me in the eyes and says: there are no social structures on the African continent, and take that from a man who has killed more Africans than you can ever imagine. I leave him, and my beer, behind. Yet Monrovia is a small place and I see him from time to time, hanging out with his 'white' brothers, as a Liberian would typically say. Within a few months he no longer walks around but drives a car, and then he starts to import heavy equipment from abroad. I hear he scored a big European Union contract to refurbish roads.

Notes

1 In reality partly the private interests of big men within state bureaucracy. See my and others' work on Big Men and networks (Utas 2012).

2 Security work forms part of international regimes of labour and its deep structural inequalities.

3 Typically local populations get no say and little pay when international mining conglomerates establish themselves in a country like Liberia or Sierra Leone. One may therefore be hesitant to join such a company. On the other hand a well-designed Corporate Social Responsibility project may at times limit the damage and in its small way give benefits to a population that cannot prevent land exploitation anyway.

4 See Lombard (2016), but also Käihkö and Utas (2014), for more about the conflict in CAR.

Bibliography

Alao, C. A. (2013) 'Islamic radicalisation and violence in Nigeria', in J. Gow, F. Olonisakin and E. Dijxhoorn (eds), *Militancy and Violence in West Africa*, London: Routledge, pp. 43–89.

Bøås, M. (2014) 'How seven Norwegian small warships ended up in the hands of a former Niger Delta militant', Blog, WordPress.com.

Brabazon, J. (2010) *My Friend the Mercenary*, Edinburgh: Canongate.

Buur, L., S. Jensen and F. Stepputat (2007) 'The security–development nexus: expressions of sovereignty and securitization in southern Africa', Uppsala/Cape Town: Nordiska Afrikainstitutet/HSRC.

Christensen, M. M. and M. Utas (2008) 'Mercenaries of democracy: the "politricks" of remobilized combatants in the 2007 general elections, Sierra Leone', *African Affairs*, 107(429): 515–39.

De Waal, A. (2009) 'Mission without end? Peacekeeping in the African marketplace', *International Affairs*, 85(1): 99–113.

Duffield, M. (2002) 'War as a network enterprise: the new security terrain and its implications', *Cultural Values*, 6(1/2): 153–65.

— (2012) 'Risk management and the bunkering of the aid industry', *Development Dialogue*, 58: 21–37.

Fanthorpe, R. (2001) 'Neither citizen nor subject? "Lumpen" agency and the legacy of native administration in Sierra Leone', *African Affairs*, 100: 363–86.

Gberie, L. (2005) *A Dirty War in West Africa: The RUF and the destruction of Sierra Leone*, Bloomington: Indiana University Press.

Hansen, S. J. (2013) *Al-Shabaab in Somalia: The history and ideology of a militant Islamist group, 2005/2012*, New York: Oxford University Press.

Hönke, J. (2010) 'New political topographies. Mining companies and indirect discharge in Southern Katanga (DRC)', *Politique africaine*, 120(4): 105–27.

Jensen, S. (2007) 'Policing Nkomazi: crime, masculinity and generational conflicts', in D. Pratten and A. Sen (eds), *Global Vigilantes*, London: Hurst, pp. 47–68.

Jourdan, L. (2011) 'Mayi-Mayi: young rebels in Kivu, DRC', *Africa Development*, XXXVI(3/4): 89–111.

Keen, D. (2005) *Conflict and Collusion in Sierra Leone*, Oxford: James Currey.

Käihkö, I. and M. Utas (2014) 'The crisis in CAR: navigating myths and interests', *Africa Spectrum*, 1/2014: 69–78.

Lombard, L. (2016) *State of Rebellion: Violence and Intervention in the Central African Republic*, London: Zed Books.

Lund, C. (2006) 'Twilight institutions: an introduction', *Development and Change*, 37(4): 673–84.

Obi, C. I. (2010) 'Oil extraction, dispossession, resistance, and conflict in Nigeria's oil-rich Niger Delta', *Revue canadienne d'*études du développement [Canadian Journal of Development Studies], 30(1/2): 219–36.

Pratten, D. and A. Sen (2007) *Global Vigilantes*, London: Hurst.

Roitman, J. L. (2005) *Fiscal Disobedience: An anthropology of economic regulation in Central Africa*, Princeton, NJ: Princeton University Press.

Shearer, D. (1998) *Private Armies and Military Intervention*, Adelphi Papers 316, Oxford University Press for the International Institute for Strategic Studies.

Themnér, A. and M. Utas (2016) 'Governance through brokerage: informal governance in post-civil war societies', *Civil Wars*, 18(3): 255–80.

Ukiwo, U. (2007) 'From "pirates" to "militants": a historical perspective on anti-state and anti-oil company mobilization among the Ijaw of Warri, Western Niger Delta', *African Affairs*, 106(425): 587–610.

Utas, M. (2012) 'Introduction: Bigmanity and network governance in African conflicts', in M. Utas (ed.), *African Conflicts and Informal Power: Big Men and networks*, London: Zed Books, pp. 1–34.

Utas, M. and M. Joergel (2008) 'The West Side Boys: military navigation in the Sierra Leone civil war', *Journal of Modern African Studies*, 46(3): 487–511.

Vlassenroot, K. and F. van Acker (2001) 'War as exit from exclusion? The formation of Mayi-Mayi militias in Eastern Congo', *Afrika Focus*, 17(1/2): 51–77.

About the editors and contributors

Paul Higate is reader in gender and security at the School for Sociology, Politics and International Studies. He has written on the gendered sub-field of military masculinities in respect of those leaving the armed services, United Nations peacekeepers, and most recently private military and security contractors. He is currently looking at the experiences of former soldiers who travel to fight ISIS in Syria and Iraq.

Mats Utas is a senior lecturer in the Department of Cultural Anthropology and Ethnology at Uppsala University. He is the editor of African Conflicts and Informal Power (Zed, 2012).

Rita Abrahamsen is professor in the Graduate School of Public and International Affairs at the University of Ottawa. She is the author (with M. C. Williams) of *Security Beyond the State: Private Security in International Politics* (2011) and *Disciplining Democracy: Development Discourse and Good Governance in Africa* (Zed, 2000), as well as numerous articles in peer-reviewed journals.

Peter Albrecht is a senior researcher at the Danish Institute for International Studies (DIIS). He has authored and co-authored several books and articles on security in Sierra Leone and beyond, including *Reconstructing Security after Conflict: Security Sector Reform in Sierra Leone* (2011) and *Securing Sierra Leone, 1997–2013: Defence, Diplomacy and Development in Action* (2014), and was co-editor of *Policing and the Politics of Order-Making* (2015). Peter has worked on and off for over a decade in Sierra Leone, as a researcher and consultant.

Maya Christensen is a researcher at the Danish Institute Against Torture (DIGNITY). She holds a PhD from the University of Copenhagen, and has conducted long-term ethnographic research on militia mobilization and security outsourcing in Sierra Leone. Her current research focuses on urban violence prevention in sub-Saharan Africa.

Tessa Géraldine Diphoorn is currently an assistant professor at the Department of Cultural Anthropology at Utrecht University. She has conducted extensive fieldwork on security and violence in diverse localities, such as South Africa, Kenya, Sri Lanka and Jamaica. Her book *Twilight Policing: Private Security and Violence in Urban South Africa* is based on her research on private security in Durban.

Commander Marcus Mohlin is an active-duty naval officer currently working at the Swedish Defence University. He is a former submarine officer and has also served with the United Nations in Angola and with NATO/SFOR in Bosnia-Herzegovina. Commander Mohlin has also been engaged as a NATO expert and has travelled in several of the former Soviet republics within the framework of the NATO Defence Education Enhancement Program (DEEP). He holds a doctorate from the Finnish National Defence University in Helsinki and has published several articles and chapters on military strategy and private military companies.

Jacob Rasmussen has conducted ethnographic research in Kenya and South Africa, mainly in Nairobi and Johannesburg. His research deals with issues of security, policing and crime, and urban politics and service delivery. His publications cover a range of issues related to the interplay of non-state security and politics.

William Reno is the author of *Corruption and State Politics in Sierra Leone* (1995), *Warlord Politics and African States* (1999) and *Warfare in Independent Africa* (2011), as well as other works on the politics of conflict. His recent work focuses on the impacts of the collapse of states on the organization and behaviour of armed groups that operate in these environments. Other recent projects include the study of changes in civil–military relations in African states and the study of how different military establishments in Africa approach counter-insurgency campaigns.

Peer Schouten is a postdoctoral fellow at the Danish Institute for International Studies, a research associate at the International Peace Information Service, and editor-in-chief of *Theory Talks*. He has extensive field experience in the Democratic Republic of Congo and South Sudan, both for academic research and as a consultant to NGOs working on human rights in the mining sector. He is editor, with Ned Lebow and Hidemi Suganami, of *The Return of the Theorists: Dialogues with Great Thinkers in International Relations* (2016) and has published widely on the intersections of mining, infrastructure, conflict and international politics in Africa.

Michael C. Williams is professor in the Graduate School of Public and International Affairs at the University of Ottawa. He is the author (with Rita Abrahamsen) of *Security Beyond the State: Private Security in International Politics* (2011), *The Realist Tradition and the Limits of International Relations* (2005) and *Culture and Security: Symbolic Power and the Politics of International Security* (2007).

Index